MIDWEST
ROAD TRIP
ADVENTURES

ISBN 13: 978-0-9846938-2-5

Library of Congress Control Number: 2020949150
Printed in the United States of America
First Printing: 2020
18 17 16 15 14   5 4 3 2 1

Edited by Gemma Peckham
Cover design by Dragan Bilic

SOMETHING OR OTHER PUBLISHING
Info@SOOPLLC.com
For bulk orders e-mail: Orders@SOOPLLC.com

CONTENTS

The eleven of us are beyond excited to share the information on the following pages with you! We love traveling and finding hidden gems and treasures right in our own backyards as we live and work in the states we cover. The group connected as members of The Midwest Travel Network, a consortium of writers and bloggers who specialize in the region.

"Sharing stories about the Midwest falls perfectly into the laps of Midwestern writers," says anthology author and Midwest Travel Network co-owner Lisa Dunham Trudell. "We live here. We work here. Most of us grew up here. It's more than just a place to us; it's home. We know the attractions and love sharing stories about them. Who better to tell the stories of the Midwest than the people who live in its backyard?"

One thing we have all learned from quarantine and Covid-19 is the simple fact that the future of travel is going to be different than what we were used to. Smaller crowds, road trips, and getting back in touch with nature are all critical as we finally get to leave our homes and venture out again. We are returning to the era of the great American road trip again—finding joy in the areas around us and what it has to offer. It is becoming more about the journey, than the destination.

This book takes travelers along some of the most storied highways and byways in the nation, including The Great River Road and Route 66. Stops include historic lighthouses along the shores of Lake Erie in Ohio, canyons in Kansas, crystal clear springs in Michigan, Underground Railroad history in Illinois, Mount Rushmore in South Dakota, and authentic fish boils in Wisconsin's Door County. Movie fans can visit the ballpark from *A League of Their Own* in Indiana or tour Iowa covered bridges showcased in the *The Bridges of Madison County*.

That all being said, why would we write a book to encourage you to visit?

Building on agritourism, eco-friendly practices, embracing their local natural features, and encouraging unique small businesses all begins to feed on each other and creates an environment that draws people. Those people bring their money and help build the economy. That leads to more jobs, increased housing, and a rapidly growing and thriving economy. THAT is the power that YOU can bring to our own country: first of all, by keeping up to seventy percent of your travel budget local, supporting the very people that are your neighbors. At the same time, you eat delicious things, see incredible sights, and learn more about people in your own community. It is a win-win for everyone.

We all have treasures from our own state to share with you in this book and have great adventures. We have organized this book by state, in alphabetical order, to make your adventure planning easier. Each chapter will tell you a little more about the incredible things you can expect inside that state's borders so you know where to stay, what to see and do, and where to eat.

Whether you find yourself admiring the brightly lit night sky of Wisconsin's Door County's Peninsula State Park, looking at the World's Largest Painting on an Easel, or even visiting the tiniest town in the United States, we hope our adventures help you create your own!

Dannelle Gay

Curator

ILLINOIS

I llinois is a land of prairies, rolling hills, farmland, and industry. Founded in 1818, the "Land of Lincoln" has been home to four US presidents, including Ulysses S. Grant, Ronald Reagan, Barack Obama, and Abraham Lincoln. Eighty percent of Illinois is farmland, but with Chicago in the northeast corner, the population exceeds twelve and a half million people.

Portions of four of the country's most famous scenic highways run through the state, making Illinois a road-tripper's dream. Route 66 begins its storied adventure in downtown Chicago, and the National Road has been bringing travelers all the way from Maryland to the Mississippi River since the early nineteenth century. Speaking of the Mississippi, an explorer can get a taste of that thoroughfare—also the state's western border—with a drive along the Great River Road. And for additional spectacular riverside motoring, the Ohio River Scenic Byway is a winding trail of history and scenic views.

I'll introduce you to these historic routes and point out several of the best places to stop along the way. We'll visit one of the most important archaeological sites in North America, see plenty of "World's Biggest" attractions, and stand where Lewis and Clark began their journey. From the booming metropolis of Chicago to the small city of Metropolis, from land that feeds the world to innovation that changed it, you'll get a taste of the state's complexity, variety, and good ol' Midwestern heart.

Basic Illinois Facts
- The state capital, its third, is Springfield.
- The state motto is "State Sovereignty, National Union," and its slogan is "Land of Lincoln."
- The state nickname is the Prairie State.

- Like Ohio and Indiana, the state bird is the northern cardinal.
- The state reptile is the painted turtle.
- There are seven National Scenic Byways in the state.

Fun Illinois Facts

- Appropriately, the Land of Lincoln was the first state to ratify the Thirteenth Amendment to the Constitution, abolishing slavery.
- Brownies, ice cream sundaes, and Twinkies were all invented in Illinois. McDonald's and Dairy Queen both began in the Prairie State, too.
- The world's first skyscraper was built in 1885 in Chicago.
- Abraham Lincoln wasn't the only tall man from Illinois; Arnold Pershing Wadlow from Alton, at 8 feet, 11.1 inches tall, was the tallest man in history.

Route 66

Route 66 is the stuff of movies, music, and lore. It's part of the American vernacular and epitomizes the freedom of the open road. The route became official in 1926, providing many small towns with access to significant national roadways for the first time. That decision means that today, anyone driving Route 66 can skip the homogeneity of the highway and see what the US is really like.

That's especially true in the Prairie State. From its beginnings in downtown Chicago, to its crossing of the Mississippi River into St. Louis, Route 66 in Illinois is 301 miles of Americana. This journey will take you into the heart of numerous historic and quintessentially American communities.

Route 66 changed course over the years, and these alignments are well marked in Illinois. If you're short on time, I-55 will take you from one attraction to the next, but the fun of driving one of the country's most historic byways is in following its original path. Keep your eyes peeled for wayside exhibits, which tell some fascinating stories about the history of the route. There's something to see at almost every turn, and before you know it, you'll be crossing the Mississippi.

*This itinerary begins in **Chicago** and heads west. If you're coming from Missouri, start at the end of this section and work your way backwards.*

Begin your Route 66 adventure with a hearty breakfast at **Lou Mitchell's** on Jackson Boulevard in Chicago's Loop. Known for its big portions and fresh donut holes, this diner has been a staple since it opened in 1923, three years before Route 66 came to be. loumitchells.com

After breakfast, you'll have to do a block-wide U-turn to get to Adams Street, but that's just practice: you'll be making lots of sharp turns as you follow the convoluted path of this historic drive. Before you start driving west, take a moment to visit **Buckingham Fountain**. This iconic ornamental landmark was completed the year after Route 66 was established, after local art patron and philanthropist Kate Buckingham donated funds to Chicago for its construction in honor of her brother, Clarence.

Navigating through Chicago toward the southwest suburbs, you'll start to see brown Historic Route 66 signs. These are your friends, and they will guide you all the way to the Mississippi River. You'll have to pay close attention, though—Route 66's alignment often changed, and navigating through all of those towns means it's not a straight path. There's usually only one sign per turn. Miss it, and you could end up backtracking.

As you drive through the town of **Berwyn**, notice the four wayside exhibits and the number of businesses with Route 66 in their names. This will give you a sense of the pride that Illinois takes in the Mother Road. Berwyn is also home to the oldest White Castle on Route 66—it's been serving sliders since 1939. whyberwyn.com

Plan to spend some time in **Joliet** because, in addition to Route 66, Lincoln Highway cuts through the town; it's also along the Illinois and Michigan Canal National Heritage Corridor. Stop at **Route 66 Park** to browse the informational kiosks and admire the public art, including an old gas pump. Take a short stroll to an overlook of the Des Plaines River and the old **Collins Street Prison**, which you might recognize from *The Blues Brothers*. Jake and Elwood themselves dance on the roof of **Rich & Creamy**, a seasonal ice cream shop that anchors the park. Leave the park and cross the river to visit the **Joliet Area Historical Museum and Route 66 Welcome Center**, then swing by the **Rialto Square Theatre**. The oldest vaudevillian theatre on Route 66, it dates back to the same year as the certification of the Mother Road. visitjoliet.com

Stretch your legs, and maybe even glimpse some bison, at **Midewin National Tallgrass Prairie**. This global treasure is the largest open space in the Chicago area, and was previously farmland, as well as the site of explosives manufacturing and storage. Now it's a massive recreational area of thousands of acres with miles of trails. (And bison. Did I mention bison?) fs.usda.gov/midewin

In **Wilmington**, you'll see one of the most photographed landmarks of Americana: the **Gemini Giant**. This fiberglass sculpture is one of four "Muffler Men" on Route 66 in Illinois—so named because several of the 1960s originals advertised muffler shops. The Gemini Giant wears a space helmet and carries a rocket, and attracts visitors to **The Launching Pad** restaurant, which reopened after a two-year renovation in 2019. Inside there's a Route 66 Welcome Center, a mini-museum, a gift shop, and a diner serving Chicago-style hot dogs. geminigiant.com

After your photo op with the giant, continue to **Braidwood** and the **Polk-a-Dot Drive In**. There, you can snap some pics with Elvis and Superman, and those Blues Brothers make another appearance. Before you leave, swing through the drive-through for a burger and chili cheese fries.

Dwight is another town that will grab your attention. Make your first stop **Ambler's Texaco Gas Station**. The official Dwight Visitor Center, it's completely run by volunteers. The cottage-style filling station was built in 1933 and pumped gas until 1999, making it the longest-operating gas station along Route 66. There are picnic tables and wayside exhibits, including highlights of Dwight's other historic spots. Head into town to see a Frank Lloyd Wright–designed bank and the Chicago and Alton 1879 Railroad Depot, home to the **Dwight Historical Society Museum**. dwightillinois.org

The **Standard Oil Gasoline Station** in **Odell** is one of the reasons to skip I-55 and drive the original route. Built in 1932, this restored landmark is on the National Register of Historic Places. Not ten minutes away is another quick photo op: an advertisement for **Meramec Caverns** on the side of a barn. There's even a pull-out so you can get a decent photo. odell-il.com

The next community is a centerpiece of the Route 66 experience. **Pontiac** truly celebrates the Main Street of America, with lively murals, six wayside exhibits, and the **Route 66 Association Hall of Fame and Museum**. Don't miss the **1875 Livingston County Courthouse**, a gorgeous red and white building restored in 2012. Abraham Lincoln, memorialized with a statue on the south side of the building's square, frequently visited the courthouse prior to his presidency; those visits contributed to the building's listing on the National Register of Historic Places. visitpontiac.org

Be careful as you drive through **Towanda**; one old route alignment is called **Dead Man's Curve**, and for good reason. The sharp turn was only eighteen feet wide, and caught many road-trippers unawares. It won't be long after you've rounded that bend that you'll be in **Bloomington–Normal**. These two-for-the-price-of-one cities have a few things going for them. There's **Sprague's Super Service Station**, a two-story Tudor revival built in 1930–31 that now houses a gift shop and information center; the **Cruisin' with Lincoln on 66 Visitors Center** inside the McLean County Museum of History; and **Miller Park Zoo**. If it's time to replenish your road trip snack stash, stop in at the **Beer Nuts Factory and Company Store**. visitbn.org

If you're driving from March through August, pull into **Funks Grove Pure Maple Sirup**. The Funk family has been tapping sap since 1824. Why's it spelled with an *i* instead of a *y*? In the 1920s, the preferred spelling according to Webster's was "sirup," and when Hazel Funk died, she requested that the family company continue to abide by Webster's recommendation. funkspuremaplesirup.com

Atlanta, population 1,619 in 2018, may be a small town, but it's big enough for a Muffler Man. Here, you'll find **Bunyon's Statue**—another one of the route's giants. Originally located at Bunyon's hot dog stand in Cicero, the nineteen-foot-tall man holding a huge hot dog now has his own plaza in Atlanta. After getting a look at the bun-toting giant, loosen up your limbs with a visit to the **Route 66 Arcade Museum**, which is packed with old pinball and video games. On your way out of town, check out the **Atlanta Public Library and Clock Tower**. Built in 1908, it's one of few octagonal libraries in Illinois. atlantaillinois.org

Your next community is **Lincoln**, the only town named for the President while he was still living. Downtown, the **Courthouse Square Historic District** is a time capsule; most of the buildings are at least one hundred years old. In the center of the square is the **Logan County Courthouse**, built in 1905. A visit to the **Postville Courthouse State Historic Site** is another trip back in time. The building is a reconstruction, erected in 1953, and inside replicates what the original would have looked like in the mid-1800s when Lincoln used to visit. Fans of "World's Largest Things" won't want to miss the **Railsplitter Covered Wagon**. Recognized by Guinness World Records as the "World's Largest Covered Wagon," the vehicle is piloted by Abe Lincoln, who sits in the driver's seat and welcomes all to this roadside attraction. destinationlogancountyil.com

It's time for **Springfield**! You'll want to spend a whole day in the state's capital. In addition to being the seat of government, the **Illinois State Capitol**, and the **Illinois State Museum**, this city of more than one hundred thousand is also home to the **Illinois State Fairgrounds**, **Lincoln Home National Historic Site**, and **Abraham Lincoln Presidential Library and Museum**. If you're hungry, visit the place that invented the corn dog; **Cozy Dog Drive In** has been serving up that venerable fair food on a stick since the 1940s. Frank Lloyd Wright fans will want to tour the **Dana–Thomas House**, and hunters of giants will find the third Illinois Muffler Man at **Lauterbach Tire and Auto Service**. Before you continue your journey, take a spin through the first drive-thru window (allegedly) in the US at **Maid-Rite Sandwich Shop**. While their specialty has been loose meat sandwiches since the 1920s, this spot should not be confused with the Iowa-based chain. Even though they have the same name and a similar menu, they're not connected. visitspringfieldillinois.com

Those trusty Route 66 signs are about to give you a real treat. Follow the pre-1930s alignment and south of Chatham, they'll direct you to 1.4 miles of **Original Historic Route 66 Brick Road**. Driving this stretch, another listing on the National Register of Historic Places, is like hopping into a time machine.

The old mining town of **Virden** is known for more than coal; it was a hotbed of labor rights in the late 1890s. A fatal battle took place here during a mine strike, and it's memorialized in a wayside exhibit and at **Virden Miner's Riot Memorial**. After Virden, you'll get to drive an even older section of the route. There's a stretch of concrete pavement that was constructed around 1920; it was originally old Illinois Route 4 before becoming Route 66. virdenchamber.com

Carlinville was also a mining town, but it had another claim to fame: bootlegging. From 1926–31, Route 66 cut through the town, bringing rumrunners and gangsters from Chicago. Rumors have it that Al Capone himself used to secretly visit and stash liquor in an area barn. Prior to Prohibition, another scandal rocked the town: an 1867 project to build a new courthouse, funded by $50,000 in bonds and taxes, had run up a cost of $1.3 million by 1870. Today's visitors can see this "**Million Dollar Courthouse**" and take a tour of the **Carlinville Historic Square**. carlinville.com

If you take the newer, eastern alignment from Springfield, you'll drive through **Litchfield**. Catch a movie at the **Skyview Drive-In**, which has been screening movies since 1951 and is the last remaining original drive-in movie theater on the Illinois stretch of Route 66. Browse the stacks at the **Litchfield Carnegie Library Building**, constructed in 1904. You can also learn about the area at the **Litchfield Museum & Route 66 Welcome Center**. Make sure you grab some baked goods to go from **Jubelt's Bakery & Restaurant**, which first opened in Mt. Olive in 1922 and moved to Litchfield thirty years later. visitlitchfield.com

You're nearing the Mississippi River, but there are still a few things you'll want to check out. **DeCamp Station** in **Staunton** is a historic roadhouse that once provided all the amenities an early road-tripper could want: a place to sleep, a dance hall—and a brothel. In 1930, gangsters robbed the place of slot machines, guns, alcohol, and cash, then escaped in their black sedan. Photos on the wall give you a glimpse of the old dance hall. decampstationil.com

Edwardsville has been around longer than all but two other Illinois cities. Incorporated in 1818, the same year the state became official, the town has three different historic districts: the **Downtown Historic District**, the **St. Louis Street Historic District**, and **Leclaire National Historic District**. cityofedwardsville.com

Take the Historic Route 66 Spur for your final stop at the **Old Chain of Rocks Bridge**. With one end on Chouteau Island in the Mississippi (which is still in Illinois) and the other in Missouri, this historic crossing is now a 1.6-mile pedestrian trail. The bridge, with its unique thirty-degree bend, is part of a network of more than three hundred miles of trails on both sides of the river.

You did it! From Chicago to the Mississippi River, you've driven Illinois's Route 66. To continue your Mother Road journey, pick up I-270 and cross the river on the New Chain of Rocks Bridge. Or, head east on our next Scenic Byway, the Historic National Road.

The Historic National Road

On March 29, 1806, the federal government authorized the construction of a new road to enable expansion from the east into the western territories. The National Road, first known as the Cumberland Road, began in Maryland with an original goal of reaching the Ohio River at Wheeling, West Virginia. Later plans stretched that goal through the Illinois Territory to the Mississippi River, but due to lack of funding, the road fell sixty miles short at Vandalia, Illinois in the 1830s. Since roads from Vandalia to St. Louis, Missouri already existed, there was no further Congress-funded construction on the National Road. Settlers swarmed the thoroughfare and headed west, earning it the nickname "the road that built the nation." Between 1830 and 1840, the population of Illinois doubled.

In 2002, the route was designated the Historic National Road and includes the section from Vandalia to St. Louis, making the Illinois portion of this historic roadway 164 miles from border to border. As you follow this drive that's more than two centuries old, look for white signs with a red, white, and blue emblem above the words "Historic National Road."

This itinerary begins at the Missouri border. If you're coming from Indiana, start at the end of this section and work your way backwards.

Since the Illinois section of the Historic National Road ends at the **Eads Bridge** in East St. Louis, we'll start there. Built in 1874, the Eads was the first bridge across the Mississippi River south of the Missouri River. Its innovative large-scale application of steel, along with foundations one hundred feet below water level, influenced the construction of future bridges, including the Brooklyn Bridge. Eads Bridge is the oldest remaining bridge on the Mississippi, and is listed on the National Register of Historic Places.

Your next stop takes you even further back in time—way back. **Cahokia Mounds State Historic Park**, just over five miles west of the town of **Collinsville**, is a UNESCO World Heritage Site that preserves the remnants of a civilization that thrived between 700 and 1300 AD. It's considered one of the most important archaeological sites, if not the most important, in North America, and is the largest Native American site north of Mexico. cahokiamounds.org

Something else that's really big in Collinsville? The **World's Largest Catsup Bottle**. The W.E. Caldwell Company built the 170-foot-tall water tower to supply water to the Brooks Catsup plant in 1949, and in a brilliant marketing move, it was decided that the tower should resemble the company's catsup bottles. This decision was so effective that the landmark is now listed on the National Register of Historic Places. discovercollinsville.com

As you drive east, you'll be following in the wheel ruts of some of the state's earliest Swiss settlers. In **Highland**, visit what was once a stage-coach stop, built in 1840, at the **Kaeser Park and Museum**. Also in town, the **Louis Latzer Homestead** is an homage to the man who perfected condensed milk, preventing spoilage in the days before refrigeration was common. highlandillinois.com

Greenville, which dates back to 1815, is one of the oldest towns on the Historic National Road. It's got more than age going for it; it was also an important point along the **Underground Railroad** during the 1840s. Here, Rev. John Leeper helped slaves find passage to freedom, using his milling business as cover; Rev. George Denny built a secret room in his home to hide refugees; and Dr. Henry Perrine also provided assistance to the people seeking freedom. In 1855, Stephen Morse founded what is now **Greenville University** as Almira College. The school was funded in part by his wife's inheritance, and Morse named it for her; it became one of the few places in the country where women could get an education. Educated women seemed to be the norm in Greenville; the following year, the **Greenville Ladies Library Association** was established, and gradually built its collection of literature, which was housed in various locales in the town. In 1900, the Association enlisted the support of the city to find a permanent home for the books; noted philanthropist Andrew Carnegie donated $11,000, and **Greenville Public Library** opened in 1905. greenvilleilchamber.org

Many National Road itineraries begin (or end, depending on the direction) at the town of **Vandalia**. The story goes that the feds ran out of money and the state government didn't want to pay to extend it. Vandalia was the state capital at the time and the buck, and the macadam, stopped there.

As you near the former terminus, take the two-lane that parallels I-70—otherwise, you'll miss the **Kaskaskia Dragon**. Situated at the entrance of an RV park, this roadside attraction invites tourists to drop in a token and make the dragon breathe fire at a stalwart (although slightly rusted) knight. In town, stop at the 1836 **Vandalia State House**, the fourth (and oldest remaining) Illinois state capitol building. This is where Abe Lincoln began his political career; he also made his first public protest against slavery here. The square in front of the building is the site of one of twelve *Madonna of the Trail* sculptures celebrating the spirit of pioneer women that were erected along the National Old Trails Highway in 1928 and 1929. vandaliaillinois.com

Once you head east out of Vandalia, you are on the original National Road. Take a short detour to the **Dr. Charles M. Wright House** in **Altamont**. Built in 1899 for Wright, a wealthy local doctor and banker, it's a preserved piece of Effingham County history, and one of only two sites in the county on the National Register of Historic Places. Three generations of Wrights lived in the Italianate-style, eighteen-room house, and it's still furnished with many of their belongings. wrightmansion.org

Ready for a nature break? Pull into the **Ballard Nature Center**. This outdoor oasis offers miles of hiking trails, a visitor center, a fishing pond just for kids, and a shelter. It's the perfect place for a picnic and to stretch your legs before you jump back in the car. ballardnaturecenter.org

After you've soaked up some fresh air, keep heading east to the **Old Effingham County Courthouse**. This distinctive building with its mansard roof is the second landmark in the county on the National Register of Historic Places, and it houses a transportation and military museum. visiteffinghamil.com

Your next stop, **Teutopolis**, is only three miles away. If you think the town's name sounds German, you'd be correct. After an extensive search, a committee of German settlers intentionally chose this land in central Illinois as the perfect place to establish their community, founding the "City of Teutons" (city of Germans) in 1839. Franciscan friars arrived in 1858 and established a monastery, which is now the **Monastery Museum**. facebook.com/monasterymuseum

If you're into covered bridges, keep an eye out for signs west of **Greenup**. You'll want to exit US 40 to take Cumberland Road, one of the older alignments, to see the **Cumberland County Covered Bridge**. If it seems new, that's because it is: this reconstruction of the original opened to traffic in 2000. Wayside exhibits tell the story of not only the bridge itself and its predecessors at this spot on the Embarras River, but also of the National Road itself. Drive through the bridge, follow Cumberland Road into Greenup and look for the **Historic Greenup Depot**. Although it also looks new, this building was constructed in 1870. It's been moved multiple times and now houses a train museum. villageofgreenup.com

Have your camera ready, because your next stop is **Casey**. The town motto, "Big Things in a Small Town," is literal. Guinness World Records has recognized several objects here as the world's largest, including the World's Largest Mailbox and the World's Largest Birdcage. visitcaseyillinois.com

Casey can't claim all of the biggest things in Illinois, though. The **World's Largest Gavel** is located at the **Clark County Courthouse** in **Marshall**, seventeen miles farther down the road from Casey. Take some time to walk around the courthouse square; there's a Veterans Memorial, a statue of Abraham Lincoln, and a bandstand dating back to 1929. Inside **Harlan Hall**, an historic opera house across the street from the courthouse, is an interpretive center for the National Road. marshall-il.com

It's pretty incredible to think you've been driving on a road that was conceived of and constructed more than two hundred years ago. From a UNESCO World Heritage Site to a fire-breathing dragon to the world's largest collection of world's largest things, this 164-mile Illinois stretch packs a lot into every mile.

Ohio River Scenic Byway

The 188-mile stretch of the Ohio River Scenic Byway in Illinois provides a nearly encyclopedic glimpse into the state's past. During this drive along the southern border, you'll see the oldest bank built as such in Illinois, visit the site of a prehistoric civilization, follow the Trail of Tears, and pass stops on the Underground Railroad. There are pirates and superheroes, Native Americans, explorers, soldiers, and miners. The road flows through lush forests and over rolling hills along the winding river, providing natural beauty, unique geology, and scenic overlooks.

There are several spurs along this route and you'll want to take them. Look for the Ohio River Scenic Byway Illinois signs featuring a blue river, green hills, and a skyline and ferry in black.

This itinerary begins at the Kentucky border. If you're coming from Missouri, start at the end of this section and work your way backwards.

Your journey begins with a spur from Shawneetown to **Old Shawneetown**. Right on the Ohio River, this is the oldest town in Illinois, despite the constant threat of flooding and the shrinking of the town as a result. A massive flood in 1937—the last of a series that decimated the low-lying community—prompted the creation of a new Shawneetown a few miles inland. A few historic attractions remain in the original town, but after all of that flooding, they're in bad shape. The most impressive landmark is a three-story Greek

Revival building with massive columns and the word "BANK" emblazoned above the entrance. Opened in 1841, the **Shawneetown Bank** is the oldest building in Illinois that was constructed specifically as a bank. Despite its status as a state historic site, it's not open to the public—but it's still worth taking a look from the outside.

Old Shawneetown seems like it's landlocked until you climb the stairs to the top of the levee and get a view of the Ohio River. At the base of the earthworks, read the wayside exhibits detailing visits by Lewis and Clark, who are represented here by cutouts. The explorers stopped by in 1803 with about twenty men to stock up on salt for their epic journey. Before you head back to the main route, swing by the **John Marshall House Museum**. In the 1970s, the building was reconstructed to its '30s-era configuration using the original bricks from 1808. The home was the location of the first bank chartered in Illinois and is listed on the National Registry of Historic Places because of its archaeological significance.

From Shawneetown, drive into the **Shawnee National Forest** and the **Garden of the Gods Recreation Area**. You'll want to get out your hiking gear and maybe even set up camp; this is one of the most beautiful places in the state. If you don't have time to stick around and you just want a quick gander at Anvil Rock, Camel Rock, Table Rock, and other hoodoos and sandstone formations, there's a quick quarter-mile trail to a lookout. fs.usda.gov/shawnee

Another unique geological site is Cave-in-Rock, about a half-hour drive from Garden of the Gods. Thousands of years ago, the Ohio River carved a fifty-five-foot-wide cave out of the bluff, which made a perfect hideout for pirates, fugitives, and other ne'er-do-wells in the late 1800s. Today, it's the centerpiece of **Cave-in-Rock State Park** and lends its name to the nearby town. The cave is accessed from a trail of stairs down to the riverbank from the park's main parking lot. All Illinois state parks are free, so it's easy to visit. If you're hankering to set foot in Kentucky, head into town and board the **Cave-in-Rock Ferry**, which is also free, and it will take you across the Ohio River. www2.illinois.gov/dnr

Nearby **Elizabethtown**, like many early settlements, started with a tavern. In 1809, James McFarland moved to the area. Three years later, he built a tavern and named the town that sprung up around it after his wife. That tavern became the **Rose Hotel**, which today operates as a bed and breakfast. It's been listed on the National Register of Historic Places since 1972. From the hotel's veranda overlooking the Ohio River, you can see **E-Town Restaurant**, a barge turned floating restaurant that's known for its fresh catfish. facebook.com/VillageofElizabethtown

After you've left E-town, as it's called by the locals (and not just the restaurant), take a spur on IL-34 to see **Rosiclare**. Originally called Pell's Landing after its first official European settler, William Pell, the riverfront community became a mining hotbed when Pell discovered hefty deposits of the mineral fluorspar, also known as fluorite. You can learn about the state's official mineral at the **American Fluorite Museum** in town. Fun fact: fluorescence is named for the mineral fluorite, which was found to emit blue light. cityofrosiclare.com

Most of Golconda is designated as the **Golconda Historic District**. There are several buildings from the 1800s, including the 1872 **Pope County Courthouse**. Look for a large stone monument on the north side of the square, which honors Sarah Lusk, the "brave pioneer woman" who was the founder of the town and the operator of the first ferry across the Ohio in this location. Also in the historic district is the **Buel House**, which was built in 1840 and owned by the same family until 1986. mainstreetgolconda.org

Before you get back on the Ohio River Scenic Byway, it's worth taking a side trip on IL-146 to **Dixon Springs State Park**. Formerly a Native American camping grounds, then a reservation, the land was settled in 1848 by William Dixon. Because of its mineral-enriched waters, it gained popularity as a health spa. Today, visitors hike and spot unique birds amid impressive rock formations. www2.illinois.gov/dnr

The route to the park is part of the **Trail of Tears**, so called because between 1837 and 1839, Golconda was the crossing point for thousands of Cherokees during their removal from their native lands—a harrowing journey that many Native Americans did not survive. To get back to the byway, look for Trail of Tears Road across from Dixon Springs State Park and you'll be driving a portion of their original route.

Another spur, right in the southeast pocket of the state, leads to **Kincaid Mounds State Historic Site**. The earthen mounds here are the remains of an agricultural society that farmed the Ohio River Valley from around AD 1050 to 1400. University of Chicago archaeologists excavated the mounds between 1934 and 1944, and their methods set standards for future archaeological studies. You can't walk the grounds, but there is a raised platform with information kiosks. kincaidmounds.com

Back on the Byway, entering **Metropolis**, your first stop should be **Fort Massac State Park**. There's a replica of an 1802 fort and the Visitor Center highlights the region's history, including the lives of the original inhabitants; the French fort built in 1757; and the 1778 trail of Colonel George Rogers Clark, which was followed by his younger brother William Clark and his pal Meriwether Lewis in 1803. Recreational opportunities include hiking, boating, fishing, camping, and picnicking. When you leave the park, look to your left and you'll see **Big John**, a well-preserved fiberglass giant welcoming you to the grocery store of the same name. And in a town named Metropolis, of course there's a Superman! Get your photo with the Man of Steel in **Superman Square** before getting back on the road. metropolistourism.com

Thirty-five miles east along the byway from Metropolis, just beyond Mound City, is a Civil War–era burial ground. Established in 1864, the **Mound City National Cemetery** began as an internment spot for wounded soldiers who died in the nearby hospital, and honors both Union and Confederate soldiers. There are 8,262 soldiers buried in the cemetery, 2,759 of whom are unknown. cem.va.gov/cems

Your last stop on the Ohio River Scenic Byway is **Cairo**. Once a thriving steamboat port and a strategic location during the Civil War, this southernmost city in Illinois suffered economic and population declines as the ferry business went away with the advent of the railroad and automobile. You can see some of the early riches in historic mansions **Magnolia Manor** and **Riverlore**, which sit across the street from one another in Cairo's Historic Park District. The **Custom House Museum** showcases artifacts from the town's marine and military past. South of Cairo is Fort Defiance Park. This former military fortification, located at the confluence of the Mississippi and Ohio Rivers, is as far south as you can go in Illinois.

Following the Ohio River Scenic Byway is more than a pretty drive. It's a look into events that shaped both the state of Illinois and the nation.

Great River Road

For 550 miles, the Great River Road follows the contours of Illinois's western border. From Cairo at the southernmost tip of the state, to East Dubuque at the northern end, this scenic byway captures the romance of the magnificent Mississippi River and the history of the towns that sprung up along its shores. As you drive, you'll encounter the National Road and Route 66, both featured in this chapter, as well as the Lincoln Highway. The western end of the Ohio River Scenic Byway is Cairo, so that's where we'll begin our exploration.

To navigate when you drive this epic byway, look for signs displaying a pilot wheel with a steamboat in the center.

This itinerary begins at the Missouri border. If you're coming from Iowa or Wisconsin, start at the end of this section and work your way backwards.

At 279 feet above sea level, **Fort Defiance Park** is the lowest point in Illinois. This land at the confluence of the Ohio and Mississippi Rivers was originally the site of **Camp Defiance**, a strategic location for the Union Army during the Civil War. The park is not well maintained, but seeing the two rivers converge makes a visit worth it. As you drive through Cairo, stop at the **Custom House Museum** to get some insight into why this area was so important.

Your next stop will be in **Thebes**. The southern third of Illinois is known as Little Egypt and, like Cairo, this town was named for its Egyptian counterpart. Thebes was the county seat from 1846 until 1859, and the **Thebes Courthouse** has overlooked the Mississippi River since 1848. The sandstone building, added to the National Register of Historic Places in 1972, is the home of the Thebes Historical Society; visitors can see one of the mid-nineteenth-century courtrooms where Lincoln practiced law. The building's wayside exhibit claims that Dred Scott—a slave whose lawsuit for freedom lasted a decade and became a landmark US court ruling— was "imprisoned here in the dungeons" during his fight for freedom. thebescourthouse.com

Don't be surprised if you start craving spinach as you near **Chester**. The creator of Popeye, Elzie Crisler Segar, was born in this town and based many of his characters, including the "Sailor Man," on people he met during his childhood. See a bronze statue of Popeye at the **Elzie C. Segar Memorial Park**, and look for Wimpy, Olive Oyl, Bluto, and others throughout the town. chesterill.com

Take a quick detour over the Mississippi at the Chester Bridge to visit the **Kaskaskia Bell State Historic Site**. When the bell was cast in 1741 by King Louis XV of France, Kaskaskia was on the east side of the Mississippi River, but flooding caused the river to shift in the late 1800s, eventually making Kaskaskia the only Illinois town west of Old Muddy. The town was the capital of the Illinois Territory from 1808 to 1819, and was briefly the original capital of Illinois state before the center of government moved to Vandalia. www2.illinois.gov/dnrhistoric

Back on the east side of the river is the **Fort Kaskaskia State Historic Site**. Built around 1759 by the French, it became an important stop for George Rogers Clark during the Revolutionary War. Today, only earthworks remain of the fort itself, but there's an overlook and picnic site, a large campground, and Garrison Hill Cemetery, which contains the remains of many of Kaskaskia's early settlers. www2.illinois.gov/dnrhistoric

Continue your French Colonial history lessons at **Fort de Chartres State Historic Site**. The site was the location of four successive French forts and is four miles west of Prairie du Rocher. The National Historic Landmark is a recon- struction of portions of the last fort and contains a restored powder magazine, believed to be the oldest building in Illinois, according to the official website. fortdechartres.us

Farther north in what is now **Collinsville**, Illinois, is what was once the largest city in North America. **Cahokia Mounds State Historic Site** is the location of a pre-Columbian city that covered six square miles. Seventy of the site's more than 120 man-made earthen mounds remain, including the largest in the Americas. Occupied from around AD 700–1350, historians estimate that the peak population here was approximately twenty thousand—about the same as London at the time. By the time the French arrived in the 1600s, the people who had built the massive mounds were gone, but the Cahokia tribe had taken up residence. Today, Cahokia Mounds is a UNESCO World Heritage Site with an impressive interpretive center that tells the story of the original inhabitants and those who followed. If you've driven the National Road, you've probably already visited, since US 40 cuts right through the site. cahokiamounds.org

Lewis and Clark buffs will love the next three destinations. The **Lewis and Clark State Historic Site** is located where the Mississippi and the Missouri Rivers meet, at Hartford, Illinois. The park commemorates Camp Dubois, also called Camp River Dubois, where the explorers mustered and trained in the winter of 1803–1804 before their search for a western passage. The site possesses both a replica of their fort and a fourteen-thousand-square-foot exhibit space. campdubois.com

Just one mile north on the Great River Road, you can't miss **Confluence Tower**. Visitors can take elevators to the top for views of the meeting of the rivers from 50, 100, and 150 feet. confluencetower.com

About three miles north of the tower is another **Camp Dubois**. This smaller site also has a replica of the Lewis and Clark fort, and volunteers occasionally turn it into a living history museum with reenactments of life at the camp.

Following the Mississippi, you'll reach the **National Great Rivers Museum** at **Melvin Price Locks and Dam**—the place to visit for an in-depth look at the Mississippi River. A US Army Corps of Engineers site, the museum covers everything from the river's geological and cultural history to its status as a transportation thoroughfare. Inside are interactive exhibits, and outside you can see how the mighty river is harnessed and watch barges make their way through the locks. mvs.usace.army.mil

One of the most significant stops on the Underground Railroad was **Alton**. Its location on the Mississippi just upriver from St. Louis made it a crossing point from a slave state into a free state. Visit the **Lyman Trumbull House**, a National Historic Landmark, to honor the man who co-authored the Thirteenth Amendment, abolishing slavery. Also in town is the **Elijah P. Lovejoy Monument**, which commemorates one of the nation's most prominent and vocal abolitionists; the publisher was murdered by a pro-slavery mob while he tried to protect his printing press. It's the tallest monument in the state, but another monument in Alton that'll make you look up is the **Robert Wadlow Statue**. Wadlow was the tallest man in history of the world, and the 8-foot, 11.1-inch statue is life-size. cityofaltonil.com

With its nineteenth-century stone homes along narrow streets overlooking the Mississippi River, picturesque **Elsah** is the definition of charming. The entire village is on the National Register of Historic Places, and was voted the top scenic spot in Illinois in the Illinois Top 200 project. Stop at the **Village of Elsah Museum** inside the Village Hall for a look at this river town's past. escapetoelsah.com

Grafton is situated where the Illinois River drains into the Mississippi, and it's got the feeling of a riverboat town. Summer visitors can take advantage of the **zipline** and nearby **Pere Marquette State Park**, and winter guests will marvel at the plethora of eagles that winter in the area. It's also a great place to stop for a bite or a drink, with multiple restaurants and wineries. Dine right on the river at **Grafton Oyster Bar** or **The Loading Dock**, and sip on wine or beer with a view at **Grafton Winery and Brewhaus**. graftonlodging.com

About forty minutes up the road, take a nature break at the **McCully Heritage Project**. This nonprofit is a 940-acre nature preserve with trails for hiking, biking, and horseback riding. See turtles poke their heads out of their shells, throw a line into the two ponds, pitch a tent at one of the primitive campsites, and have a picnic in the pavilion. There's also a nineteenth-century log cabin. Since it's a nonprofit, bring some cash to drop into the donation box, or donate some money online. mccullyheritage.org

Aspiring archaeologists will want to stop in nearby **Kampsville** for a visit to the **Center for American Archeology Museum**. After that, drive directly west back to the Mississippi, head north for an hour, and you'll end up in

Hannibal, Missouri, the childhood home of Samuel Clemens (better known as Mark Twain). caa-archeology.org

Back in Illinois, allow some time in **Quincy**, because there's a lot to see in one of America's Most Artistic Towns, according to Expedia. Begin at **Villa Kathrine**, a Moorish mansion that's not just beautiful, it's also the home of the **Quincy Area Convention and Visitors Bureau**. The villa has overlooked the river since the early 1900s. Inside is a harem, courtyard, and a reflecting pool, and tours are offered by appointment. Within the town are four different National Historic Districts, as well as several museums. The **Eells House** honors prominent abolitionist Dr. Richard Eells, the **John Wood Mansion** was the home of the city's founder and the state's twelfth governor, and the **Quincy Museum** shows visitors how the movers and shakers of 1890 lived. seequincy.com

Take the spur in **Warsaw** to visit the **Fort Edwards State Memorial**. The monument is an obelisk that overlooks three states: Illinois, Missouri, and Iowa. The memorial was erected in 1914 to commemorate the construction of the fort a century earlier, although the fort wasn't actually built until 1816–17, so the timing was a little off. warsawillinois.org

The stretch of Great River Road between Warsaw and **Nauvoo** is one of the most beautiful parts of this drive. The road hugs the river, and it's one of the Mississippi's narrower stretches, so you can practically wave to Iowans. The **Historic Nauvoo Visitors Center**, a National Historic Landmark; and the **Joseph Smith Historic Site** celebrate the Mormon pioneers who bought the town of Commerce in 1839. They renamed it Nauvoo the next year, and by 1844, the population had swelled to twelve thousand. The town's success was short-lived and tensions increased with neighboring communities as well as within. After Joseph Smith—founder of the Latter-day Saints—destroyed a newspaper that denounced both polygamy and his leadership, he and his brother Hyrum were arrested for inciting a riot. While the two awaited trial in Carthage, they were murdered by the townspeople. Less than two years later, Brigham Young led the Mormons west. You can stay near the historic attractions at **Hotel Nauvoo**, located in an 1841 residence, and visit **Baxter's Vineyards**, the oldest winery in Illinois. beautifulnauvoo.com

The **Quad Cities** (actually five cities, not four) straddle the Mississippi River, and comprise Davenport and Bettendorf in Iowa; and Rock Island, Moline, and East Moline in Illinois. If you are near this area in the evening, stop at **Rock Island**'s aptly named **Sunset Park**. Also in Rock Island is **Black Hawk State Historic Site** where, in addition to enjoying hiking trails, visitors can view exhibits at the **Hauberg Indian Museum** that tell the history of the Sauk and Meskwaki peoples. Also on site is the **Refectory**, which highlights the Civilian Conservation Corps, the group that created the hiking trails and much of the Watchtower Lodge, as well as planted many of the trees that shade the park today. To the north of town, on Arsenal Island, is the **Rock Island Arsenal Museum**—the second oldest Army museum after West Point. The nearby Mississippi River Visitor Center, also on the island, gives spectators an excellent view of **Lock and Dam 15**. In **Moline**, see the history of farm machinery at the **John Deere Pavilion**. visitquadcities.com

Thirteen miles north, take time for a quick photo op in **Port Byron** with **Will B. Rolling**, a thirty-foot cyclist atop a penny-farthing bicycle. portbyronil.com

Speaking of bikes: if you brought yours with you, take a spin with a side of archaeology at **Albany Mounds State Historic Site**, twenty minutes past Port Byron. The site was the location of a large Native American community around two thousand years ago, who buried their dead in earthen mounds. Despite the loss of several mounds due to farming, construction, and excavation, this location remains the biggest Hopewell culture mound group in Illinois. albanymounds.com

You can't miss the Dutch heritage in **Fulton**: the town has its own authentic windmill. Built in the Netherlands expressly for Fulton and dedicated in 2000, **de Immigrant Windmill** overlooks the Mississippi atop a berm on the flood control dike. It's a working mill and visitors can buy stone-ground flour in its gift shop. As you drive around town, you'll see signs for Lincoln Highway, which passes through Fulton on its east–west journey across the United States. North of town, **Lock and Dam 13** has an observation deck, picnic tables, and a boat ramp. cityoffulton.us

With more than 240,000 acres in four states over 261 miles, the **Upper Mississippi River National Wildlife and Fish Refuge** is a sprawling habitat for birds, fish, and other animals. You can see a portion of this Global Important Bird Area on the next leg of your Great River Road trek, north of Ayers and south of Savanna. Its location within the Mississippi Flyway, a migratory corridor for waterfowl and shorebirds, makes it a birding hot spot. Fishing is allowed and there are canoe access points. fws.gov

If you're traveling during summer and in need of a frosty treat, stop at **Shivers Ice Cream Shoppe** in **Savanna**. You can't miss it: there's a pair of giant double-scoop waffle cones right on Main Street. savanna-il.us

Work off your dairy indulgence with a hike in **Mississippi Palisades State Park**. You're now in the Driftless Area, a rocky terrain of bluffs and ravines that the glaciers missed. The 2,500-acre park has fifteen miles of trails and is a National Natural Landmark. If you're short on time (or energy), there are easily accessible lookout points. www2.illinois.gov/dnr

As you continue north, keep an eye out for **Blackjack Road**. This Great River Road Spur is a fun drive, with two lanes winding and curving through the hilly landscape to some of the region's most scenic spots. **Chestnut Mountain Resort** is a playground overlooking the Mississippi with ziplines, segway tours, a river cruise and an alpine slide. In the winter, it's known for skiing and snowboarding, and has almost twenty ski runs. The inn has on-site restaurants, an indoor pool, and a sauna, among other amenities. chestnutmtn.com

A little farther up Blackjack is the more intimate **Goldmoor Inn**, a romantic bed and breakfast that's known for its fine dining and amazing sunset views over the Mississippi. goldmoor.com

A short detour leads to **Casper Bluff Land and Water Reserve**, which protects the Aiken Mound Group, a collection of fifty-one mounds dating back to AD 700, including the last known remaining thunderbird effigy in Illinois. Near Galena, you can see for fifty miles on a clear day from **Horseshoe Mound Preserve**. It's located four hundred feet above the Mississippi, providing views of Galena just a few miles away, as well as Iowa and Wisconsin. jdcf.org

A word of caution before you enter **Galena**: you may never want to leave. As you pass stately mansions and enter downtown through open floodgates. Those floodgates were once a necessity, but now serve as a look into the town's past. (as long as there's no threat of flood at the time), you'll see why it's considered one of the most charming towns in America. Main Street is filled with great restaurants, unique boutiques, and historic buildings. You can tour the **1826 Dowling House** and stay in the **1855 DeSoto House Hotel**, Illinois's oldest operating hotel. There are multiple wineries in the area—several with downtown tasting rooms—and **Galena Brewing Company** serves up craft beer. Across the Galena River, you'll see Grant Park and, just down the street, the mansion for which it's named. Ulysses S. Grant was from Galena, and after he returned from the Civil War, the town gave him a home. The **Ulysses S. Grant Home State Historic Site** is a National Historic Landmark and is open to visitors. It's part of the **Galena Historic District**, which has more than one thousand contributing properties. Before resuming your journey, head east on US 20 for a stop at **Blaum Bros. Distilling Co.**, then go a little farther for a few rounds of golf, a pontoon ride on Lake Galena, and some farm-to-table dining at **Eagle Ridge Resort & Spa**. visitgalena.org

The northernmost town on the Great River Road in Illinois is East Dubuque. The toughest part about reaching this community is deciding whether you want to continue west across the Mississippi into Iowa, or if you want to go north into Wisconsin—each state has its own section of the Great River Road. Iowa and Wisconsin are both included in this book, so you can read about what you can expect to see before making your decision. Or, choose to see it all! They don't call this scenic route "great" for nothing.

Theresa L. Goodrich is an Emmy-winning author and the force behind thelocaltourist.com, a site dedicated to telling in-depth stories of magnificent, quirky, and unique places. A passionate member of the Midwest Travel Network, Theresa is slightly obsessed with writing, road trips, camping, and history. She's turned these interests into the Two Lane Gems book series, first-person travelogues highlighting the beauty and diversity of the United States.

In 2020, she published Living Landmarks of Chicago, *a non-traditional guidebook featuring fifty of the Windy City's historic landmarks. She's driven, often literally, to inspire you to get off the interstates and explore the towns and communities that make this country, and especially the Midwest region, a constant and welcome surprise.*

Learn more about Theresa at theresalgoodrich.com and follow her on social media @thelocaltourist.

INDIANA

I ndiana is a flourishing Midwest state that was founded in 1816. It is known to many as "The Hoosier State," and houses roughly 6.85 million people. There is a lot to discover in this beautiful state, which is recognized for its state parks, gigantic tenderloins, Hoosier hospitality, the Indy 500, a fantastic state fair, lakes, caverns, trails, and rich history.

I was born and raised in Indiana, the Hoosier state. I've grown to love everything here, from the cornfields to the State Capitol. Indiana is full of beauty, from our ample state parks, hiking, and nature, to our bustling college towns and inviting metropolitan areas.

Whether you are on the hunt for waterfalls, tenderloins, sugar cream pie, fossils, caves, or even murals, you can find it in Indiana. The highways and byways of this state lead to treasures and trails full of adventure and exploring—with plenty of good eats and local favorites along the way.

Ready to eat a tenderloin bigger than your face? How about stomping through some creeks to find fossils? Maybe tour a historical figure's birthplace? Or explore caves and caverns? An Indiana road trip brings these adventures, and much more. But perhaps the best incentive to take a road trip through Indiana is the "Hoosier hospitality" that local business owners display, which contributes to the state's tourism brand: "Honest-to-Goodness Indiana."

We'll explore the Historic National Road, American's first and most crucial highway. I'll introduce you to small towns with significant experiences and friendly communities. Up in northern Indiana, we'll dip our toes into Lake Michigan and explore Amish country. And of course, no road trip in Indiana is complete without venturing through the historic south.

I suggest checking the local counties and businesses for policies that may affect hours and access to all road trips.

Basic Indiana Facts:
- The state capital of Indiana is Indianapolis.
- Indiana's motto is "The Crossroads of America."
- Indiana's state bird is the cardinal.
- Indiana's state flower is the peony.
- There are eleven Indiana highways and byways to explore.

Fun Indiana Facts
- It was a hot summer in 1816 when forty-three delegates to Indiana's first constitutional convention worked together to form Indiana's constitution. It was so hot that they wrote the law outside, under the shade of an elm tree. That elm tree is known as the "Constitution Elm," and is located off of Indiana's Ohio River Scenic Byway.
- Indiana is known for basketball; however, the first professional league baseball game took place in Fort Wayne, Indiana, in 1871.
- It's no secret that Indiana is full of cornfields—it produces more than 20 percent of the US popcorn supply! Popcorn king Orville Reden-bacher grew up in Brazil, Indiana.
- The first US city to ever use streetlights was Wabash, Indiana, in 1880.

Indiana's Historic National Road (US Highway 40)

The Historic National Road is America's first national highway. In the early 1800s, it became a critical road for pioneers, and hundreds of wagons journeyed across it daily. The pioneers started settling into towns and building businesses, eventually earning this route the name "The Main Street of America." In Indiana, the Historic National Road is known as US Highway 40, and is sometimes also referred to as US Route 40.

Starting in 1811, it took more than twenty years to complete the National Road, which began in Maryland and ended in Illinois. In the 1920s, the route became known as US Highway 40, and in 2002, it was designated the Historic National Road. The highway travels across much of the United States and crosses through Indiana, connecting Ohio to Illinois. From the east, the highway enters Indiana from Ohio, and travels west to Indianapolis and Terre Haute before entering Illinois.

The entire Indiana Historic National Road is 144 miles in length. For this road trip, we'll venture through my favorite section: the seventy-two miles from Richmond to Indianapolis. We start at the Old National Road Welcome Center in Richmond, Indiana, and end at the Indiana State Museum in Indianapolis, Indiana. This drive travels through small towns, the countryside, and Indiana's state capital. I would recommend two to three days for this road trip in order to see everything.

Travel tip: If you'd like to take this road trip further, you can continue the Historic National Road through Indiana, Ohio, and Illinois.

We begin this road trip in **Richmond**, Indiana, a town known for its pre–Civil War history and its biking trails, and for being home to one of many of Indiana's waterfalls. At the **Old National Road Welcome Center**, you can pick up a free copy of the Richmond–Wayne County Visitors Magazine in the twenty-four-hour foyer. The center also has a gift shop with items from local artists. visitrichmond.org

If you are interested in camping or a cabin stay, the **Natural Springs Resort**, just across the border in **New Paris**, Ohio, is less than three miles from the Old National Welcome Center. In addition to modern cabins and a freshwater lake, the resort also has a beach, a swimming pool, and a general store; and offers fishing, kayaking, and scuba diving. The inflatable obstacle course on the lake and golf cart rentals will make your stay even more fun and accessible. naturalspringsresort.com

Food and history enthusiasts will want to stop at Richmond's **Historic District Depot** for local restaurants, entertainment, and flair. Four blocks make up the District Depot, which is packed with historic landmarks dating back to the 1860s, murals, antique shops, galleries, live music venues, and pubs. richmonddepotdistrict.com

Downtown Richmond has plenty to do, see, and eat. Grab some drinks at **Roscoe's Coffee Bar and Tap Room**; they've got a great Nitro Cold Brew or lattes made with organic, fair-trade beans. With custom drink flavors like Horchata, Nutty Professor, Zebra Cake, Iron Man, and Butterbeer, you can't go wrong. Roscoe's also has a full food menu with sandwiches, salad, and breakfast offerings. The **Tin Lizzie Cafe** has been voted Best Hospitality and Best Lunch in Wayne County. The eatery is located in one of the oldest buildings in downtown Richmond, and serves sandwiches, wraps, and comfort foods. They have daily specials, as well. Check out the Humphrey Bogart and Marilyn Monroe murals on the interior walls of the cafe while you're there—two of several murals that are located downtown. roscoescoffee.com; thetinlizziecafe.com

Ullery's Homemade Ice Cream makes real, handcrafted ice cream in its downtown Richmond shop. This family-owned creamery was featured on the Food Network show *Carnival Eats*, after gaining attention for its limited-edition "Burst of Freedom" sundae—red, white, and blue ice cream with popping candy, served in a waffle bowl. The store offers cones, sundaes, affogatos, root beer floats, hand-dipped milkshakes, malts, and old-fashioned sodas. ullerys.com

The **Cardinal Greenway**, Indiana's largest rail-trail, runs through Richmond and connects to the Whitewater Gorge Trail and the White River Greenway. **Thistlewaite Falls**, a beautiful man-made waterfall, can be accessed from the trail. The falls were created in 1954 by a man named Timothy Thistlethwaite, who dammed the river, creating the waterfall, and built mills at the site. Although the mills no longer remain, you can still find history here—in the form of ancient fossils! Bring an old pair of tennis shoes or water shoes to walk along the river and play in the falls; it's an excellent opportunity to do some creek-stomping and fossil hunting.

Travel tip: After visiting the falls, head back to US Highway 40 by taking the Sim Hodgin Parkway and stop at the White-water River Swinging Bridge on the way. It crosses the river to the Veterans Memorial Park and offers views of the Weir Dam.

Traveling west, you'll hit **Cambridge City**, where you'll find antique shops, cozy eateries, and historic homes. In 1831, the first pioneers arrived in Cambridge City, and the city was platted in 1836. Are you an antique collector, or interested in shopping? **Antique Alley** is part of two antique trails in Wayne County, and is known for being Indiana's best antique shopping experience—and Cambridge City is home to eleven antique stores on the route!

After you've worked up an appetite from shopping, swing by one of Cambridge City's many eateries. For such a small town, there sure are plenty of dining options. You can indulge in baked goods at **King's Cafe & Bakery**, including jumbo cinnamon rolls (baked fresh daily!). The cafe serves breakfast and lunch, and dinner on the weekends. The **No. 9 Grill** also has some great dining options in a lovely environment—the old Rhim's Grocery building, which has been restored and repurposed into a restaurant specializing in steaks, burgers, and salads. kingscafeandbakery.com; no9grill.com

Rest easy and enjoy a good night's sleep at the **Lofts on Main** in Cambridge City. These luxury guest rooms are available for short- and long-term stays, and are located in a renovated 1890s historic building. With 850 square feet of living space, there is plenty of room for two to four people to make themselves at home; there are full kitchen and dining areas, a washer and dryer, and a king bed. theloftsonmain.com

In between Cambridge City and Knightstown, there are a few overnight stay options available as well. The **Newhouse Family Inn** in **Lewisville** was once a 1893 schoolhouse and is now a quaint bed and breakfast. The inn rests on the schoolhouse's original foundation, and has three rooms available for travelers along the Highway 40 route. newhousefamilyinn.com

Next stop: Hoosier basketball and film history! In tiny **Knightstown**, Indiana, sits a gym called the **Hoosier Gym**. It reminds me of my elementary school gym; it's a straightforward structure with a lot of history. In 1985, the movie *Hoosier* was filmed at this very location, and since then, the gym has famously attracted eighty thousand visitors a year. It is generally open to the public six days a week, and admission and tours are free. In Knightstown, the **Block & Brew** is a family-friendly bar and grill with a pub-style menu, including steaks, sandwiches, and their famous fries (they also serve up some delicious fish 'n' chips!). thehoosiergym.com; blockandbrew.com

Heritage, great coffee, good food, and outdoor recreation are all on the list for **Greenfield**, Indiana—just fifteen minutes down the road from Knightstown. After shooting some hoops at the Hoosier Gym, you'll be ready to satisfy your appetite at **The Mug** restaurant. The Mug serves up delicious "farm-to-curb" food, drive-in style! This place gives me all the warm-fuzzy nostalgia of a drive-in restaurant, combined with complete satisfaction for good eats. Pull up and a Mug Hop will greet you and take your order, and bring your food right to your car! There is no need to get out of your vehicle (but you're welcome to use their outdoor seating if you'd prefer). The Mug uses pasture-raised, drug-free meat to create a variety of burgers, sandwiches, and hot dogs. themug.com

Don't forget to grab dessert at **Greenfield Chocolates**, located right along 40 in historic downtown Greenfield. You must try their Giant Sugared Pecan Clusters, made with homemade caramel and high-quality chocolate. You can also grab some artisan truffles, caramel, and toffee while you are visiting. greenfieldchocolates.wordpress.com

If you need a caffeine boost, you're in luck: coffee is plentiful in Greenfield! With two coffee shops right along 40, there is ample coffee and espresso. Stop by the **Greenfield Grind** for handcrafted espresso drinks and coffee or a bite to eat. Explore a little farther north to visit **Hitherto Coffee and Gaming Parlour**, where you can enjoy coffee and browse their excellent selection of tabletop games—or play demo games from their game library. thegreenfieldgrind.com; hithertocoffee.com

While in downtown Greenfield, stop by the **Hancock County Veterans Park**. It's one of the most inviting and loveliest memorial parks I've visited, full of memorials to Hancock County veterans. Be sure to also make a mandatory stop at the **James Whitcomb Riley Boyhood Home and Museum**. This historic home is where the "Hoosier poet" James Whitcomb Riley grew up. The story of the original Little Orphant Annie who Riley immortalized in poetry is also part of this home's history—you can take the tour to learn more! Many unique pieces and heirlooms are on display, and the home has a beautiful garden area in the back. greenfieldin.org

If you are seeking overnight camping and RV spots or cabin rental accommodations, **S&H Campground** is just what you need: a clean and family-friendly campground just west of Greenfield. They have loads of amenities, including a family fun park, cafe and concessions, modern bath facilities, a pool, laundry facilities, a lake, and free hotspots. sandhcampground.com

Coming to the end of our adventure along the eastern side of Indiana's US Highway 40, we continue onward to our final destination: **Indianapolis**. Indianapolis is in the middle of Indiana's Old National Road, and is home to many great restaurants and museums. The **Irvington Historic District** is right along the highway, and is a neighborhood founded by noted abolitionist lawyers Jacob Julian and Sylvester Johnson in the 1870s. Driving through, you will see beautiful historic homes, parks, and streets. irvingtondevelopment.org

Travel tip: US Highway 40 will turn into
Washington Street as you enter Indianapolis.

Wyliepalooza Ice Cream Emporium is a great ice cream stop in Indianapolis, with tons of flavors to choose from, including unique offerings like Exhausted Parent, Fat Elvis, and Snap-O-Lantern. If you can't tell, this is a fun establishment; the owners are a mother-and-daughter team, and the shop is named after the younger daughter. For lunch, swing by the **Rock-Cola 50s Cafe** for an authentic 1950s diner experience. This diner is known for its authentic rock 'n' roll atmosphere, Choc-Ola soda, and giant grilled tenderloin sandwiches. wyliepalooza.com; rockcolacafe.com

The historic **Steer-In Diner**, established in 1960, is a good option for lunch or dinner. This landmark drive-in diner is known for its original recipes and was featured on Food Network's *Diners, Drive-ins, and Dives* in 2011. If you are interested in pizza, you can't go wrong with **Jockamo Upper Crust Pizza**, a family-owned pizzeria serving pizza made from scratch (and, incidentally, where the idea for Wyliepalooza Ice Cream Emporium was hatched). steerin.net; jockamopizza.com

Lastly, we head to downtown Indianapolis, passing by the Bankers Life Fieldhouse indoor arena, and the Soldiers and Sailors Monument—an Indiana icon on Monument Circle. East of here is **White River State Park**, where you'll find a number of attractions, including **Indiana State Museum** and its next-door neighbor, the **Eiteljorg Museum**. The Eiteljorg is an Native American and Western Art Museum that I definitely recommend checking out, and the Indiana State Museum is a must-see part of Indiana history. I wish that all Indiana road trips could begin or end here, at the museum that showcases Hoosier history through exhibits, hands-on experiences, and stories. Before leaving the museum, take a walk along the White Water River, or enjoy a picnic in one of the park's lovely green spaces. indianamuseum.org; eiteljorg.org; whiteriverstatepark.org

If you're looking for a place to spend the night in Indianapolis, the **Crowne Plaza Indianapolis** is a unique hotel experience. What makes the Crowne Plaza so interesting is that the hotel is built inside the historic Union Station, built in 1888, and much of the original structure is still visible. The hotel is known for its impressive structures, most notably the station's Grand Hall, where you can still see remnants from WWI. Hotel rooms sit among iron beams and original stained glass—some are even 1920s Pullman train cars that still stand in the middle of the hotel. There aren't many places where you can spend the night in a real train car on the original tracks of a historic train station! crowneplazaindydowntown.com

The Indiana Lincoln Highway Byway

Named after the sixteenth US president, the original Lincoln Highway was conceived by Carl G. Fisher (who also helped cofound the Indianapolis Motor Speedway) to allow coast-to-coast transportation, including a section across northern Indiana. The highway was the country's first paved transcontinental route, and it connected New York to San Francisco. In 2011, the Indiana section of the highway was designated a byway, leading to its current rhyming descriptor: the Indiana Lincoln Highway Byway. This byway has two routes: the older route travels from Fort Wayne to Goshen, on to South Bend, and then across the state to northwest Indiana; the new, shorter route travels from Fort Wayne to Warsaw, Plymouth, and finishes in the same place as the longer option. For this road trip, we will be moving along the older course and adding a detour to Lake Michigan.

The Indiana Lincoln Highway Byway is just over 120 miles in length, and traverses farmlands and bustling cities, including South Bend, as well as visiting the beach. I would recommend three to four days for this road trip in order to see a good amount of everything it has to offer.

Travel tip: If you'd like to take this road trip even further, you can continue on the Lincoln Highway Byway through Ohio and Illinois.

We start near downtown **Fort Wayne** with a visit to the **Historic Old Fort**. The original fort was constructed by American troops in 1815 to defend against Native American uprisings, but was abandoned only three years later; in 1976, a reconstruction of the historic fort was erected at a site only a quarter mile from the original. The fort is open for walk-throughs, but the interiors are closed to visitors; admission is free. **Promenade Park** is just across the St. Marys River, and is one of Fort Wayne's newest and most interactive parks. The park features a café, kids' canal, riverboat rides, an amphitheater, swings, playground, walking trails, and kayak rentals. fortwayneparks.org

Fort Wayne has many great museums that I recommend checking out if time allows. If you're traveling with kids, **Science Central** is a great stop that enables kids to explore, learn, and have hands-on experiences in a science-based environment. The **Fort Wayne Museum of Art** is another great attraction, featuring American art from the nineteenth century to today, with a focus on exhibits that promote the diversity of artists and their artworks. sciencecentral.org; fwmoa.org

Don Hall's Old Gas House is an excellent stop for lunch or dinner, and is known for great burgers, steaks, and seafood. The Old Gas House is a long-standing Fort Wayne restaurant, having served the community for more than sixty years. The restaurant is located along the St. Marys River, in a building that was originally a nineteenth-century gas plant. If you want a more casual dining experience, **Fort Wayne's Famous Coney Island** has the best Coney dogs—ask one of the folks who eat the one million or so hot dogs that are sold here each year—and has been around since 1914! donhalls.com; fortwaynesfamousconeyisland.com

After hanging out in downtown Fort Wayne, we'll make our way back to the Historic Lincoln Highway Byway by taking US Route 33 north towards **Churubusco**. You'll notice something pretty quickly about this place: there are turtle sculptures scattered all around town. There is even a festival in Churubusco every June called Turtle Days. But why? Well, in the late 1800s, several people claimed to have seen an enormous turtle living on a farm in Churubusco. Those sightings led curious sightseers, anxious to get a glimpse of this gigantic turtle, to pass by the property and prompted a frenzy among the media and the townspeople. Although the turtle's existence was never proven, it was nicknamed "Oscar"—after the original owner of the farm, who first claimed to have seen the creature—and is now the city's mascot!

While you're passing through Churubusco, stop by the **Magic Wand Restaurant** for ice cream or a Magic Burger. This establishment is a small-town diner that has been in operation since 1964, and its vintage look and atmosphere will have you believing you've stepped back in time to a local diner from a different era. buscomagicwand.com

The next stop is the **Kimmell House Inn** in **Kimmell**, Indiana—a great place to rest, relax, and enjoy the elegant tea room (reservations for the Victorian Tea are required). Ready for a night's sleep? The Inn has four cozy guest rooms and serves a full, hot breakfast every morning. The Kimmell House is adorned with antiques and historical pieces, and is listed on the National Register of Historic Homes. kimmellhouseinn.com

After Kimmell, you will continue your northwest drive on US 33 towards Elkhart County. **Ligonier**, Indiana has a Visitor Center near Main Street that was originally a 1920s filling station—stop here for history and local information. You can also find murals, a coffee shop, and the **Ligonier Historical Center** on Main Street in town. The **Grounded Coffee House** is located in the lower level of a downtown building on Main Street. If you are looking for hot coffee, a cold frappe, or some lunch, Grounded Coffee is a great choice, known for its espresso drinks, frozen drinks, paninis, and soups. ligonier-in.org

Goshen, Indiana—the "Maple City"—will be our next stop. Goshen is located in the heart of Amish country, and is known for its famous

Green River drinks (a popular Midwest lime-flavored soft drink), the Old Bag Factory, walking paths, and popular downtown First Fridays events. Goshen's First Fridays are held the first Friday evening of each month with live music, children's activities, food trucks, and events in the downtown section of Goshen. I grew up in Goshen, and it's hard for me to limit the number of things to do here to just a few paragraphs. I'll start with one of my favorites: Mexican food. For terrific Mexican, you'll want to make a stop in Goshen—this town has some of the best in Indiana! **El Camino Real** serves up authentic Mexican food and drinks, including a darn good chimichanga! mycaminoreal.net

*Travel tip: If you'd like to stretch your legs and get some physical activity in, **Fidler Pond** in Goshen is an excellent stop for walking, fishing, and renting kayaks or canoes. It is located right along US 33/Lincoln Highway.*

The **Old Bag Factory** is a great stop for shopping, eating, and taking photos. This beautiful brick building is a sight to behold! Built as the Cosmo Buttermilk Soap Factory in 1896, and then being taken over by the Chase Bag Factory in 1910, this landmark was abandoned in 1982. Only two years later, it was restored to life and over the years has been filled with antique shops, artisans, and eateries. These days, there's also an escape room, an event center, and a pottery shop. Locals and tourists from all around the country are drawn to Goshen to visit the Old Bag Factory. oldbagfactory.com

Downtown Goshen has a lot to offer, with ample food, shopping, and specialty stores. I suggest grabbing a coffee and strolling around downtown to browse; you'll find a specialty popcorn shop, chocolates, trendy boutiques, a bookstore, markets and artisans, a music store, and much more. For shopping energy, **The Electric Brew** serves up freshly roasted coffee, specialty drinks, bakery items, and lunches. Located inside a historic downtown building, it has a cozy vibe that encourages gathering with friends, and families will love the children's play area and ample seating. After grabbing some coffee or food, stop in next door at **Ignition Music Garage**, a vinyl record store and concert venue, to browse a selection of records and CDs, turntables, audio gear, and more. theelectricbrew.com; ignitionmusic.net

For dinner, **Pizzeria Venturi** on the next block over is always a great option with its Neapolitan pizza and delicious desserts, and is named among Yelp's Top 50 Restaurants in Indiana. eatventuri.com

While in **Elkhart County**, take advantage of the **Heritage Trail Audio Driving Tour**. There are few easier ways to include a tour in your road trip than to listen as you drive, as you do with this ninety-mile tour through Elkhart County. You can start the tour in Goshen or Elkhart, Indiana, and discover Amish heritage and historical sites from your vehicle. A free CD or USB and map can be picked up at the **Elkhart County Visitor Center**, or the tour can be downloaded online. visitelkhartcounty.com

Elkhart is known for its railroads, and was an essential connection between the north and the south in the 1800s. Because of this, the town is the perfect place for the family-friendly **National New York Central Railroad Museum**—a preservation site of national railroad history. The small museum is built in an old train station, and its walk-through exhibits showcase train models, displays, cabs, and engines. elkhartindiana.org

Travel tip: The Lincoln Highway changes from US 33 to Old US 20 in Elkhart. Old US 20 takes you into South Bend.

Half an hour from Elkhart, in **South Bend**, grab some breakfast or lunch at the **Yellow Cat Cafe**. It's named after the owners' favorite cat, who lived for twenty-one years on the family farm. They say Yellow Cat Cafe is "a place where you can come and feel at home, a place where everyone knows your name, and a place where laughs and memories are made." A hidden gem with some of the best biscuits and gravy, burgers, and a pie case. For dinner, **Woochi Japanese Fusion and Bar** is a delicious option for sushi and Asian food. As "one of the top 10 fine dining destinations in the Great South Bend region," Woochi is known for its fresh, made-to-order sushi, and melding of Japanese, Chinese, and other Asian dishes. yellowcatcafe.com; notjustsushi.com

Travel tip: South Bend has great restaurants and diners; there are many options along Old US 20 in the Mishawaka and South Bend area.

If you are passing through downtown South Bend in the evening, the **River Lights Plaza** is an impressive sight—a public art display in the form of water and lights. From half an hour before sunset until sunrise, the St. Joseph River lights up. Until midnight, enjoy the interactive light sculptures—you can activate the light through sensors in the sculptures—that create colorful cascades of water. downtownsouthbend.com

The **Studebaker National Museum** is a 55,000-square-foot automobile museum that showcases vehicles related to Studebaker's history, as well as associated industrial artifacts. Famous exhibits, such as the carriage that transported Abraham Lincoln to Ford's Theatre on the night of his assassination, and other presidential carriages, can be found at the Studebaker National Museum. The museum is family-friendly, featuring a Super Service Station interactive play area for children. studebakermuseum.org

If you're staying in the area, a perfect place to rest is the **Oliver Inn** in South Bend. This bed and breakfast provides a luxurious and pampering stay. The historic mansion and beautiful gardens, live piano music, and homemade breakfast are inviting, and the evening refreshments are a bonus. If you are traveling with a family, the Josephine Ford Suite and the Carriage House are both equipped with two bedrooms. oliverinn.com

The next stop is **New Carlisle**, which became a popular city in the 1850s when the South Shore Railroad came to town. Today, the historic downtown, listed on the National Register of Historic Places, offers visitors a glimpse of preserved nineteenth-century mansions, several restaurants, and antique shops. Check out **New Age Baking Company** for the best (and largest) donuts! They also make brownies, cookies, cinnamon rolls, muffins, pies, and pizzas. It's an essential stop to grab some road trip treats. newage-bakingcompany.com

This road trip takes a slight detour off of the National Lincoln Highway and continues on US 20 to **Michigan City**. You'll want to follow Michigan Road into Michigan City instead of continuing east on US 20 toward Illinois. Our road trip will end in Michigan City, a city full of great stays, good eats, a zoo, a lighthouse, and gorgeous views of Lake Michigan.

Are you ready for some beach time? The **Washington Park Beach** is ninety-nine acres of lakefront land, with two miles of Lake Michigan shoreline, and includes a zoo and the **Michigan City Lighthouse**. A marina, concessions, restrooms, shelters, picnic tables, and splash pad are available at this beach park. Bring a volleyball to take advantage of the beach volleyball nets, or poles to do some fishing. It's a great place to take the kids, but note that pets are not allowed. The park is open from 5 a.m. until 9 p.m. daily. emichigancity.com

There are several excellent overnight options in this city to choose from, so I'll be highlighting three specific stays.

Serenity Springs is a great overnight option in Michigan City for couples. Located on eighty-five acres of wooded land, it has the coziest cabins available for a romantic night (or more!). Each cabin is equipped with a sunken whirlpool tub, fireplace, private porch, complimentary bikes, and other recreational options such as horse-drawn carriage rides, fishing, and campfires. serenity-springs.com

The **Brewery Lodge** is a unique and modern experience: a twelve-suite boutique hotel attached to a craft beer and wine bar, on forty wooded acres. In addition to its luxury suites, the Brewery Lodge also has a Supper Club offering brunch and dinner, complimentary breakfast to guests, and special events. Guests can fish on the property's pond, and the lodge is located just down the road from Lake Michigan. brewerylodge.com

The **Bridge Inn** offers family-friendly, private suites. This bright and cheery inn is near an old train bridge on the Lake Michigan waterfront, and is close to the beach, restaurants, and activities. Two-bedroom suites are available for families and large groups, and include a kitchenette. For dining, the **Bridges Waterside Grille** next door is a great outdoor option, offering outdoor, dockside seating, live music, and a nice-sized American and seafood menu. The Bridge Inn is within walking distance of Washington Park Beach and the Michigan City Lighthouse. bridgeinnmc.com; bridgeswatersidegrille.com

If you are looking for more road-tripping adventures, jump on **Michigan's US 12 Heritage Trail**, which runs through Michigan City (check out the Michigan chapter in this book for more details). You can also continue the Lincoln National Highway Byway road trip across the Midwest by following the route west through Illinois, or east through Ohio (check out the Ohio and Illinois chapters for more details). The Indiana Lincoln Highway Byway certainly offers a variety of scenic views, and options to further advance your road trip into the three surrounding states of Ohio, Michigan, and Illinois.

Indiana Highway 7 & 46

I've put together an Indiana Highway 7 & 46 road trip that is not technically a byway, but it is a fabulous road trip option in Indiana. The route is great for all seasons, but is exceptionally beautiful in the fall. The two Indiana state parks on this trip have some of the most beautiful fall foliage displays. If you are interested in nature and good food, this is the road trip for you!

This road trip travels from Madison to Columbus along Highway 7, and then over to Nashville along Highway 46 (these are all towns in Indiana, despite their common names with places in other states). Beginning in Madison, you'll get a glimpse of the Ohio River Scenic Byway and waterfalls at Clifty Falls State Park. In Columbus, you'll find great eats and art culture. The road trip ends in Nashville, where you can explore Brown County State Park, and enjoy antiques, art, inns, and Nashville restaurants. The route is just over seventy miles long, and I would recommend two to three days for this road trip, depending on the number of stops you want to make.

Travel tip: In Madison, your route crosses with the Ohio River Scenic Byway, giving you plenty of road-tripping options in this region.

Clifty Falls State Park in **Madison** is known for its gorgeous waterfalls and hiking trails. There are four waterfalls in the park, and all require hiking except Big Clifty Falls. There is a paved walkway to the viewing point for the Big Clifty Falls, and from there, you can access more rugged trails that lead to the other waterfalls, ravines, rock formations, creeks, and rock stairs.

Be sure to wear comfortable shoes for hiking. Campsites are available to book, and there are plenty of lovely picnic spots in the park. Additionally, the **Clifty Inn**, located inside the park, is an excellent stop for dining or staying overnight. A swimming pool and tennis courts are also located in the park. in.gov/dnr

Downtown Madison is full of boutiques, restaurants, and coffee shops. While you are downtown, check out the ornate 1876 cast-iron Broadway Fountain—it offers a beautiful photo opportunity. For a morning pick-me-up, the **G.H. Coffee Company** has a vast coffee menu—the lattes and mochas come recommended!—as well as gelato, sandwiches, pastries, and artisan pizzas. It has a cozy downtown atmosphere with very affordable prices. Another great option is **Red Pepper Deli Cafe**, located in a 150-year-old building in downtown Madison. It is family-run, and offers a wide array of sandwiches, paninis, salads, soups, and wraps. The sandwiches are made to order and served fresh, either hot or cold. It's a great lunch spot! ghcoffeeco.com; theredpepperdeli.com

There are eight house museums in Madison, including the famous **Lanier Mansion State Historic Site**, an 1844 Greek Revival home and National Historic Landmark. You can tour the mansion and its lovely landscaped gardens. To take in more of Madison's history, go on a walking tour; there are several guided tours, including riverfront, historical, and cultural tours. Madison was also an important link in the **Underground Railroad**, and there are fascinating self-guided tours of the sites where slaves were assisted to freedom. Don't miss **Georgetown**, a neighborhood in Madison across the river from Kentucky, where abolitionists risked their lives to help rescue slaves. visitmadison.org

As you leave Madison and head north on Highway 7 toward Columbus, there are several opportunities to explore nature. Big Oaks National Wildlife Refuge, Guthrie Woods Nature Preserve, Monarch Butterfly Garden, and Muscatatuck Park are great for hiking, scenic views, and picnics along Highway 7. **Big Oaks Wildlife Refuge** has fifty thousand acres of land boasting more than two hundred bird species, forty-six mammal species, and thirty-two caves—there is so much to see! The refuge is open to the public on specific days of the week (check in advance) for fishing, hunting, photography, and wildlife viewing. fws.gov/refuge/big_oaks

Columbus is known for its art and architecture. Throughout the city, there are public art displays and sculptures, and the popular **Miller House and Garden** is a great mid-century modern home with landscaped geometric gardens. More outdoor splendor can be found at the beautifully designed, award-winning **Mill Race Park** in downtown Columbus—a riverfront park known for fishing, picnics, skateboarding, and its amphitheater. The park has two lakes, an observation tower, and a covered bridge, and is lauded for its landscape architecture. columbus.in.us

Don't leave Columbus hungry! There are ample options in the downtown area, including the **Zaharakos Ice Cream Parlor**, named the number one ice cream shop in Indiana by Thrillist.com. The parlor has been open since 1900, and serves homemade sodas, desserts, and ice cream; there are also dining options for lunch and dinner. For coffee, the **Lucabe Coffee Co.** brews its caffeinated drinks using locally sourced beans, and has teas, handcrafted espresso drinks, smoothies, and bakery items available. The cafe has a creative children's play area for kids as well! Indoor and outdoor seating is available. zaharakos.com; lucabecoffeeco.com

ZwanzigZ Pizza and Brewing is a family-friendly establishment that offers a famous lunch menu. The legendary lunch combo here is the best deal in Columbus (a slice of pizza, two breadsticks, dipping sauce and unlimited soda refills for $4.99) and is available on weekdays. This is a great place to take the family or visit with friends, with indoor and outdoor seating available, affordable prices, and a great selection of specialty pizzas. For a more adult environment, visit the **4th Street Bar & Grill**—the local pub where you must be twenty-one or older to dine. The bar has a vast menu that goes above and beyond your average bar food; I recommend the burgers and fish tacos. zwanzigz.com; 4thstreetbar.com

For the ultimate foodie experience, take a detour to **Edinburgh**, just a few miles from Columbus. The **Edinburgh Diner** serves the biggest tenderloin I've ever seen! Legend has it that the tenderloin was first created and became famous in Indiana, but there are claims to its origins all over the

Midwest. Whatever its origin story, Indiana is known for having some of the best tenderloins in the country! The diner itself is a dive, but people come from all over to experience the food. (812) 703-5086

A luxurious stay in Columbus is available at the **Inn at Irwin Gardens**. This historic bed and breakfast has five rooms and suites for overnight stays. The beautiful gardens are open to the public on certain days with limited hours; you'll want to check these times in advance. Reservations are also available for a guided house and garden tour. irwingardens.com

For camping and cabin accommodations, as well as the **Abe Martin Lodge**, head to **Brown County State Park**. Upon leaving Columbus, take Highway 46 west towards Nashville, and you will soon arrive at the entrance of this state park, known for its scenic rolling hills and many trails. One of the highest points in Indiana is located inside the park at Weed Patch Hill, at 1,058 feet in elevation. **The Little Gem Restaurant** is a rustic and whimsical restaurant inside the Abe Martin Lodge, with a buffet and outdoor patio seating offered. All guests staying overnight at the lodge, or in the cabins, will receive wristbands to the indoor aquatic center—which features a zero-entry pool, slide, a lazy river, fountains, and a hot tub. in.gov/dnr

After a day in the park, relax or shop in downtown **Nashville**. This small town is a popular Indiana destination between Columbus and Bloomington, with plenty of things to do. The charming streets are lined with shops, antiques, cafes, and boutiques. You will also notice plenty of art studios and galleries; Nashville is where the Brown County Art Colony was formed, and evidence of the town's artistic heritage is everywhere you look. And, as with all country towns, it's full of home-cooked comfort foods, snacks, and gifts— including an ample amount of kettle corn, fudge, jams, and candies.

The **Story Inn** is Indiana's oldest country inn, offering a unique dining and lodging experience in a preserved nineteenth-century village. The Blue Lady Room is rumored to be "haunted," making it one of the most popular rooms at Story Inn. There are eighteen unique, distraction-free lodging options to choose from, and a restaurant and tavern on the property. The **Brown County Inn** offers lodging in updated rooms, and breakfast, lunch and dinner are served seven days a week in the Harvest Dining Room.

The Cornerstone Inn is another lodging option in Brown County—once a small bed and breakfast, it offers guest rooms, a lodge, a log cabin, an apartment, and a historic home. storyinn.com; browncountyinn.com; cornerstoneinn.com

Hard Truth Hills is a family-friendly restaurant and distillery located on over three hundred acres of wooded property in Nashville. Aside from the great food and drinks, Hard Truth Hills offers live music in an outdoor amphitheater, as well as ATV tours that take guests to tasting spots throughout the forested property. There is also a beautiful outdoor terrace with outdoor games, a fire pit, picnic tables, and lots of seating. Visitors at the property's **Big Woods Restaurant** get picturesque views of the surrounding woods while enjoying campfire-themed favorites, barbecue, burgers, tacos, and flatbreads. hardtruthhills.com

Indiana's Ohio River Scenic Byway

The Ohio River Scenic Byway in Indiana covers just over three hundred miles, and travels east–west between Lawrenceburg and Mount Vernon. This byway primarily uses State Road 56 and State Road 66, and can be accessed from both Ohio and Illinois. It travels across the entire southern part of Indiana, bringing the history of the Underground Railroad and Indiana's first constitution to life. Because of its length and many experiences, we won't be visiting the entire byway for this road trip; instead, we'll start in historic New Albany, and end in Evansville.

The Ohio River was the primary way for pioneers to travel west around the early nineteenth century, and it became the hub of the industrial and transportation revolution. Today, the river lends its name to the winding byway that takes visitors along State Route 66, past historical farms and architecture, scenic views of the Ohio River, and forested hillsides. The byway is rich in history and nature, with stops at caves, Lincoln's boyhood home, Underground Railroad stations, and more.

The route that we're taking is more than 130 miles long, and travels from New Albany to Evansville. I would recommend three to five days for this road trip in order to explore its full itinerary.

Travel tip: This road trip can begin or end close to the Highway 7 & 46 Road Trip that begins in Madison, Indiana (only an hour from New Albany).

We begin our road trip in **New Albany**, a historic southern Indiana city that was an essential part of the Underground Railroad system in the nineteenth century. The **Town Clock Church** in downtown New Albany was an Underground Railroad station during the Civil War. Today, rooms and small openings in the basement remain as they were when freedom seekers hid during their journey north. Don't miss checking out the **Underground Railroad Gardens** in the back of the church—there is a small plaza with public art, a sculpture, and a gazebo (the ceiling is lined with the original clock from the clock tower). townclockchurch.org

Another historical find in New Albany is the **Division Street School**, one of the first elementary schools for African American children. Opened in 1885, the school operated for more than sixty years before Indiana school desegregation began. Now a museum, the school is also used as a history center to teach all local children about segregation and African American history. (812) 786-2019

The **Culbertson Mansion State Historic Site** is one of many historic mansions in New Albany. This twenty-thousand-square-foot mansion was built by renowned philanthropist William Culbertson—once considered the wealthiest man in Indiana—in 1867. The mansion was sold to a historical society for $24,000 in 1964, shortly after which it became an Indiana State Museum. Today, you can tour the beautifully restored home, which is a centerpiece of New Albany's history. indianamuseum.org

Traveling out of New Albany, take State Road 62 to stay on the Ohio River Scenic Byway, and head to **Corydon**. You may want to reserve an entire day or more just for this town—there is a lot to see here! We'll start with its legacy as the first state capital, before it moved to Indianapolis in 1825. The entire downtown area of Corydon is brimming with historical buildings to check out, including the **Corydon Capitol State Historic Site**. Walking tour maps are available at the Blaine H. Wiseman Visitor Center.

After your architectural tour, take a walk to the **Constitution Elm**, located just down the road from the Capitol. In 1816, forty-three delegates to the Constitutional Convention signed Indiana's First Constitution under this elm, and the trunk remains for visitors to view today. indianamuseum.org

While in downtown Corydon, you can grab lunch at **1816 Modern Kitchen & Drinks**, located in a historic Italianate building, built in 1892. This farm-to-fork restaurant specializes in Southern comfort foods and drinks. After lunch, pick up a coffee from **KentJava Bar**. They have flavored lattes and a seasonal Espresso Tonic (espresso with tonic and just a hint of orange), which is my favorite. For something sweet, and a bit on the funny side, head across the street to **Butt Drugs**, where you can enjoy hand-scooped ice creams, old-fashioned sodas, Buttshakes, and other treats. Butt Drugs has been serving Corydon since 1952 as a pharmacy and old-fashioned soda fountain. Be sure to check out their "Buttique" while you're there for some fun gifts and sassy apparel. 1816kitchen.com; kentjavabar.com; buttdrugs.com

Those overnighting in Corydon can stay at the **Kintner House Inn**, an 1873 Italianate brick bed and breakfast. The inn has fifteen guest rooms, each with a private bathroom and full breakfast included. If you are looking to camp, the **O'Bannon Woods State Park** offers a range of campsites. This state park is encompassed by the twenty-six-thousand-acre Harrison–Crawford State Forest. From here, you can visit the Wyandotte Caves, go hiking, and climb the O'Bannon Woods Fire Tower for scenic views of the park and state forests. kintnerhouse.com; in.gov/dnr

Continue traveling along State Road 62 to **Leavenworth**. It's a tiny town, but it has a few gems you'll want to check out. Upon entering the town, there is an Ohio River Scenic Byway roadside stop with information about the region, and a small picnic and playground area. In 1931, the city of Leavenworth was swept away by floods, and afterward the town was rebuilt on top of a bluff.

In 1948, the **Overlook** opened as a cafe and grocery store in Leavenworth. Now, the Overlook is a restaurant that seats up to 160 people, and it's a great place to grab some lunch or dinner. It occupies the top floor of what used to be a chicken hatchery, sitting right on the Ohio River, and offers magnificent views, particularly from the patio that overlooks the river. The restaurant offers various menu options, including house specialties like seafood, steaks, and fried chicken. If you want a more casual dining experience and drinks, you can eat at **Walter's Pub**, which is located in the basement of the Overlook. theoverlook.com

Stephenson's General Store has been in Leavenworth since the early 1900s and serves as a general store, hardware store, and cafe. Need some groceries, a cold drink, maybe some nuts and bolts, or lunch? You'll find that all and more when you step back in time at Stephenson's. (812) 739-4242

*Travel tip: Take a detour to visit **Marengo Caves** in Marengo. Here, you can take a tour of the caves, camp, or rent a cabin.*

The next suggested stop takes a detour from the Ohio River Scenic Byway, but it's worth it for those interested in history . . . or Christmas. Yes, Christmas! **Santa Claus**, Indiana, is a touristy stop for those who love Christmas year-round. It's fun, has a water and amusement park, and is great for anyone traveling with kids. If you'd like to stop overnight, I recommend the **Lincoln Pines Lakefront Resort**, which is between Santa Claus and Lincoln City. Lincoln Pines is a thirty-acre resort with modern cabins, a lake, a splash pad, a game room, and a pool, and it's located near the Lincoln Boyhood National Memorial and Lincoln State Park (RV and camping spots are available). staylincolnpines.com

The Lincoln Boyhood National Memorial is the historic part of this detour. This memorial is where Abraham Lincoln spent his boyhood (from the ages of seven to twenty-one) and where his mother was buried. Admission is free, and guests can visit the Memorial Building and Memorial Court, featuring sculpted panels depicting significant periods in Lincoln's life. Also on the site are the foundation of Lincoln's boyhood cabin, Abe's mother Nancy Lincoln's gravesite, hiking trails, and the Lincoln Living Historical Farm, where rangers portray life as it was in the 1820s, dressing in period clothing and performing activities including arts and crafts, farming and animal husbandry. **Lincoln State Park** is across the street and has RV and camping spots available, as well as a beach and water activities. There are plenty of picnic tables, as well. nps.gov

Jumping back onto the byway and stopping in **Rockport**, you'll find the **Rocky Side Park**. This hidden and narrow park is tucked under a bluff in Rockport, along the Ohio River. You'll first notice a staircase leading up the side of the cliff, which visitors can climb to get a view. It's a bit narrow and rugged, and it's warping with time, so use your discretion for safety. In the park is the Lankford Cave, home to the first settlers of Rockport in 1808. Rocky Side Park is a great spot to picnic, bike, and relax.

Our next stop is **Newburgh**, Indiana. Located just east of Evansville, Newburgh is a destination filled with shopping, restaurants, historical charm, and several annual celebrations. The **Tin Fish Restaurant** is known for its award-winning crab cakes and great seafood. If seafood isn't for you, **Knob Hill Tavern**—Newburgh's oldest—offers an extensive menu of American food, Italian subs, and pizza. tinfishnewburgh.com; knobhilltavern.com

This road trip ends in **Evansville**, but not before taking a day to venture around the city, exploring its sites and eateries. First, head to the downtown arts district (Evansville has five arts districts) and strike a pose with the "Greetings from Evansville" mural in Self.e Alley. Also in the downtown region, admire the many classic Victorian homes, or enjoy one of the six museums. One of those museums, located on the Ohio River, is the **LST-325**, the last fully operational WWII Landing Ship Tank (LST) in the United States. Guided tours of the ship are offered seasonally. lstmemorial.org

Bosse Field is home to the Evansville Otters, but it is also famous for being the filming site for the movie *A League of Their Own* in 1992. Additionally, it is the third-oldest baseball stadium still in use in the United States, after Fenway Park and Wrigley Field! If you arrive during the baseball season, you may want to check the schedule, grab some tickets, and take in a game at this iconic stadium. evansvilleotters.com

If animals are more your thing than baseball, Evansville's **Mesker Park Zoo and Botanic Garden** is a great option. This is Indiana's oldest zoo, which offers hundreds of animals, forty-five scenic acres, a lake, and a botanic garden. Mesker Park Zoo is open every day of the year. meskerparkzoo.com

I highly recommend **Parlor Doughnuts** in Evansville for breakfast, snacks, and coffee options. Parlour makes huge, layered doughnuts that are unique and delicious. Additionally, there are excellent coffee options with beans that are roasted locally at Parlor's flagship location. For lunch, check out the **Bru Burger Bar** in downtown Evansville, which has taken over a former Greyhound Bus Station and turned it into a unique dining experience (don't forget to grab a picture outside the iconic building!). For dinner, I suggest **Cork 'n Cleaver**. This restaurant has been around for more than thirty years, and is a favorite Evansville eatery known for its award-winning salad bar and steaks. parlordoughnuts.com; bruburgerbar.com; evansvillecork.com

For more road trip adventures, continue west on the **Ohio River Scenic Byway** road trip through Illinois, or east along the remainder of Indiana's byway and on to Ohio's Ohio River Scenic Byway.

Jamie Ward is the writer and owner behind the travel and lifestyle blog Cornfields & High Heels. Her love for travel takes her from the west coast to the east coast, north to the south, through tiny towns with cornfields, and bustling cities with skyscrapers. She is a member of the Midwest Travel Network and frequently writes about her Midwest adventures. Jamie resides in the central Indiana area with her husband and children, and enjoys road trips, finding waterfalls, and visiting new coffee shops. She specializes in writing about her home state of Indiana, affordable travel and tips, and destinations for families and couples.

Learn more about Jamie at:
fieldsandheels.com
instagram.com/fieldsandheels
facebook.com/fieldsandheels
twitter.com/fieldsandheels

IOWA

I am thrilled that I have the opportunity to share my home state with you. Together, we will explore these byways, which will inspire you to hop in your car to take a scenic drive. I have found it challenging to choose a favorite route, as I have driven all of these byways and I find something new and beautiful each time I hit the road.

Around every bend in the byways, Iowa has beautiful valleys, cliffs, waterways, and roads that lead to something beautiful. From the flatlands in the North Central part of the state to the rolling hills in the Southwest, Iowa will surprise you. Each season is very distinct in Iowa, giving you the opportunity to drive the scenic highways and byways at any time of year.

Iowa is home to approximately 3.1 million people and produces more corn and eggs than any other state. Iowa also has a diverse economy, with agriculture leading the way.

Basic Iowa Facts
- The state capital is Des Moines.
- The state motto is "Our liberties we prize and our rights we will maintain."
- The state nickname is the Hawkeye State.
- The state flower is the wild rose (or wild prairie rose).
- Iowa is home to eighty-three state parks and recreation areas.
- Fourteen byways cross the state of Iowa, and two are designated as National Scenic Byways.

Fun Iowa Facts
- Sac City is home to the world's largest popcorn ball. It weighs in at 9,370 pounds. Visitors can view this masterpiece on Main Street at the Sac City Museum.

- The last known hotel in the world designed by Frank Lloyd Wright is in Mason City. The Park Inn Hotel hosts guests from all around the world.
- The World's Largest Truck Stop is located along I-80 near Walcott, in eastern Iowa.
- The World's Largest Strawberry stands fifteen feet tall in Strawberry Point.

I hope you will explore Iowa and find things that surprise you. There are hidden gems all across the state that are waiting to be uncovered. So, jump in your car and begin your journey through the wonderful state of Iowa.

The Glacial Trail Scenic Byway

Situated in Northwest Iowa, the Glacial Trail Scenic Byway is a thirty-six-mile loop that is likely to surprise many travelers. Most of Northwest Iowa is relatively flat, but this glacial area proves that there is a little variation in the topography of the state. Stop at the **Prairie Heritage Center** near Peterson to learn about the byway and get a grip on the scenic drive that awaits you. If you're lucky, the bison will be near the Heritage Center—head to the observation tower for a view of the small herd that resides there. You will also find several archaeological sites near the byway, and museums that tell the stories of a place in time that dates back to AD 1000. obriencounty.com

The rolling hills of Iowa come to life as you drive through the valleys and maneuver the road's curves. The best tip that I can give is to experience this route during each of the four seasons because it promises a vibrant show of color for each month on the calendar. The Glacial Trail Scenic Byway is a small loop that sits alone, but it makes an incredible gateway drive to the Loess Hills National Scenic Byway when you travel into Iowa from the northeast.

Loess Hills National Scenic Byway

Situated on the western border of Iowa, the Loess Hills National Scenic Byway covers nearly 200 miles. To me, this is the granddaddy of Scenic

Byways in Iowa. It has something for everyone, including a huge range of majestic views along the route. This beautiful drive begins north of Sioux City, and comes to an end near St. Joseph, Missouri. Let's start our scenic drive north of Sioux City.

This scenic byway alone can easily be built into a week-long road trip, but there are also sixteen scenic loops that branch off of it. Some of these loops are paved, some are not, and whether you explore all of them or none, or something in between, is completely up to you. Weather and the amount of time you have will likely determine how many of these scenic loops you take on your drive.

Hop on Highway 12 near Akron, and you will be on the Loess Hills National Scenic Byway. As you leave town heading south, you will notice hills appearing in the landscape, and the Big Sioux River to the west, across which is South Dakota.

Westfield is Iowa's westernmost city, and it is home to the **Loess Hills Interpretive Center**. This is an excellent place to start your journey, as it is a good place to learn about the topography of the area. You will see the sign to an excursion loop as you head south: the Butcher Road Connection. This loop is four miles of gravel and offers outlooks over the three-thousand-acre **Broken Kettle Grasslands Preserve**—Iowa's largest remaining prairie, and a great place to spot bison. The signage along the byway is prominent, which makes this route easy to navigate. westfieldiowa.com/loess.htm

To the east of Butcher Road is the Ridge Road Loop, which takes you to the **Five Ridge Prairie Reserve**. Here, you will find spectacular views of Iowa and South Dakota, as well as a stunning combination of prairie and woodlands. These two gravel loops are close together, and the panoramic views that they offer are unique to the Loess Hills National Scenic Byway.

Continue south on Highway 12 to **Stone State Park**, on the northwest side of Sioux City. You will see a sign to Stone Park Loop, a three-mile paved loop that runs through Stone State Park. This offers a great opportunity to view the cliffs and valleys of this state park. This state park is known for its beautiful hiking trails, so it's not uncommon for drivers to share part of this byway with a hiker or two. I have personally recently fallen in love with this state park, as it offers some of the best hiking trails in Iowa. The cliffs, views of the scenic byway, and forests offer beautiful scenery. bit.ly/stonestatepark

After exploring the northern prairie region, continue on Highway 12 to **Sioux City**—the fourth largest city in Iowa, and a place that will keep you busy for days if you choose to stay a while. As you approach, you'll reach the **Dorothy Pecaut Nature Center**, where prairie grasses, 150-year-old oak trees and sweeping views across the landscape are certainly worth a stop. facebook.com/DorothyPecautNatureCenter

A little farther south is an attraction that railroad enthusiasts will love: the **Siouxland Historical Railroad Association**, with exhibits that include old rail tracks and locomotives from the past one hundred years. You can also visit the **Mid America Museum of Aviation and Transportation**. Visitors can expect a history lesson on transportation history from the roads to the skies. Experience the moving tribute to United Flight 232, which crash-landed en route from Denver to Chicago at Sioux Gateway Airport in 1989. This crash is noted as the fifth-deadliest in American history, more than 184 lives were saved that day after an engine failed and disrupted hydraulic flight controls. siouxcityrailroadmuseum.org; midamericaairmuseum.org

Leaving Sioux City, the byway travels on a ten-mile stretch of the Inter-state Highway system—I-29—which is a little unique in itself. I have never driven on a scenic byway in any state in the United States, where I have driven on an Interstate Highway. Within a few miles, we were back on a two-lane highway, the scenic byway.

About an hour out of Sioux City, traveling south from Smithland, you will find yourself near the **Lewis and Clark State Park Visitor Center**. Visitors can see a full-sized reproduction of Lewis and Clark's keelboat, along with other historic vessels that were used during the same time frame. Boating, fishing, hiking, and camping are popular activities in this state park. iowadnr.gov

There are also three excursion loops in this area that you may want to explore. Wilderness Loop, Preparation Loop, and Larpenteur Memorial Road Connection are all linked to the Loess Hills National Scenic Byway. These loops traverse some of the twelve thousand acres of state-owned land in the Loess Hills State Forest, so you will find some of the Loess Hills' best views as you drive.

Nearby **Preparation Canyon State Park** is home to one of the best overlooks of the hills' interior region. Picnicking is popular in this park, as the views of the ridges of the Loess Hills are dramatic. Hiking is very popular, as there are several trails in this state park. Each time I have visited this state park, it is quiet. This remote state park is where you can easily connect with nature and surround yourself in a beautiful natural setting in Iowa. iowadnr.gov

Continuing south, on Highway 183 you will pass through **Pisgah**, the home of the **Loess Hills State Forest Visitor Center**. Follow the signage for the byway in this area, as you travel a few miles and make a few turns now and then. This area is not flat and you will be weaving in and out of curves along the road. The rolling hills will lure you in, with breathtaking views as you drive the byway. Orchard Ridge Loop and Sawmill Hollow Loop offer some fun, near off-roading experiences. Sawmill Hollow Loop is classified as a low-maintenance "B" road, which means it's not well-maintained.

Traveling farther south, you'll reach the **Hitchcock Nature Center**, which is located on 1,300 acres that offer beautiful views of the Loess Hills. Here is where you will want to take out your binoculars and look towards the sky. This facility is home to the Hitchcock HawkWatch, which is one of twenty-five Hawk Watch stations in America. Few primary hawk-viewing stations are listed in the Hawk Watch stations in America. In the fall, hawks are abundant and you can spend hours watching hawks in this nature center. If you only have time to stop in one nature center along this route, this is the one that I would recommend exploring. With 1,300 acres and a large viewing area for birding, you can easily spend all day here. pottconservation.com

The Hitchcock Loop is also in Council Bluffs—the partially paved road heads west on I-680. This is a forty-minute loop off of the main route of the byway. **Lewis & Clark Monument Scenic Overlook** is along this route, which features a monument of them that overlooks the Missouri River. There are also several hiking trails in this area that highlight the path that Lewis and Clark took. Several experiences such as the rail museums, scenic overlooks of the Missouri River, and historical sites await you, as you drive this loop.

Continuing on your journey, you enter the **Council Bluffs**—a metropolis in southern Iowa. Here, a treat awaits railroad buffs. The **Union Pacific Railroad Museum** is where the history of rail travel in this region comes to life. With two railroad museums in Council Bluffs, you will have the opportunity to learn a lot about rail travel in the United States. uprrmuseum.org/uprrm

The **Rails West Museum** is located on Main Street in Council Bluffs and is popular with railroad enthusiasts. The restored railroad depot was built in 1899 for the Chicago Rock Island and Pacific Railroad. The depot has been renovated and was placed on the National Register of Historic Places in 1995. The museum showcases dining car silverware, ticket stubs, and collections of newspapers that showcase the transitioning of railroads from passengers to hauling freight in the United States. thehistoricalsociety.org/museums/railswest.html

Another fun activity in Council Bluffs is to cross the **Bob Kerrey Pedestrian Bridge**, which links Iowa with Nebraska. Be sure to place one foot in each state while the Missouri River flows beneath you. omaha.net/places/bob-kerrey-pedestrian-bridge

Once you have traveled through the city of Council Bluffs, you head back into more remote areas of the Loess Hills National Scenic Byway. The endless rolling hills take center stage again as you maneuver the road's curves, which always seem to lead to another perfect view. June and July are prime times to travel this route, as the wildflowers and crops are at the perfect color and height.

Just half an hour south of Council Bluffs is the Pony Creek Loop, which begins north of Glenwood and takes you through **Pony Creek Park** before linking back to the national byway south of Glenwood. This park offers boating, fishing, a virgin prairie, and a viewing area of the Loess Hills. In 1971, it was listed on the National Register of Historic Places. Two prehistoric Plains Indian earthen lodges in this park are what led to this national recognition. In 2012, the Davis Oriole Earthlodge Site was also designated as a National Historic Landmark.

Almost immediately after finishing the Pony Creek Loop, you can hop on the Waubonsie Loop. A highlight of this route is the countryside **Waubonsie Church**. Here is where the first Religious Organization in Mills County was. The first preachers here were Cannon and Witten, of the Methodist Church. When you enter the thirty-nine-acre park, **Mile Hill Lake**, you will find a handicap-accessible beautiful scenic overlook and a peaceful ten-acre lake where you can toss your fishing line into the waters. Fishing is popular in this lake. Fishermen can expect to catch large bass, crappie, and channel catfish. mycountyparks.com

The southern part of the Loess Hills National Scenic Byway wraps up near Iowa's southern border. Pleasant Overview Loop provides excellent birding opportunities, so have your binoculars handy. Spring Valley Loop is a three-mile gravel road that offers some caving that is unique to this route. If you see a trail that looks enticing, lace up your hiking boots and go exploring. You might come across some stone outcroppings, which are not often seen in this area of Iowa. As you complete your drive, the rolling hills and beauty of the area offer a time of reflection.

Western Skies Scenic Byway

Also in western Iowa, the Western Skies Scenic Byway connects with the Loess Hills National Scenic Byway, meeting Highway 183 between Pisgah and Council Bluffs.

You can start this east-west byway adventure towards the southern end of the Loess Hills National Scenic Byway experience. At the beginning of this route, I enjoy stopping at the **Harrison County Historical Village**, which is located north of Missouri Valley on US-30 and is a step back in time, boasting an original log cabin, general store, and school from the 1800s. The Village is also home to the Iowa Welcome Center, which offers Iowa keepsakes, history, and treasures to take with you. Once you hop out of your car, head to the lookout point, where you have an epic view of the surrounding area. Summertime brings wildflowers and lush, green fields of corn and soybeans.

As you head east, the route to the towns of **Logan** and **Woodbine**, which are just eight miles apart, offers rolling hills and a fun, scenic drive. Between the two towns, you'll turn off US-30 at Interstate 44 to continue on the byway—but I recommend a quick stop at the lovely community of Woodbine, with its carefully refurbished historic downtown. Back on the byway, a fun find just a little off of the route is **Prairie Rose State Park**. This beautiful park offers 422 acres of outdoor paradise nestled in Iowa's scenic hills. It's located three miles south of Harlan (which is worth a visit for its historic downtown), and offers fishing, boating, hiking, and picnicking, as well as numerous campsites for all types of campers. bit.ly/iowastateparks

Be sure to visit the **Historic Downtown Harlan Courthouse**, as it is listed on the National Register of Historic Places. A fun time to visit Harlan is during Christmas. The lighting of the Shelby County Christmas tree is held every year on the Saturday following Thanksgiving.

Heading east, **Elk Horn** is my favorite place to visit on the Western Skies Scenic Byway, because of its unique European heritage. This village and the neighboring town of **Kimballton** make up the most extensive rural Danish community outside of Denmark. Here, you can see an authentic, working Danish windmill, which in itself is a popular reason for many travelers to visit Elk Horn. The **Museum of Danish America** shares the history of the area, and it also offers one of the finest genealogy centers in the United States. danishmuseum.org

While you're in Elk Horn, enjoy an award-winning pork tenderloin on Main Street at **Larsen's Pub**—trust me, your belly will thank you. Stay connected with this eatery through their Facebook page.

As you drive this scenic byway, you will fall in love with the rolling hills and authentic Iowan farm views. Not only that, but you might be struck by an interesting phenomenon: there is a good chance that the driver of any car you meet on the two-lane road will give you a wave—just a couple of fingers lifted off the steering wheel in acknowledgment, but a lovely gesture. It's become such a known thing in Iowa that there's now a term for it: the Farmer Wave. Yes, there's something to be said about the friendliness of the people of Iowa.

White Pole Road Scenic Byway

As you reach the end of the Western Skies Scenic Byway, you'll realize that you're close to the eastern end of the **White Pole Road Scenic Byway**, which runs parallel to I-80. This byway is just twenty-six miles of road between Adair and Dexter, but it has plenty of attractions along the way.

This drive surprised me, as I have driven I-80 numerous times and never realized what White Pole Road was. I was excited to begin the trip—maybe because the smiley face on **Adair**'s yellow water tower makes it impossible to be in a bad mood. It won't be long, and history will come to life while driving this byway.

Hop on this route today and enjoy the seven hundred white telephone poles that line the road. The road is fun, as it's not flat. There are rolling hills and white poles to keep you entertained as you drive this scenic byway.

On July 21, 1873, Jesse James and his gang made the first train robbery of a moving train in the American West, just outside of Adair. Today, there is a historical park and historical marker (a metal wheel) at the site, near the White Pole Road Scenic Byway.

Bonnie and Clyde made their names well known along this route as well. They were involved in a shootout near **Dexter** in 1933. There is a historical marker on Dexfield Road in Dexter that recaps the story in a park, near the byway. A year later, in 1934, Bonnie and Clyde robbed a bank in **Stuart**, taking approximately $2,000. The site is marked with a sign on the hair salon that stands where the bank did at one time. A short month later, their crime sprees came to an end, as they were gunned down by police officers in the South.

The White Pole Road Scenic Byway played a large part in Iowa's history, having been part of the route known as the Great White Way, which helped connect Iowa with the east and west coast before the Interstate highways came into play. It was once part of a route that connected America from coast to coast. This route originally went from Des Moines to Council Bluffs. The white poles were in place for travelers to know they were still on the correct route. Today, hundreds of white poles remain.

Covered Bridges Scenic Byway

After finishing the White Pole Road Scenic Byway in Dexter, head southeast and you'll find yourself surrounded by the countryside made famous by the book and movie *The Bridges of Madison County*. To enjoy this unique, picturesque slice of Iowan Americana, take a trip on the **Covered Bridges Scenic Byway**.

The Covered Bridges Scenic Byway is not really a straight-shot road; it's more of an adventure in the region to discover the six remaining covered bridges, with **Winterset** and its authentic Americana historic downtown at its heart. The town square in Winterset is stunning come summertime, adorned by a beautiful courthouse. You can also visit the **John Wayne Birthplace & Museum** and the **Iowa Quilt Museum**.

The John Wayne Birthplace & Museum features the life of Marion Robert Morrison, known as John Wayne. He was an American actor and filmmaker who starred in several Western films. His personal life, as well as his professional life, is featured in the museum and birthplace. His briefcase, schedule, and 1972 Pontiac Grand Safari station wagon are on display. johnwaynebirthplace.museum

The Iowa Quilt Museum features several quilts and old sewing machines. Quilt enthusiasts will appreciate the work that has gone into these beautiful works of art. The current exhibits change every few months, featuring special prints and colors. iowaquiltmuseum.org

Stop in at the **Madison County Chamber of Commerce Welcome Center** in Winterset to inquire about any road closures. Many of the bridges are on gravel roads on the Covered Bridges Scenic Byway, so if the weather's bad, you might have to sit some of them out. Regardless of the weather, you can enjoy lunch on the Town Square at the **Northside Cafe**, where Robert Kincaid offered Lucy Redfield a seat at the counter in *The Bridges of Madison County*. bit.ly/northsidecafe

After exploring lovely Winterset, let's hop in the car and begin driving this beautiful byway. Just outside Winterset, you can visit the **Cutler–Donahoe Bridge** at **City Park**. This historical bridge was built in 1870 and moved to its current location at the entrance to the Winterset City Park, in 1979. The Cutler–Donahoe Bridge and a stone bridge in this park were both used in the movie, *The Bridges of Madison County*. bit.ly/cutlerdonahoe

I would then suggest taking a short drive over to the **Imes Bridge** in St. Charles. Stop at the **St. Charles Visitor Center**, and from there, take a short drive or walk to see the bridge. The bridge was built in 1870 and is eighty-one feet long, making it the oldest of the remaining covered bridges. bit.ly/imesbridge

Follow the signs for the byway to the **Roseman Covered Bridge**, which is also referenced in *The Bridges of Madison County* movie and book. If haunted experiences are your thing, hang out at this covered bridge for a period of time. Many people have reported unusual experiences while walking their dogs across the Roseman Covered Bridge. Their dogs have become frightened and won't continue to cross the bridge. bit.ly/rosemanbridge

Hogback Covered Bridge lies in a valley north of Winterset. It is still in its original location—unlike some of the other bridges, which have been moved during the last century—and was renovated in 1992. Stroll through this bridge and you will view a corn or soybean field through the exit of it. Sunset is a particularly stunning time to visit this nearly one-hundred-foot wooden bridge, as the western skies turn to red, orange, and yellow. bit.ly/hogbackbridge

Nearby **Cedar Covered Bridge** is seventy-six feet long, and it is the only covered bridge you can drive across today. This bridge is on the cover of the book, *The Bridges of Madison County*, and in the story, it's where Francesca Johnson goes to meet Robert Kincaid to help him take photos. This bridge was renovated in 1998. What I love about the renovations is that the bridges get updated, but they remain authentic. If you look at the bridge floors, they are the real deal—the reason that these bridges were covered in the first place was to protect the expensive timber that was used for the flooring. cedarcoveredbridge.com

Holliwell Covered Bridge is the last of the six covered bridges to visit on the byway, and it remains on its original site over the Middle River, southeast of Winterset. History buffs will appreciate this span, which was built in 1880 and renovated in 1995. bit.ly/holliwellbridge

While driving the roads between all of the bridges, you will find yourself immersed in the idyllic countryside surrounding these famous structures. Pack a picnic lunch and enjoy the Iowan landscape.

Each time I have driven the Covered Bridges Scenic Byway, I have altered my route a little. I tend to get drawn in by the flowers, rivers, and streams that follow the road. Explore the area, and don't be afraid to take minor diversions from the byway, as you can pick the trail back up relatively easily.

Historic Hills Scenic Byway

Southeast Iowa's **Historic Hills Scenic Byway** is, in my opinion, the most overlooked scenic byway in the state of Iowa. With 105 miles of charm and historic communities, this route gives you a new appreciation of Iowa. Machinery enthusiasts of all ages will appreciate this area of Iowa. You will find several old combines, tractors, and plows peppered along the byway in fields. It's as though this byway is still in the early 1900s, with all of the agriculture history that can be spotted as you drive along the byway.

This adventure begins in **Moravia**, which is referred to as the Gateway to Rathbun Lake—an impressive recreational lake surrounded by stunning scenery and two state parks. **Rathbun Lake** is home to hiking trails, an outdoor playground, a swimming beach, and an eighteen-hole championship golf course. With eleven thousand acres of water and 150 miles of shoreline, this lake is a fun place to experience nature.

As you continue east, you will travel through the **Drakesville** area, which is home to numerous Amish and Mennonite families. Take in the beautifully kept farms and local Amish businesses, and keep your eyes peeled on the roads for a horse-drawn buggy or two.

Farther along the route, plan to spend a few hours in the **Villages of Van Buren**, which center around the town of **Keosauqua**. The county where you'll find these eleven villages has no fast food restaurants—or even stop lights!—making a visit here a real step back in time. Stop in at the small town of **Bentonsport**, with its lovely historic district, where several artisan shops are sure to inspire the art lover in you. The whole region is fantastic for cycling, so if you've got a bike with you, get out of the car and enjoy the numerous trails, getting some exercise while you explore the byway. villagesofvanburen.com

North of the Van Buren region is a stop that is an absolute must: the **American Gothic House and Center**. It's located just outside of **Eldon**, and offers a free visitor's center where you can learn all about Grant Wood, the artist behind the iconic painting *American Gothic*, which satirically depicts the Midwestern character. Be sure to dress up in the world-famous attire with a pitchfork and straight face for your own classic Grant Wood photo recreation of this classic. americangothichouse.org

Should you travel this byway in the fall, I'd highly suggest that you join in the fall festivities at **Appleberry Orchard**, which is just beyond Donnelson at the official end of the byway. Appleberry is the oldest working orchard in the state of Iowa, and brings fall to life with a corn maze and even pig races throughout the season. And if you're looking for a completely unique experience, watch the Pumpkin Chunker shoot a pumpkin a ridiculously long way into the air. appleberryorchard.com

Iowa Valley Scenic Byway

The **Iowa Valley Scenic Byway** offers seventy-seven miles of awesome experiences in southeast Iowa. At the eastern end of the byway you will find the Amana Colonies, and at the western end is Iowa's only Native American Community, the Meskwaki Settlement. As you traverse the byway, you will travel through the communities of Amana, Marengo, Ladora, Belle Plaine, Chelsea, Tama, and Toledo.

Delivering everything from shopping for handwoven baskets and beautiful furniture, to enjoying family-style cooking, this byway is one not to miss. I'd encourage you to spend time in each community as you follow the Iowa Valley Scenic Byway signage.

I like to begin in the east, at the **Amana Colonies**, which comprise seven villages that were founded by German immigrants in 1855. These villages all offer a space where road-trippers can take a break and step back in time. Handmade Iowa quilts and antiques can be found in the **Fern Hill Gifts and Quilts Shop**. You can also view craftsmen building and designing authentic Amana Furniture in the **Amana Furniture and Clockshop**. The knowledge and skill that these craftsmen have, has been in their families for several generations.

The **Ox Yoke Inn**, in Amana, is where families have gathered for years to share a family-style meal. The inn has been serving up home-cooked meals since 1940. Wait times can be quite long here, so I would encourage you to call ahead to inquire about table availability. oxyokeinn.com

Belle Plaine sits in the middle of the byway and is home to a beautifully restored Main Street, which includes the historic **King Theatre**. The architecture has been well-maintained, and it adds to the historic look of Main Street. History continues as the Lincoln Highway crosses through Belle Plaine. **Preston's Station Historic District** has been a vital part of the community since 1923. Today, the fourth generation, helps keep this district welcoming to everyone that comes to town. prestonsstation.com

Chelsea lies north of Belle Plaine and is home to several antique shops. Folks that enjoy birding will find the **Otter Creek Marsh State Wildlife Area** a fun experience. Trumpeter swans can be seen taking flight throughout the year. This quaint town of under three hundred (2010 census) will welcome you as you drive into town.

Another fun find that's a little detour from this byway is **Traer Salt & Pepper Shaker Gallery**, about half an hour north of Chelsea. Here, you can surround yourself with more than thirty-two thousand salt and pepper shakers—who knew that was something that people might want to do?

Another intriguing attraction towards the western end of this byway is the **Matchstick Marvels Museum** in **Gladbrook**. The museum is home to more than seven million ordinary wooden matchsticks that have been made into life-like sculptures. matchstickmarvels.com

Grant Wood Scenic Byway

The Grant Wood Scenic Byway is an eighty-mile route connecting Stone City in Iowa's eastern region to Bellevue on the Mississippi River. This scenic byway showcases the Iowa scenery that inspired Grant Wood to create the artwork that is well known around the world. This route is a relatively easy drive—it's all pavement for easy driving, and it's also easy on the eye, with a beautiful view out of every window of your car. The beauty of the region, while wonderful, can also be a time suck—if you are like me, you will want to pull the car over at every given opportunity to capture the perfect photo.

Begin your route in **Stone City** and travel east to the Mississippi. Stone City is home to the **Stone City General Store Pub**, which has a large outdoor deck overlooking the river. Grant Wood's colorful painting, titled *Stone City, Iowa*, lives on here.

A little farther east is **Anamosa**, home to the **National Motorcycle Museum**. Anyone with interest in bikes of any sort could spend an endless amount of time in this museum, which houses more than 450 vintage and new motorcycles, as well as fascinating, high-quality exhibits of all things motorcycle-related. nationalmcmuseum.org

A visit to Anamosa—especially because you're traveling on the Grant Wood Scenic Byway—would not be complete without stopping at the **Grant Wood Art Gallery**. Wood was born in Anamosa, and this volunteer-run space is dedicated to preserving and promoting his history and his art in this beautiful part of Iowa. grantwoodgallery.org

As you continue east on this byway, you will find several mom-and-pop restaurants waiting to serve you a home-cooked meal. Iowans are known for baking great pies, so if you come across a pie shop, put on the brakes. Pie shops come and go, so grab an opportunity when you can.

About forty-five minutes down the road from Anamosa is **Maquoketa**— home to the **Maquoketa Caves State Park**. This state park is one of my favorites in Iowa, and caving in this area is a one-of-a-kind experience. Depending on your athletic ability, you can get a great workout—not to mention an adventure of a lifetime—walking, and at times crawling, through the network of caves. The best tip that I can give you is to wear clothes that you can toss in the dumpster when you are done caving for the day, and take a headlamp to help you see the beauty of the caves as you explore. There is a campground in this state park with reservable camping cabins and campsites. bit.ly/maquoketacavessp

The Maquoketa area also offers fantastic picnicking spots. As a road-tripper, you'll surely have camp chairs on hand; pull them out, set them up where you have a great view, break out your picnic lunch, and congratulate yourself for a road trip well-done.

As you continue eastward, you will arrive in **Bellevue**. I highly recommend a night of lodging at the Inn at Potter's Mill. You can stay in an old, rustic grist mill that produced flour for more than 126 years, from 1843–1969. It has all of the amenities that you would expect in the twenty-first century, along with the historical features of the mill. You can also indulge in a bowl of one of Iowa's best bread puddings at the restaurant on site. Now that you've reached Bellevue, the end of this route, enjoy the views of the mighty Mississippi River and reflect upon Grant Wood, and the legacy he has left in this beautiful region. pottersmill.net

Delaware Crossing Scenic Byway

North of the Grant Wood Scenic Byway is a thirty-six-mile paved and gravel loop road, known as the **Delaware Crossing Scenic Byway**. You can join this route where it best fits your itinerary. Outdoor enthusiasts will fall in love with this area, as Delaware County has more than a dozen parks to enjoy.

A lovely way to make sure you scan the scenery as you drive is to keep your eye out for the painted "barn quilts" that adorn the barns that dot the countryside—there are more than seventy to be spotted. Quilts are painted on barns, which add beauty to these historic buildings which are vital to Iowa's economy. Animals and hay often take up space in the barns that dot the countryside.

Start your loop in **Manchester**, home to **Bailey's Ford Nature Center and Wildlife Exhibit**, and the **Manchester State Trout Hatchery**. If you have never visited a hatchery, do it. They are fascinating places, as there are thousands of fish swimming in one place. It's also fun to learn about all of the fishing experiences in Iowa. Manchester is a short hop off of the byway, but well worth the stop. bit.ly/fishhatchery

As you continue to drive the byway, you will come to the town of **Delaware**. The **Delaware Speedway** is open during the summer months. If you want to take a break from driving your car, why not enter the races and drive a go-kart on a dirt track? delawarespeedwayllc.com

Driving along, you will arrive at **Lake Delhi Recreation Area** in **Delhi**. Many Iowans say that this lake is one of the "best kept secrets in Iowa." It is nine miles long and fishermen come from miles around. Black Crappie,

Channel Catfish, Northern Pike, and Walleye can be caught in this lake. iowadnr.gov

A little detour from the northernmost part of the loop takes you to **Backbone State Park**—the oldest state park in Iowa, which offers more than two thousand acres of forested bluffs. The rocky cliffs here are unique to this area, and they offer spectacular views throughout the park. With more than twenty miles of hiking trails, you will want to grab some water and a snack and hit the trails. Camping cabins and campsites can be reserved, as well. iowadnr.gov/Places-to-Go/State-Parks

River Bluffs Scenic Byway

The **River Bluffs Scenic Byway** is a little north of the Delaware Crossing Scenic Byway and is 109 miles long. It encompasses Fayette and Clayton Counties in Northeast Iowa and is a route that you can easily spend one full week exploring. Yes, I said one whole week! I recently drove this byway and was reminded of why this area of Iowa is so loved. It's not heavily populated, yet it offers a stunning drive with endless attractions.

This byway links up with the Great River Road National Scenic Byway in both Marquette and Guttenberg, along the Mississippi River. From those two towns, it forms a loop into eastern Iowa, featuring parks, caves, campgrounds, hiking, water trails, and spectacular views.

We'll start at the northeasternmost point of this byway. Only five minutes north of the riverside town of **Marquette** is **Effigy Mounds National Monument**—the only national monument in Iowa—which is home to more than two hundred prehistoric burial mounds. This park offers a glimpse into human life in the Archaic period, between 10,500 and 2,800 years ago. It's a fascinating place to visit. and each time I have been there over the years, I've seen and learned something new. nps.gov/efmo

As you venture around this loop, you will drive through thirteen little towns that together make up the area that is often referred to as "**Little Switzerland**." On the Mississippi, McGregor, Marquette, and Guttenberg all offer historic districts that distinctly define them as landmark river towns. Inland, a fun find on my most recent time traveling this route was the covered bridge in **Froehlich**. This town is also home to the 1890s **Village Museum**, which occupies the site where the first successful gasoline tractor was built. It's a quaint stop, and I'd highly recommend enjoying a picnic lunch here, as well. froelichtractor.com

Heading to the west and farther inland, the road meanders along the byway as you approach **Clermont**. Historical architectural enthusiasts will love this town, which is home to **Montauk**, a mansion built in 1874 by William Larrabee, Iowa's twelfth governor. You can schedule a guided tour at Montauk, but if you're more of a solo explorer, take yourself on a self-guided walking tour that features eighteen historical sites in Clermont. bit.ly/montaukmansion

At the northwesternmost point of the loop, stop at **Goeken Park**, which overlooks the Turkey River Valley and Eldorado. While surveying the scenery, you might notice a church steeple in the distance. I also saw several church steeples on my most recent drive through this area, and thought to myself, "Wow, this could also be the Church Steeple Byway." bit.ly/goekenpark

Now you're coming down the back straight of the River Bluffs Scenic Byway. Along this section is **West Union**, home to the **Barrel Drive-In**. The movie venue has an actual drive-up drive-in; you order your food from your car, and then it is delivered to your vehicle. I highly recommend that you indulge in the broasted chicken (for those who are not from the Midwest, this is chicken that is fried and pressure-cooked at the same time). In my opinion, this is an award-worthy broasted chicken meal that you won't find elsewhere. This, in itself, makes this byway worth the drive! facebook.com/barrelwestunion

South of West Union, **Fayette** is home to the **Big Rock Country Club**. If you have your clubs in tow, call ahead to reserve a tee time. bigrockcountryclub.org

The **Volga River State Recreation Area** is also near Fayette and offers two campgrounds, one is an equine campground, and the other is for campers. The Volga River meanders through the area and offers kayaking and canoeing experiences. The area along the river is rugged and rough, yet beautiful. I visited on a summer day and found the park very busy, with kayakers floating down the river. Folks were on their horses riding the trails and hikers had hit the trails. This is an all-year-round park that offers cross-country skiing in the winter and hunting for deer and wild turkey during different times of the year.

Red fox, raccoon, skunk, muskrat, and even a fox or two can be spotted in this park. The wildlife is abundant, also including red-tailed hawks and great horned owls. Bring your binoculars and enjoy the view.

This byway has something for everyone, and if you take the time to slow down and embrace Iowa, this will be a memorable drive for you and your family.

Driftless Area Scenic Byway

The **Driftless Area Scenic Byway** is a paved route in Northeast Iowa, which includes fourteen miles of gravel. The 144-mile road meanders through the beautiful towns of Decorah, Harpers Ferry, Lansing, New Albin, Postville, and Waukon, zigzagging across this area of Iowa. The landscape came to be, from being surrounded by glaciers from years past. You will find majestic lime bluffs and winding river bottoms carved by the Mississippi, Yellow, and Upper Iowa Rivers. The outdoor activities here are endless, from hiking to horseback riding, camping, and kayaking. You could spend a whole month in this area in the great outdoors.

Summertime is extraordinary in this region, but once fall rolls around, the foliage and autumnal scenery through your car's windshield will take your breath away.

We'll start this drive at the western end, in the Norwegian community of **Decorah**. This town is great for water-lovers, with fifteen canoe access points into the Upper Iowa River, and numerous trout streams. In fact, trout-fishing is great in Iowa—be ready to toss in a line at any given point along this route, but first, make sure you have a current state of Iowa fishing license on hand. The **Decorah Fish Hatchery** is definitely worth a visit, and while you're there, keep an eye out for the famous Decorah eagles—bald eagles whose nesting area is near the hatchery. visitdecorah.com/business/decorah-fish-hatchery

As a Norwegian, I found **Vesterheim, The National Norwegian-American Museum & Heritage Center** to be a top-notch museum. Not only does it offer beautiful displays of rosemåling and woodcarving, but it also provides presentations on Norwegian foods—anyone hungry for *lefse* or *rommegrot?* For years, I would not touch my Mother's homemade *rommegrot*, until I experienced it at this museum.

When you're done at the museum, stroll Decorah's main thoroughfare, **Water Street**, and grab a bite to eat at **Mabe's Pizza**—you won't be disappointed. Campgrounds, hotels, cabins, and several Airbnb properties offer lodging in this area of the byway. vesterheim.org

Nature lovers are also spoilt for choice in and around Decorah. The **Decorah Prairie and Butterfly Garden** is an area of prairie plants, created for visitors wanting to learn about the native flora of the prairie, as well as to preserve the area's pollinators—including butterflies. It's spectacular in summer and should not be missed. bit.ly/decorahprairiegarden

Dunning's Springs Park is where you'll find the most popular trail in Decorah, leading to a stunning two-hundred-foot waterfall—perhaps the most photographed place in Decorah. Why not add a selfie in front of the falls to your photo collection? Also nearby is the fascinating **Decorah Ice Cave**, where you can see ice for most of the year. bit.ly/dunningssprings

A trip to Decorah, when in season, would not be complete without a stop at the world-famous **Whippy Dip**. This ice cream shop serves up some of the most sought-after soft-serve ice cream in Iowa. A simple vanilla or chocolate ice cream cone are the two most popular menu items. The ice cream will melt in your mouth and leave you longing for your next visit. It operates on a seasonal basis, as it is closed during the late fall through early spring. bit.ly/whippydip

Continue east on to **Waukon**, as your drive takes you into the bluffs, and through exceptional wildflowers in the summertime. **Empty Nest Winery**, on the western edge of town as you approach, is in a beautiful setting and offers breathtaking views of the countryside. A one-hundred-year-old family barn here has been transformed into a winery; folks travel for miles to see it, and enjoy wine, craft beers, hard ciders, and free popcorn.

There is signage along the byway that makes this great spot easy to find. emptynestwinery.com

Another one of my favorite stops in Waukon is **WW Homestead Dairy**. Indulge in some premium home-style ice cream and stock up on the dairy's famous cheese curds for the road. I'm not a coffee drinker, but I hear that many folks enjoy their gourmet coffee, as well. wwhomesteaddairy.com

Around twenty minutes east of Waukon, **Lansing** is a small town that I have fallen in love with over the past couple of years. The river views and the views from **Mount Hosmer** are fantastic. Follow the signs in town to the Mount Hosmer Overlook, and go all the way to the top. Step out of your car for a spectacular view of the Upper Mississippi River; you can see up to fifty miles of the river valley from here. There are picnic tables in this area, and it's a nice place to spend a few hours relaxing in the great outdoors. The drive to the top is short and steep; stay to the right going both up and down, as there are hairpin curves. mylansingiowa.com/mt-hosmer-lookout-and-park

Horsfall Lansing Variety Store is a must-have experience while in town. You can find anything and everything imaginable in this store. The items are packed in, with no obvious rhyme or reason. It's important to note that they only take cash for payment. On one of my last visits to this store, I found my most recent Rand McNally atlas on a table out front on the sidewalk.

The **Driftless Area Education and Visitor Center** in Lansing is an excellent place to educate yourself on the area. The center offers travel advice as well as interpretive displays, which explain the Driftless Area. The visitor center sits beneath limestone bluffs with scenic river views. There is no entrance fee to visit. allamakeecountyconservation.org

A highlight for me in the Driftless Area recently was taking a ride on **Roller Coaster Road**, south of Lansing on the way to Harper's Ferry. Google "Roller Coaster Road" when you're in the area, and you will find yourself driving one of the most fun roads in Iowa. Hint: The name speaks for itself.

This scenic byway is a handy gateway to other driving routes; portions of it connect with the Great River Road National Scenic Byway and the River Bluffs Scenic Byway. For a unique opportunity to get to know more about the area, stay in a bed and breakfast, and enjoy local foods with a local. If you choose to drive this byway and remain in your car, you will see a lot. If you hop on a trail, toss a fishing line in a stream, camp under the stars, float in a canoe, or hike on a path, your experience will be epic. Tourism directors across this area of Iowa continue to tell me that their visitors are surprised when they visit. If you experience the great outdoors along this byway, you'll find yourself thinking that it's just as good as out West!

Note **New Albin** and **Harpers Ferry** are another two beautiful stops on this byway, and they are also components of the Great River Road Scenic Byway—see the following section for more information on these lovely townships.

Iowa's Great River Road National Scenic Byway

The Iowa section of the **Great River Road National Scenic Byway** is part of a three-thousand-mile-long federal, state, and county road network. This scenic byway runs down the eastern border of Iowa, parallel to the Mississippi River. It's one of two national scenic byways in the state, with the other one being the Loess Hills National Scenic Byway. All 328 miles of Iowa's contribution to the Great River National Scenic Byway offers fantastic views and experiences. This drive also connects with several byways along the route, including the Driftless Area Scenic Byway, the River Bluffs Scenic Byway, the Grant Wood Scenic Byway, and the Historic Hills Scenic Byway. You could easily plan one EPIC road trip along the Great River Road National Scenic Byway in Iowa, and experience several of these scenic routes on one major adventure.

Let's start in the north and travel south. As you drive, you will notice that the landscape continually changes, yet the river never does. The **Upper Mississippi National Wildlife and Fish Refuge** runs the length of the Mississippi along your route. This 240,000-acre refuge spans Minnesota, Iowa, Illinois, and Wisconsin. This area offers some of the best views you will find in Northeast Iowa. Multitudes of birds, fish, and even elusive river otters can be seen here. Along the Iowa stretch, you can stop at Visitor Centers at Prairie du Chien and Thomson, both in Illinois, but literally right across the river from Iowa.

New Albin, Iowa, is the northernmost town along the Great River Road National Scenic Byway in Iowa. The fourteen-mile **Reno Bottoms Canoe Trail**—a popular paddling spot for folks to enjoy Iowa's waterways—is just north of town (technically in Minnesota, but we'll allow it). There are plenty of launch sites here, and if you feel like it, you can paddle from Reno Bottoms to New Albin (just get someone to meet you at the end with the car!). mylansingiowa.com/reno-bottoms

Lansing is the next town that you will come upon, and it is one of the places where you can join up with the Driftless Area Scenic Byway—in fact, the Driftless Byway connects up with this route at New Albin, Lansing, and Harpers Ferry. Lansing is a river town that is home to a historic **Main Street**—recognized as a national historic district—and spectacular views of the Mississippi River from nearby **Mount Hosmer**.

Continuing south, you will enter the town of **Harpers Ferry**. As you approach, look out and up; bald eagles are a common sighting as you travel this scenic byway alongside the Mississippi. **Effigy Mounds National Monument** is nearby, which is also accessible through the River Bluffs Scenic Byway (see the River Bluffs section for more information on this fascinating site). Harpers Ferry is a great place to rent a boat and head out into the Mississippi River's beautiful waters. **Bluffview Park** offers picnic opportunities, featuring grills and tables. bit.ly/harpersferryia

Marquette and **McGregor** lie south of Harpers Ferry. Make time to stroll each town's **Main Street** for a memorable walk through a historic river town. Several antique shops line the streets, which make for a fun afternoon of antiquing. One of my favorite book and gift stores in the Midwest is here; **Paper Moon Indie Book and Gift Store** is located in Marquette. Customer service, books, and toys in a fun atmosphere are what you will experience, all within one block of the Mississippi River. papermoonbooks.com

Just past McGregor, which is worth a stop for its unique small businesses and historic streets, is **Pikes Peak State Park**—a great place to enjoy a picnic lunch. Spread out a blanket and break out the picnic basket—the grassy area that overlooks the Mississippi River here boasts incredible views, and you can claim "your" spot to have a chilled-out alfresco lunch. There are beautiful hiking trails throughout this state park, as well as a campground that offers reservable sites. bit.ly/pikespeaksp

In **Guttenberg**, just twenty minutes south Pikes Peak, you can experience the granddaddy of all fish hatcheries: the **Guttenberg Fish Hatchery**, located in historic downtown Guttenberg. Here, millions of fish eggs are collected, fertilized, and hatched before they are transported to rearing stations and distributed to Iowa's lakes and streams. You can also attend educational programs and fishing clinics throughout the year. bit.ly/iowafishhatcheries

Leaving Guttenberg, be sure to follow the signs in this area and do not miss the **Guttenberg Roadside Overlook**, as this is where the Mississippi River and the Wisconsin River join. Anytime you are driving the scenic byways in Iowa, it's easy to get caught up in the scenery and miss the signs along your route. If you do miss the turnoff for this overlook, it's worth turning back around to experience.

As you approach Dubuque, you will see **Balltown**. This is one of Iowa's smallest communities, and the home to Iowa's oldest restaurant and bar, **Breitbach's Country Dining**—a fantastic place to get a meal and experience real, local hospitality. The restaurant is owned by sixth-generation Breitbachs—for 120 years, the same family has doled out great food and good times. breitbachscountrydining.com

Next is **Dubuque**, but just before you arrive in this little city, take the time to visit the **Dubuque Heritage Trail**, which claims to be the Upper Midwest's most scenic all-season trail. This thirty-mile trail follows a historic railroad route. The route runs along the Little Maquoketa River Valley, which lies near several farmsteads. The rugged beauty in this area offers some outstanding outdoor experiences, which is surely why thousands of bicyclists and hikers take to this region every year.

There is a small fee to use the Dubuque Heritage Trail, which is worth every dime spent. From picnicking to fishing, there is something for everyone. The trail is an ADA Accessible area, and there are public restrooms nearby. bit.ly/dubuqueheritage

When you reach Dubuque proper, plan to explore—here, you can have the ultimate Mississippi River experience. Spend part of your day at the **National Mississippi River Museum & Aquarium**, and learn about the history of the river and how it continues to play a large role in the United States of America's economy. You can also peep in on some cute and creepy (snakes and spiders!) critters that are housed here. The museum sits on the riverbank and is a short walk to Dubuque's famous Riverwalk. rivermuseum.com

On the southern side of the city, the **Mines of Spain State Recreation Area** offers scenic views, as well as numerous outdoor activities. With more than 1,400 acres of birdwatching, hiking, canoeing, and educational opportunities, you can easily get lost (in a good way) in this beautiful eastern Iowa area. minesofspain.org

Bellevue is a short drive south on the byway, and here is where you can join the **Grant Wood Scenic Byway** if your inner artist is keen for some sightseeing. Outdoor enthusiasts will appreciate **Bellevue State Park**. With more than seven hundred acres of hiking trails and scenic views from above the Mississippi River, this state park is a favorite of many. During the warmer months, enjoy the butterfly garden and the wildflowers that are in full bloom.

Twenty minutes on, the **Green Island Wildlife Management Area** near **Sabula** offers more incredible wildlife experiences. If you look at a map of Iowa, you'll see that this region is at the extreme easternmost tip of the state. There are more than 3,700 acres of land to explore nature; hunting, fishing, and birding are prevalent here. The National Audubon Society lists Green Island as one of the top birding areas in the United States. bit.ly/greenislandwma

Once you travel through Sabula, you will approach **Clinton**, Iowa. As with all of these byways, the signage is excellent; before you reach Clinton, keep an eye out for signs pointing you to the North Overlook at **Eagle Point Park**. Your views along the river here are panoramic, so take it all in, and then head to Clinton. The historic districts within the community are great for strolling— I'd recommend exploring the marina and riverfront, and all of the amenities that surround them. As with any river town, my favorite pastime here is finding a bench near the river, and settling in to watch the boats and barges float by. bit.ly/eaglepointpark

Camanche is not very far from Clinton; follow the signage and you'll know when you have arrived. The **Mississippi River Ecotourism Center** here is not only educational, but it also offers an opportunity to camp and explore the backwaters of the Mississippi River. Guided naturalist boat tours are available; it's recommended that you call ahead to check on available seats. And if exploring one of the world's most famous rivers isn't enough, the eight-thousand-gallon aquarium here is also sure to leave you with a lasting impression. Donations keep this facility operating, and it educates tourists, as well as families, school kids, clubs, and folks of all ages—so help out if you can spare a penny or two. bit.ly/mississippiecocenter

The next passage south on the Great River Road National Scenic Byway takes you to **LeClaire**, Iowa—one of the cutest river towns that I have ever set foot in. I love the vibe: it's not too historic, and it's not too charming, it's just right! This little river town of fewer than four thousand residents plays big. The **Buffalo Bill Museum** in LeClaire is a fun stop for folks of all ages that like to explore, with exhibits including the one-room schoolhouses from the 1920s, and a look at life on the river. Also in LeClaire, take a riverboat cruise to experience the Mississippi—you can view the Great River Road National Scenic Byway from the river for a different perspective on your drive. buffalobillmuseumleclaire.com

Here, the road takes a westward direction to follow the river, and soon you'll come to **Davenport**, one of the **Quad Cities**, which actually consist of five cities: Bettendorf and Davenport in Iowa, and Rock Island, Moline and East Moline across the river in Illinois. A unique experience here is the **Figge Art Museum** in downtown Davenport. This museum is the premier art facility between Des Moines and Chicago. It boasts permanent exhibits, as well as those that rotate in and out. There are also art classes, lectures, and special events to keep visitors engaged with the artwork. figgeartmuseum.org

A fantastic thing to do while traveling in the Iowa Quad Cities area is to explore the **Mississippi River Trail**, which runs for 18.5 miles along the river between Bettendorf and Davenport. You will see riverboats, barges, and plenty of wildlife that lives in the water and near the shoreline. Make sure you check out the double-decker **Government (or Arsenal) Bridge**, built in 1896—it connects Davenport to Rock Island, and has a swing span that allows water traffic on the Mississippi to pass. There's also a newer pedestrian **Skybridge** that doesn't cross the river, but has wonderful views of it—this bridge allows people to cross River Drive between Second Avenue and Davenport's waterfront at **LeClaire Park**, where there's an observation deck with fantastic views. qctrails.org/trails/trail/mississippi-river-trail-iowa

Your byway journey continues thirty miles west, in **Muscatine**. Here, consider visiting the **Pearl Button Museum**, which tons of Iowans talk about. Muscatine is known as the "pearl button capital of the world," because it's where 1.5 billion buttons crafted from the shells of river mollusks (clams and mussels) were made annually in the early 1900s. muscatinehistory.org

The **Environmental Learning Center** is also in Muscatine. If you have not stopped at any of the environmental learning facilities along your route, this may be where you want to check one out. With two 1,200-gallon aquariums with native fish and a certified Monarch Waystation site, you can quickly learn a lot about these two species. I have always been fascinated by the Monarchs and how and why they migrate. This center is a fantastic resource for butterfly fans from all across the globe. bit.ly/muscatineelc

Heading south again as you continue to navigate the byway and the Mississippi River, you will come to **Wapello**. Here is where you can explore the **Toolesboro Mounds and Museum**, a national historic landmark that is open from sunrise to sunset. The burial mounds at the site date back to between 200 BC and AD 300, and include some well-preserved and accessible remnants of Iowa's Hopewell culture. These Middle Woodland people hunted, gathered, and gardened in the area. The site is in close proximity to the **Odessa Wildlife Complex**, where kayak enthusiasts can explore the Odessa Water Trail—a paddler's dream that winds through a 6,400-acre wetland consisting of lakes, ponds, timbered chutes, marshes, and forests. Twists and turns along some sections of the water trail are similar to your drive along the scenic byway. naturallylouisacounty.com/toolesboro-mounds-and-museum

Farther south is **Burlington**, which is home to more beautiful views of the Mississippi River. Drive **Snake Alley** while you're in town—this crooked street is Iowa's answer to Lombard Street in San Francisco, but with sharper turns—seven of them over 275 feet. bit.ly/burlingtonsnakealley

Our next stop, **Fort Madison**, is home to **Old Fort Madison**. which is the only national battlefield site in Iowa. It has been recently suggested that it is also the earliest military gravesite in Iowa. Fort Madison is the only place in Iowa where US soldiers fought and died in battle against a foreign power, during the War of 1812. The fort runs parallel to the scenic byway and the Mississippi River. oldfortmadison.org

Montrose is where you will find the **Heron Bend Conservation Area**, which lies between Fort Madison and Keokuk. The Heron Bend Park Perimeter Trail is .6 miles long and an easy hike. Several native prairie plants line the trail and offer different colors as the season's change. Take in the views of the Mississippi River while here and if you are lucky, a bald eagle will fly overhead. leecounty.org

Keokuk is where your Iowa journey along the Great River Road National Scenic Byway will wrap up. While in Keokuk, reflect on your road trip with a visit to the **George M. Verity Riverboat Museum**—a historic towboat that now houses exhibits that take you back to the riverboat era. For a fun memory, dangle your feet in the Mississippi River before saying goodbye to the Great River Road National Scenic Byway in Iowa. bit.ly/georgemveritymuseum

The **Lincoln Highway Heritage Byway** runs east–west across Iowa, between Council Bluffs in the west, and Clinton in the east. If you want to branch out beyond Iowa, you can travel this route across the country—it begins in Times Square in New York and ends in San Francisco.

This route was established in 1913, and it was the first improved transcontinental road in the state. Today, it's a large part of many Iowans' lives, as nearly two-thirds of Iowa's residents live in the counties along the Lincoln Highway route. A fun stop is the **Kate Shelley High Bridge** near **Boone**, in Central Iowa. The bridge is one of the highest and longest double-track railroad bridges in the United States. It is 184 feet tall and 2,685 feet long. Fall is an exceptional time to visit, as the trees are bursting with color. In town, buy a ticket for a seat on the **Boone and Scenic Valley Railroad**, which allows visitors to travel in vintage train cars while enjoying spectacular views, including from the 156-foot-high Bass Point Creek High Bridge, which overlooks the Des Moines River Valley. bsvrr.com/wp

Pro tip: This train ride is exceptional in the fall.

The **Jefferson Highway Heritage Byway** runs north and south through the center of Iowa. The full road came to be in 1916 to connect Winnipeg to New Orleans—hence its alternative moniker: the Pine to Palm Highway. In Iowa, the Jefferson Highway Heritage Byway runs on US Highways 65 and 69. A highlight of this road trip is a stop in **Mason City**, Iowa—also known as the home of renowned architect Frank Lloyd Wright. The **Historic Park Inn Hotel** in the downtown area is the last known hotel in the world designed by Wright. Visitors can stay in the renovated hotel for an affordable price in the city's downtown, which is filled with architecture and art. bit.ly/parkinnmasoncity

I marvel at the beauty of my home state of Iowa, and the remarkable scenic and heritage byways that allow visitors to take it all in. Once you've driven one byway, you will most likely seek out more. The people of Iowa are proud of their heritage, and they enjoy showcasing the beauty of the state. I hope you will take to the road and explore Iowa—and all of the byways in the midwest. I'm sure you will not be disappointed.

Sara Broers is a travel enthusiast residing in North Central Iowa. She is passionate about the Midwest, specifically her home state of Iowa. She has lived in Iowa all of her life, and finds it interesting that she always meets people with an Iowa story when she travels. Sara is the CEO of Travel With Sara and the co-owner of the Midwest Travel Network. She is also an auctioneer, and she prides herself on connecting people to help them tell their stories.

KANSAS

The beautiful state of Kansas gets its nickname, the Sunflower State, from the wild sunflowers that highlight its open spaces, and nearly three million people call it home.

The battle over slavery marred Kansas's early history. The undeclared Civil War started in Kansas when pro- and anti-slavery forces fought to decide whether Kansas would be a slave state or a free state. This unrest became known as "Bleeding Kansas."

Basic Kansas Facts:
- The state capital is Topeka.
- The state motto is "Ad Astra Per Aspera." It means "To the Stars Through Difficulties." Kansans cherish their motto, and they often abbreviate it as "Ad Astra."
- The state bird is the western meadowlark.
- The state flower is the wild sunflower.
- The state animal is the bison.

Fun Kansas Facts:
- Kansas is named for the Kanza tribe, also called the Kaw. It means "people of the south wind."
- Dr. Brewster Higley wrote "Home on the Range" in Smith County. It became the state's official song in 1947. The Western Writers of America listed the song as ninth in the Top 100 Western Songs of All Time.
- Smith County also holds the geographic center of the lower forty-eight states.
- Kansas grows enough wheat each year to bake thirty-six billion loaves of bread.

- Argonia elected the nation's first female mayor in 1887. She was nominated as a joke, but she won and got the last laugh.

Kansas has designated twelve highways and byways to explore, all of which are listed in the index in the back of this book. Two of them, Flint Hills and Wetlands and Wildlife, are National Scenic Byways.

In this guide, we'll explore three of the state's corners and the unique Flint Hills. Pack your suitcase, grab your keys, and let's take a drive!

Thrill at the bounty of Kansas on Land and Sky Scenic Byway

Land and Sky Scenic Byway runs through eighty-eight miles of wide-open Northwest Kansas spaces. Revel in the vast skies and the beautiful land that spreads out lavishly before you. On Kansas Highway 27, you'll marvel at the rugged canyons that form the Arikaree Breaks; relax at Soldiers Memorial County Park, a true oasis; and climb to Kansas's highest point at the top of Mount Sunflower.

Land and Sky is the nation's first agriculture-themed byway, and as you drive, you'll quickly begin to understand why. The name of the city at the byway's center, Goodland, tells you all you need to know about agriculture.

Wheat, corn, dry beans, sunflowers, and milo (also known as sorghum) grow in abundance on the Land and Sky byway. Come in late June to see the wheat waving in the wind, and in mid to late August for sunflower blooming season. Milo is a colorful crop, and you'll see a range of shades from gold to maroon to brown in the fall. In late July and early August, expect to enjoy the fruits of county fair season—the byway's three counties, Wallace, Sherman, and Cheyenne, all boast home-owned carnivals, where community members staff the rides and games.

Consider setting up your home base in **Goodland** and taking short trips into the surrounding regions. Goodland is in Sherman County, which is sandwiched between Cheyenne County to the north, and Wallace County to the south. When traveling this byway, remember that Cheyenne County observes Central Time, while Sherman and Wallace Counties are on Mountain Time.

Reserve a hotel or an Airbnb in Goodland, like the **Prairie Lodge** on a bison ranch northeast of Goodland. This Airbnb lodge allows you to take tours of the buffalo and cattle herds. On clear nights, the stars will astound you. bit.ly/prairielodge

Campers can stay at **Mid-America Camp Inn**. With ninety-one paved sites, the park offers 30- and 50-amp connections, a playground, showers, and laundry. Your phone may lead you wrong; the park is south of Interstate 70. bit.ly/midamericacamp

There are plenty of accommodation options in the other counties, as well, if you want to awaken in a different place on each day of your trip. In Wallace County, reserve a room at **Mount Sunflower Bed and Breakfast**, in **Sharon Springs**. President Theodore Roosevelt once attended church here when it was the Sharon Springs Methodist Church. mtsunflowerbedandbreakfast.com

In **St. Francis**, Cheyenne County, enjoy excellent hospitality at the **Spencer House Bed & Breakfast**. thespencerhousebandb.com

From Goodland, head thirty miles north on Highway 27 to **Wheeler**.

The **Cheyenne Valley Cemetery** stands south of the Highway 27–36 intersection, where you can either head east to Bird City, or west to St. Francis. (Google Maps shows it as Wheeler Cemetery.) At the cemetery, pay respects to Medal of Honor winner Jack Weinstein. While his courageous acts earned the Medal of Honor in 1951, Weinstein did not receive the medal until 2014, because of his "Jewish-sounding name." The medal was awarded posthumously, as he died in 2006. Ironically, he was not Jewish.

St. Francis is five miles west of Wheeler on Highway 36. At **Cheyenne County Museum**, learn about famous Cheyenne County residents Ron Evans, Apollo 17 Command Module Pilot; and Len Dresslar, Jr., the voice of the Jolly Green Giant. cncoks.us/museum

Hit the road on vintage motorcycles at **St. Francis Motorcycle Museum** (in your dreams, at least). Thirty of the bikes predate 1929, including a 1902 Orient motorcycle. stfrancismotorcyclemuseum.org

At **Quincy Gallery**, enjoy regional and local artists' works, and perhaps even choose a new piece of artwork for your home. bit.ly/quincygalleryc4c

After your indoor browsing, opt outside at **Keller Pond** and the connecting **River Walk**. Catch fish, take a walk, ride a bike, and enjoy a picnic. bit.ly/kellerpondriverwalk

At **Sawhill Park**, enjoy the playground, take in a concert at the bandshell (or stage your own), and admire the artworks. bit.ly/sawhillpark

If the day's heating up, play in the water at **St. Francis Aquatic Park**, with its interactive play structure, waterslides, and diving boards. bit.ly/sfaquatic

The heavenly aroma of fresh-roasted coffee greets guests at **Fresh Seven Coffee**, and the food and ambiance are as divine as the coffee. This relaxing cafe is all a coffee house should be. freshsevencoffee.com

The decision at **Diamond R Bar** is a hard one to make. Eat burgers first, or play pool first at this century-old eatery? While you're deciding, put another quarter in the jukebox, baby. bit.ly/diamondrbar

No one makes better sopapillas than **Park Hill Restaurant & Lounge**, a local favorite since the mid 1970s. The beef, bean, and cheese version is a winner. facebook.com/parkhillrestaurant

Before heading north to the **Arikaree Breaks**, known as the Breaks, fill up your gas tank and pick up a brochure at **Roadside Park**'s kiosk. Google Maps isn't particularly helpful when it comes to the Breaks, so download a map at bit.ly/arikareebreaksmap.

Cell phone service north of St. Francis is spotty. Ask about road conditions before you go, because some roads are inaccessible when wet.

Your journey through the Breaks will require at least three hours if you want to see all of the sights, but a full day is more fun. To visit every tour stop, take Highway 27 north from St. Francis to Cheyenne County Road W.

One look at a topographical map of northern Cheyenne County will tell you that the Arikaree Breaks are canyon country. The tightly spaced elevation lines on the map indicate the deeply eroded gashes in the ground. As you drive, watch for the round, red directional signs. Highlights include the **Cherry Creek Encampment**, where Sand Creek Massacre survivors recovered and planned revenge. Peer into **Devil's Gap** canyon. Stop for a picnic at **Sue's Picnic Table**, which overlooks another canyon. Drive a dirt road to **Colorado's lowest point**—3,315 feet—where you'll stand in the (usually dry) Arikaree River. Stand in three states at once on the **Kansas-Nebraska-Colorado Tri-Point**. On the return trip, visit **Horse Thief Cave**, which has partially collapsed, and the **Mini-Grand Canyon at Lookout Point**. Except for the encampment, the Breaks tour is on gravel roads. bit.ly/breaks8wonders

An alternative route to the Breaks, the **Ancient Indian Traders Trail** on Highway 161 north of Bird City, will keep you on paved roads. Stop at the **Round Hole Campsite** marker at the highway's intersection with Road Y. Cavalry camped here while on at least three campaigns during the wars against indigenous people. Sign the guestbook at the marker. Continue north on Highway 161 for a taste of the Breaks.

After your canyon adventure, head to **Bird City** to see what's on offer. If you love golf, tee off at the unique, nine-hole **Bird City Golf Course**, which features sand greens. bit.ly/birdcitygolf

Bird City also hosts the **Tri-State Antique Engine & Threshers Association Annual Show** in late July celebrating the rural heritage of this area; and the **Mule and Draft Horse Show** in October. You'll love the living history demonstrations. threshershow.org

When hunger strikes, eat a delicious steak supper at **Big Ed's Steakhouse** in town. bit.ly/bigedssteakhouse

From Bird City, take the byway south, back to Goodland (you're now in Sherman County—change your clocks!). Drive to the **Kidder Battlefield** on well-maintained gravel roads, east of the intersection of Road 77 and Road 75.2. From there, walk to the memorials on private property to learn a little bit about this infamous battle. In June 1867, Lt. Lyman Kidder, ten enlisted men, and scout Red Bead took dispatches to Lt. Col. George Custer. Instead of Custer, the patrol met Lakota and Cheyenne warriors. All twelve soldiers died. Custer found their bodies a few days later. The State of Kansas placed a marker at the intersection closest to the battlefield. Download a map at bit.ly/kiddermap. visitgoodland.com/kidder

The **Giant Grasshopper** stands a mile north of Goodland on Highway 27. Farmer Lloyd Harden created whimsical sculptures from used mechanical parts, and after he died, the Ihrig family preserved his nine-foot grasshopper and palm tree. They moved the grasshopper from Harden's farm to theirs and put it on display. bit.ly/goodlandgrasshopper

Enjoy Goodland's most famous attraction, the **Giant van Gogh Painting** in **Pioneer Park East**. On an eighty-foot-tall easel, the painting measures twenty-four by thirty-two feet and weighs forty-thousand pounds. The artwork inspired smaller paintings in several Goodland parks. bit.ly/giantvgpainting

Next to the painting, the **Goodland Welcome Center** offers souvenirs and information. Let your dog run at **Pioneer Dog Park** behind the welcome center. gogoodland.org

Walk two blocks to the **High Plains Museum**, home of "America's First Patented Helicopter." William Purvis and Charles Wilson of Goodland invented the helicopter in 1909. The project was beset with difficulties before funding ran out. The museum holds a replica. highplainsmuseum.org

Goodland Skate Park is in Steever Park next to the museum. Stretch your legs on **Topside Trail**, which runs from the park to **Northwest Tech**.

Enjoy watching the Tech Mavericks compete in one of nine sports. ntmavericks.com

If you're driving, turn left onto Seventeenth Street to visit the restored **White Eagle Gas Station**, which is full of petroleum memorabilia. During daylight, walk the grounds and look in the windows to catch a glimpse of history. visitgoodland.com/white-eagle

Enjoy art exhibits at the **Carnegie Arts Center** on Twelfth Street, and shop in the gift shop, where you'll find art to warm your home. goodlandarts.org

The **Ennis-Handy House**, a block away on Thirteenth Street, is supposedly haunted. A funeral home once operated there, and Edythe Handy died in the house. Tour the restored 1907 Queen Anne treasure and learn its story. bit.ly/handyhouse

Loop back up to Tenth Street, where you'll find the **United Telephone Building**—an Art Deco masterpiece. Call (785) 899-6733 for a tour. bit.ly/phonebuilding

Right across the road is **Goodland Churches Thrift Store**, where local artists painted the *History of the Opera House* mural. The artwork depicts ninety years of businesses in the building. Learn more inside the store. bit.ly/goodlandthriftstore

The **Goodland Post Office** has changed names and locations several times. Its current building, on Eleventh Street, was a government stimulus project during the Great Depression. The mural *Rural Free Delivery* hangs in the lobby. bit.ly/ruralfreedelivery

Sherman County Courthouse was built in 1931 on Broadway Avenue. Like the United Telephone Building, it's an Art Deco gem. The sculpture *They Came to Stay* on the lawn honors Sherman County's pioneers. visitgoodland.com/courthouse

Goodland Public Library, across Broadway from the courthouse, contains several artworks: *More Than Words*, a sculpture of a mother reading to her children; a reproduction of *The Gleaners* painting; and the stained glass Railroad Window. bit.ly/rrwindow

Head to the northern outskirts of the city for the free tours that teach weather and weather forecasting at the **National Weather Service Forecast Office**. Mornings are the best tour times, and the office customizes tours to the group's ages. Call (785) 899-2360 at least twenty-four hours ahead of your visit. weather.gov/gld

It's time to turn your attention to your taste buds. For heavenly spice blends, visit **Olde Westport Spice** on Main Street. Call (785) 899-2020 at least twenty-four hours ahead for a tour. Enjoy the spice blends at their restaurant, **Westport on Main**. oldewestportspice.com

Next, enjoy artisan drinks and shaved ice next door at **Terra Bona Hawai'ian Shaved Ice** (*Terra Bona* means "Good Land" in Latin). Play board games, and help put together the current community jigsaw puzzle. terrabonagoodland.com

For a snack and a caffeine kick, the biscuits and coffee are to die for at **Good Grounds Café & Bistro**, as is the pulled pork. facebook.com/goodgroundsks

If burgers, steak, and antiques are your favorites, head to **Crazy R's Bar & Grill**, a few blocks south on Main Street. Antiques are everywhere, and the food is delicious. The Ragin' Cajun burger is a local favorite, and prime rib is the ticket on Wednesday nights. bit.ly/crazyrbar

Also on Main Street, **L&T Family Restaurant** features fried chicken, and their brisket burrito is an unexpected pleasure. facebook.com/ltperla

After a day packed with exploring (and eating), spend your evening at the **Sherman Theatre**. It's a restored 1920s movie palace with twenty-first-century amenities. Come early to enjoy the theatre's original artworks, including a mural of Venice. goodlandnet.com/movies

When you've soaked up everything that Goodland has to offer, the next community on your byway tour is Sharon Springs, thirty miles south of Goodland via Highway 27. You have two stops in between. If you're looking for an oasis, well-maintained gravel roads will take you to **Soldiers Memorial County Park**, also known as Smoky Gardens. Enjoy a picnic, a nature trail, disc golf, and camping. Download a map at bit.ly/soldiersmemorialmap. facebook.com/soldiersmemorialpark

Southwest of the park, explore Kansas's high point, **Mount Sunflower**—just drive to the top of the 4,039-foot "summit." Getting there from Highway 27 takes you on twenty miles of gravel roads. Watch for the brown directional signs. You can also download a map at bit.ly/mtsunflowermap. bit.ly/mountsunflowerfb

You're on an agricultural-themed drive, so a stop at **21st Century Bean**, where a variety of legumes are processed, will give you insight into the food production of the area. Call several days ahead for a tour appointment at their plant in southeast **Sharon Springs**. Learn all about cleaning, packing, and sorting dry beans, then bring some home to eat later. 21stcenturybean.com

Don't feel like cooking beans? Grab a bite at **Town's End Tavern**, where Erin makes everything from scratch, and it's all delicious. Recent specials included bacon-wrapped filet and giant pork tenderloin sandwiches. facebook.com/townsendtav

Another great option, on the northern edge of town, is **Penny's Diner**, which takes you back to the 1950s with its checkerboard flooring, vinyl booths, and classic diner cuisine. facebook.com/pennysdinersharonsprings

Drive eight miles east, just past the city of **Wallace**, to **Fort Wallace Museum**, where you can check out a forty-foot replica of the plesiosaur that the fort's surgeon, Theophilus H. Turner, discovered east of the post. Explore the museum's grounds and find the bullet holes in **Pond Creek Station**—believed to be the oldest building in northwest Kansas—and tour other historic buildings. Admire the "**Barbed Wire Buffalo**," crafted from two miles of barbed wire. Ask about the **Guided Path to Old Wallace** tour, which explores the city's early history. ftwallace.com

Head back to town and, while walking in Wallace, enjoy some coffee and browse antiques at **The Memory Bank and Wallace Trading Company**, housed in a restored bank. bit.ly/wallacetradingco

Then, take a short stroll to admire the **1879 Kansas Pacific Railroad Superintendent's House**—one of the only two remaining of these buildings from the Kansas Pacific Railroad era, and often called the most beautiful superintendent's residence on any railroad. bit.ly/kprrsuperintendenthouse

Fort Wallace is also on the 102-mile **Western Vistas Historic Byway**. On Western Vistas, rock formations rise out of the plains, displaying remnants of the **Western Interior Sea** floor. If you have an extra day or two, take a little time to check it out. bit.ly/westernvistas

When the sea disappeared, it left a fossil-hunter's paradise. Schedule your hunt at **Keystone Gallery**, found between Oakley and Scott City on Highway 83. keystonegallery.com

Western Vistas includes **Little Jerusalem Badlands** and **Historic Lake Scott State Parks**; **Monument Rocks** National Natural Landmark; **Battle Canyon**, site of the Battle of Punished Woman's Fork; and the *Birthplace of the Legend*, a giant Buffalo Bill sculpture.

Explore the land and scan the sky for even more treasures on Land and Sky Scenic Byway. Find more shopping, golf, trails, and good times when you dig a little deeper into what this Kansas route has to offer.

Explore Kansas's "Little Switzerland" on Glacial Hills Scenic Byway

Bluffs on one side of the road and the roiling Missouri River on the other are the hallmarks of the sixty-three-mile **Glacial Hills Scenic Byway** in Northeast Kansas. When the glaciers receded from Kansas, they left the bluffs, rushing streams, and quartzite rocks colored from pink to reddish-purple. The glaciers had dragged the quartzite from western Minnesota!

The byway follows Kansas Highway 7 south from the Kansas-Nebraska line to Highways 7 and 92 in Leavenworth, on the north side of the Kansas City metropolitan area. The northern part of the byway cuts through Doniphan County, which, with its many hills and valleys, was nicknamed Little Switzerland. Besides taking in this byway's beautiful topography, you'll follow in the footsteps of Meriwether Lewis, William Clark, Abraham Lincoln, Susan B. Anthony, Amelia Earhart, Melissa Etheridge, and more. Many of the riverfront communities along the route boast Lewis and Clark markers.

Glacial Hills Scenic Byway was also a significant travel nexus. The **Santa Fe Trail, California Trail**, the **Pony Express**, and the **Atchison, Topeka, and Santa Fe Railroad** (ATSF) all came through the byway counties. These trails are well-marked. bit.ly/ksnationaltrails

For accommodation, there are a number of good options. In **Leavenworth**, stay at the lovely **Union Park Guest House**, which is elegant and right in town. unionparkgh.com

In **Atchison**, stay at **Tuck U Inn at Glick Mansion**, a former governor's home that is rich in history. glickmansion.com

Make your reservation in **Troy** at **Troy Bed & Breakfast at Windermere House**. bit.ly/troybandb

When you're ready to hit the road, start in Doniphan County straddling the 40th parallel—the Kansas–Nebraska line. At the Nebraska historical marker on the state line, cross the road to a footbridge and hike 150 feet up the bluff to the **1855 surveying marker**.

White Cloud is 2.5 miles south of the state line. On bluffs above the Missouri River, White Cloud's entire downtown is a **historic district**. bit.ly/neksnrhp

The Italianate White Cloud School holds the **Ma-Hush-Kah Museum**. Ma-Hush-Kah, or White Cloud, was the Iowa chief when Euro-American settlement began. facebook.com/mahushkah

Look for the **Wilbur Chapman Monument** at the White Cloud Community Chirstian Church. In 1913, ten-year-old Chapman sold his pet pig and donated the proceeds to a leper colony—an action that inspired the piggy bank.

At White Cloud's **Four-State Lookout**, see Kansas, Nebraska, Missouri, and, on cloudless days, Iowa. bit.ly/4statelookout

Eleven miles south of White Cloud, in **Sparks**, the **Sparks Flea Market** attracts thousands to Doniphan County each spring and fall with 450 antique dealers and plenty of great collectibles and food. bit.ly/dpfleamarket

Eight miles farther, in **Troy**, the **Doniphan County Courthouse** is a gem. Browse displays of Doniphan County history, and ask the clerk's office about the courthouse square walking tour. The interior staircases feature beautifully turned wood railings, and a small staircase on the courthouse's third floor leads to a beautiful view. *Tall Oak*, a twenty-seven-foot-tall sculpture of a Native American, carved from a burr oak tree, stands on the lawn. dpcountyks.com

Hungry? Stop at the charming **Feed Store Café** near the courthouse, and eat the half-pound stuffed Trojan horse burger and butterscotch pie. The napkins are bandanas. facebook.com/FeedStoreCafe

Doniphan County also has a fascinating barn collection. Explore the **Byre and Bluff Barn Trail** to get a good look. bit.ly/byrebarntrail

From Troy, follow Abraham Lincoln's 1859 campaign trail. At 138 E. Walnut Street, a marker commemorates his Troy visit. Lincoln entered Kansas in Elwood, twenty miles southeast of Troy. He spoke in Elwood, Troy, and Doniphan before heading south to Atchison and Leavenworth. alincolnguide.com/december-1-1859

To get to **Elwood**, take a slight detour from the byway, on Highway 36. Floods have washed away much of Elwood. The Grand-Duchy of Luxembourg donated relief funds after the devastating 1993 flood, and Elwood honors its benefactors at the log-cabin **Fort Luxembourg/Doniphan County Visitor Center**. bit.ly/fortluxembourg

Back on the byway, **Doniphan**, a ghost town, is twelve miles southeast of Troy on Mineral Point Road. The road turns to gravel and is best when it's dry. Before you reach Doniphan, turn east on 100th Road, then south on Moon Light Road for spectacular views of the Missouri River and the surrounding area at **Doniphan Cemetery**. bit.ly/doniphancemetery

Note: Plaques at the **Atchison County Courthouse** in Atchison, and at Fourth and Delaware in Leavenworth, as well as a sculpture at the **Leavenworth Municipal Building** also commemorate Lincoln's visit. bit.ly/lincolninkansas

Doniphan was a winemaking center for many years. The **Brenner Vineyards Historic District** shows how extensive the Brenners' operation was. bit.ly/brennerhistdistpdf

Head south on Mineral Point Road toward Atchison. At the Atchison County line, the road becomes River Road. South of 306th Road, River Road takes a sharp westward turn. Instead of turning, follow the field road to **Benedictine Bottoms Wildlife Area** for excellent birding. bit.ly/benedictinebottoms

Join the **Independence Creek Trail** at the bottoms. The ten-mile trail uses Atchison's levee, and it passes by the recreated **Kanza Earthlodge** on Road 314. Before white settlement, the Kanza tribe dominated much of Kansas. bit.ly/independencecreektrail

In **Atchison**, make a stop at **Benedictine College**, and admire **St. Benedict Catholic Church**'s architecture. benedictine.edu

For more architectural delights, see the church at nearby **St. Benedict's Abbey**. Barry Byrne, a student of Frank Lloyd Wright, designed the 1957 structure. kansasmonks.org

From here, River Road takes you to Atchison's **Riverfront Park**, where **Veterans' Memorial Plaza** displays memorials and a relic of the USS Arizona, which sank in Pearl Harbor on December 7th, 1941. After dark, enjoy the lights on the **Amelia Earhart Bridge**, and if you're in town in July, join the **Amelia Earhart Festival** in the park. bit.ly/atchisonriverfront

Earhart was born in her maternal grandparents' home, now the **Amelia Earhart Birthplace Museum**. The exterior looks like the house in Grant Wood's *American Gothic*. Inside, get to know the daring aviator. Mementos include a model of an Electra, the plane Earheart was flying when she and navigator Fred Noonan disappeared forever. The house is on Challis Bluff, and offers a great view of Earhart's namesake bridge. ameliaearhartmuseum.org

In the southwest part of Atchison, Earhart's statue welcomes guests at the **International Forest of Friendship**. Trees from all fifty states and many foreign countries grow here. The forest paths honor more than 1,500 honorees. ifof.org

Kansas artist Stan Herd built the ***Amelia Earhart Earthwork***—a 42,000-square-foot portrait on a hillside in Atchison—at nearby **Warnock Lake** in 1997. A viewing platform offers the best ground-based view. bit.ly/earhartartwork

All of Earhart's grandparents are buried at the **Mount Vernon Cemetery**, not far from Warnock Lake. A cemetery walking tour is one of the **Haunted Atchison** tour offerings. bit.ly/mtvernoncemetery

The **Sallie House** is the most haunted of all Atchison's ghostly dwellings. Six-year-old Sallie died at the house, which was also a doctor's office, during an appendectomy before the anesthesia took effect. Ever since, objects move, visitors are scratched, equipment stops, and the house turns cold. Stay overnight—if you dare. bit.ly/salliehouse

Learn more about all things Atchison at the **Visitor Information Center**, which occupies the last Atchison, Topeka and Santa Fe Railway (ATSF) structure standing in Atchison. The sculpture ***Working Men of the Railroads*** stands outside the former ATSF depot. Ask about Atchison's **Trolley Tours** in the visitor center, and pick up self-guided historic home tours. visitatchison.com/visitor-information

A gift shop separates the Visitor Center from the **Atchison County Historical Society Museum** and the Atchison **Rail Museum**. Outside the Rail Museum is an excellent collection of railroad cars. On weekends from June to October, ride the miniature train around the park. atchisonhistory.org

The Atchison museum includes the city's namesake Missouri Sen. David R. Atchison's "Presidential Library." Atchison was president pro tempore of the Senate in 1849. At the time, the president pro tempore was second in line for the presidency after the Vice President. Outgoing President James K. Polk and Vice President George M. Dallas's terms ended on a Sunday at noon. Incoming President Zachary Taylor refused to take the oath of office until Monday noon. In the supposed gap between Polk and Taylor, Atchison was president for a day.

Fourth of July 1804 Creek runs past the museum under a covered bridge. Lewis and Clark named the stream on Independence Day 1804. Beautiful rapids are on one side of the bridge, with a waterfall on the other side.

At **Muchnic Art Gallery**, the artistic value of the building itself is equal to the works displayed inside. The original owner collected oak, walnut, and mahogany to use in the house, and the parquet floors and carved woodwork are stunning. Carvers cut eight faces into the lower hall's newel posts; the faces are said to be the original owner's family members. atchisonart.org/muchnic-gallery-1.html

At **Farmers Market Place** between Fourth and Fifth on Main, find gorgeous mosaics on upright concrete slabs. The market is open from the third Saturday in May through the last Saturday in October. atchisonfarmers.market

There are plenty more public art projects in Atchison. Learn more here: atchisonart.org/public-art-projects.html

Hungry? Order a five-pound banana split at **Snowball Ice Cream Shop**. bit.ly/snowballicecreamshop

For a century-old taste sensation, visit **Paolucci's Restaurant**. The restaurant opened in 1894 and is still using traditional family recipes. Try A Taste of Italy or the spinach lasagna. paoluccibegley.com

If you need to pick up a few things, shop in Atchison's **outdoor pedestrian mall**. visitatchison.com/shopping

A half-hour drive west of Atchison is **Muscotah**, the home of Baseball Hall of Famer Joe Tinker. The city celebrates his life with the twenty-foot-wide **World's Largest Baseball**, a marker, and a mural. Sing "Take Me out to the Ball Game" inside the ball, which is made from an old water tower tank. The city park's monument includes two bats and a baseball, the town's name, and a plaque that honors Tinker. Chicago Cubs fans will enjoy the mural wrapped around the park's concession stand. roadsideamerica.com/tip/38003

Make your way back to Atchison. From there, heading south, Highway 7 passes the **United States Federal Penitentiary** west of Leavenworth. At night, the illuminated prison dome resembles the US Capitol. Photograph the prison across Metropolitan Ave. bit.ly/lvprison

Founded in 1827, **Fort Leavenworth** is the oldest fort west of the Appalachians. Stop at the Visitor Control Center for a temporary pass. bit.ly/ftlvvisitorgateinfo

The fort hosts numerous attractions, including three self-guided tours. The **Wayside Tour** extends into the City of Leavenworth. bit.ly/ftlvtours

Also in the fort's vicinity, visit the **Frontier Army Museum, Lewis and Clark Center, Berlin Wall Monument, The Rookery**, and **Fort Leavenworth National Cemetery**. Watch the Missouri River from the bluffs. The **Lewis and Clark Center** includes the **Fort Leavenworth Hall of Fame** and the **International Officer Hall of Fame**, plus military artifacts. bit.ly/ftlvattractions

In 1854, barely after Kansas Territory opened for settlement, Leavenworth was founded. The **Carroll Mansion** preserves early Kansas history. Enjoy the home's Victorian finery and look for the dog theme. While at the mansion, stand on the **Lincoln Steps**, where Lincoln spoke in Leavenworth. Greet the **Heroic Dog**. According to legend, the dog saved a girl in 1865 by throwing himself under the hooves of runaway carriage horses. The grateful family purchased the memorial. leavenworthhistory.org

The **Leavenworth Historical Museum Association** oversees three museums. Learn more about Leavenworth at the **First City Museum**, which features exhibits about Leavenworth's signature industries. Ride carousels at the **C.W. Parker Carousel Museum**. Fred Harvey changed travel with the Harvey House restaurant and hotel chain. Learn about Harvey, his business, and the famed Harvey Girls at the **National Fred Harvey Museum**. firstcitymuseums.org

At the **Richard Allen Cultural Center & Museum**, learn about Leavenworth's African American history. Exhibits discuss the Buffalo Soldiers, Gen. Colin Powell, and the ruins of the Bethel African Methodist Episcopal Church's Underground Railroad site. A bust of Cathay

Williams, the only known female Buffalo Soldier, is on the grounds. jazzbytheriverleavenworth.com/museum

Learn more about Leavenworth's connection to the Missouri River at **Leavenworth Landing Park**—a beautiful green sanctuary by the Missouri River. Its walking path connects to the **Wayside Tour** and the **Three-Mile Creek Trail**. bit.ly/lvtrails

There's plenty of veterans history in Leavenworth. Six Medal of Honor winners are interred at the **Leavenworth National Cemetery** as part of the **Dwight D. Eisenhower Medical Center Historic District**. bit.ly/lvnatlcemetery

Visit the beautiful Gothic-inspired **Chapel of the Veterans** nearby, and check out the three gargoyles. bit.ly/chapeloftheveterans

Singer/songwriter Melissa Etheridge was born in Leavenworth, and her lyrics often refer to Leavenworth. Download an **Etheridge tour brochure**. bit.ly/etheridgetour

Etheridge's lyrics refer to Fourth Street—and if you enjoy food trucks, you'll find a great one on Fourth, **Mido's Halal Mediterranean Grill**. Their gyros are heavenly. facebook.com/MidosHalalMediterraneanGrill

Luigi's 418 is a Leavenworth legend. The sausage pepper Parmigiana and the stromboli? Yum, yum! facebook.com/luigis418

Drink Twisted at **Z&M Twisted Vines Wines & Winery**. Besides their wines, they also offer soaps and scrubs made from wine ingredients. zmtwistedwines.com

The downtown Leavenworth historic shopping district offers a fun shopping experience with numerous specialty shops. The militaria shops are fascinating. bit.ly/lvshopping

You've only seen the tip of the iceberg of things to do on Glacial Hills Scenic Byway. Just driving the roads will make you happy—but there's so much more to see. Happy exploring!

Glacial Hills connects to the **Frontier Military Historic Byway**. Frontier Military runs north–south between Kansas City and the Oklahoma state border and Route 66. At the north end of Glacial Hills, Nebraska's **Heritage Highway Scenic Byway** begins in Brownsville, about an hour northwest of White Cloud.

Get your kicks on Route 66 and Frontier Military Historic Byway

Nostalgia and history meet on the eastern edge of Kansas. **Highway 66** runs briefly through the very southeast corner of Kansas, and Mother Road icons fill those thirteen miles. On Frontier Military's Highway 69, mining, Bleeding Kansas and the Civil War are everywhere present. We'll explore ninety miles of 66 and 69, starting at the south end of the route in Baxter Springs, and heading north to the **Marais des Cygnes National Wildlife Refuge**.

Fort Scott is near this drive's midpoint. If you're looking for a great home base for this route, stay in Fort Scott's last remaining railroad hotel, the **Courtland Hotel & Spa**. courtlandhotel.com

Orientation begins at the **Route 66 Visitor Center**, Baxter Springs. Look for the vintage Phillips 66 sign and pumps. Sign a brick inside the center before you leave. bit.ly/baxterspringsstation

For more nostalgic car culture, head to **Decades of Wheels** car museum and its on-site bistro and soda fountain, **Rita's Roost**. decadesofwheels.com

For more stomach satisfying, try the excellent brisket dinner at **Van's Steakhouse**, which one diner lauds as having "lip-smackin' good vittles." facebook.com/vansbaxter

Stand on the **Kansas, Missouri, and Oklahoma Tri-Point** on the edge of Baxter Springs. roadsideamerica.com/story/50144

Baxter Springs holds plenty of history. Learn about mining, Mickey Mantle, the Osage Tribe, and the Civil War at **Baxter Springs Heritage Center & Museum**. Mantle, a baseball Hall of Famer, played with the Baxter Springs Whiz Kids in the late 1940s. Also at the museum, examine a world-record hand-carved wooden chain and pick up walking tour brochures. baxterspringsmuseum.org

At Fort Blair in 1863, Union soldiers defeated William Quantrill's guerrillas. Visit the **Fort Blair Historic Site** to learn more. bit.ly/ftblair

Because of poor leadership, guerrillas massacred the members of a Union wagon train approaching the fort shortly thereafter. The soldiers were buried in the **Baxter Springs Cemetery Soldiers' Lot**. bit.ly/soldierslot

The impressive **Baxter Springs Bas Relief Mural**, on the south side of the American Bank, explains the city's history. bit.ly/basreliefmural

Drive three miles of the original Route 66 north of Baxter Springs in the **North Baxter Springs Historic District**. bit.ly/ksoriginal66

After six miles, walk the original **Rainbow Bridge**—the only remaining Marsh arch bridge on Route 66. It's now a pedestrian bridge, with a replacement bridge built for traffic nearby. bit.ly/66rainbowbridge

Just a little west of the bridge, and a slight detour off the highway, hunt the king of upland birds at America's largest pheasant resort, **Show Me Birds**. showmebirds.com

Back on Route 66, a great place to stop for supplies is **Eisler Bros.' Old Riverton Store**, which dates from 1925. It's the epitome of a general store, with the best selection of Route 66 souvenirs anywhere. You'll love a bottle of Route 66 Soda. The store is also a lovely place to hang out. eislerbros.com

Galena is your last stop on Route 66 before heading north. The movie *Cars* was a shout-out to Route 66. The idea for Tow Mater, one of its major characters, originated in Galena. Meet the inspirational little truck, named Tow Tater, at **Cars on the Route**—the Sheriff and other movie characters are present. Inside the former Kan-O-Tex station, choose classic burgers and fries. facebook.com/CarsOnTheRoute

A *Greetings from Galena* postcard mural adorns the wall at Main and Seventh. Nearby, a **Ghost Bike** honors the memory of two German cyclists killed in an accident. bit.ly/galenaghostbike

Galena is another name for lead ore, which is the origin of the city's name. Early settlers picked up chunks of lead on the ground, and by the 1880s, thirty thousand miners had flooded Galena. Of course, vice and crime followed. Learn about Galena's fascinating and sometimes-lurid history at the **Galena Mining & Historical Museum**. galenamuseum.org

For example, notorious madam **Ma Steffleback** robbed and murdered as many as fifty victims in Galena. Police only found two of the missing bodies. No one has discovered her ill-gotten money. bit.ly/murderousmadam

A fifty-mile piece of the Ozark Plateau juts into Kansas. Explore the natural wonders of the plateau at **Schermerhorn Park**. In the 1920s,

Route 66 travelers visited the area to wade or swim in shallow Shoal Creek, on which the park sits. In the 1930s, the Works Progress Administration built the park's entrance gate, terraces, and retaining walls. Take the wooded trail past limestone bluffs to **Schermerhorn Cave** where, according to legend, Jesse James hid out. The cave's spring houses rare salamanders, and many birds and other creatures visit the park. geokansas.ku.edu/schermerhorn-park-and-cave

A historic Boy Scout cabin became Schermerhorn's **Southeast Kansas Nature Center**. Get a hands-on education about local plants and wildlife at the center. bit.ly/schermerhornpark

When your appetite calls, head back to Galena. In a restored train depot, order the Burrito Torito at **Mi Torito Mexican Restaurant**. Dip your chips into queso fundido while you wait for your entrée. facebook.com/MiToritoMexicanRestaurant

To explore more of Route 66, take a slight detour east to **Joplin**, Missouri.

To continue on Frontier Military Historic Byway, head north from Galena on North Main, crossing Short Creek, where miners discovered lead. From there, a half-hour drive via Forest Avenue, Jackson Avenue and SE 110th Street will take you to Old Highway 96, over Turkey Creek and Spring River. Heading west on 96, you'll enter **Columbus**. While here, visit the **Cherokee County Courthouse**; the 1919 Seth Thomas clock tower on the square in front of the courthouse honors World War I service members. It's the only working clock of its kind. cherokeecountyks.gov

In the **Columbus Museum**, look for oddities like a 468-mile ball of string, a Frisco caboose, and a wye switch. bit.ly/columbusksmuseum

Pick up a **Columbus driving tour** at the museum or the chamber office. The **Community Building** features a 1940 sand sculpture by Waylande Gregory, called **R.F.D.**, and a large mural of historic Columbus. chamberofcolumbus.com

In October, enjoy the **Hot Air Balloon Regatta**. columbusdayballoons.com

Beyond the eastern edge of town, Admire T.J. Losey's elaborate monument while sitting on the benches in his family's **Columbus City Cemetery** plot. Losey, a Civil War cavalryman, long outlived his family. The missing branches on the stone tree stump that adorns his gravesite honor their lives cut too short. bit.ly/tjlosey

Head northwest from Columbus to West Mineral, stopping at **Scammon** halfway. Original stained glass windows depict Bible stories in the 1907 **Saint Bridget Church**. bit.ly/scammonchurch

Before you leave, taste the love in **Josie's Ristorante** recipes. You've never had such a delicious Italian cream cake. bit.ly/josiesristorante

In **West Mineral**, you'll find the region's biggest delight: **Big Brutus**. The world's largest electric shovel weighs eleven million pounds and stands sixteen stories high. Big Brutus stripped overburden (soil on top of ore veins). The dipper's capacity was 150 tons, enough to fill three railroad cars. Climb five stories to sit in the controller's seat. Learn more about mining in the visitor center. Campers will find showers and hookups. bigbrutus.org

Envision Big Brutus devouring the ground in the gorgeous **Mined Land Wildlife Area**, which covers 14,500 acres in the region. After the mines closed, the state reclaimed the area for habitat protection and outdoor recreation. bit.ly/minedlandwa

When the Mayer Mine No. 9 exploded on December 13, 1916, twenty miners died. Sixteen of them came from **Stone City**. The Windson family lost a father and two sons. A bank vault is all that's left of Stone City— you can see it on NW Fortieth Street outside West Mineral.

Continue north on a beautiful drive to scenic **Hudgeon Bridge**, which spans Limestone Creek. bit.ly/hudgeonbridge

Next is **Pittsburg**, whose coal boom attracted immigrants from fifty-two nations. Celebrate their contributions at the annual **Little Balkans Festival** in August. littlebalkansfestival.com

Honor the miners and their families at the **Miner's Memorial and Immigrant Park** on N. Walnut Street. Read their stories and the local miners' names. minersmemorialpittks.org

On November 9, 1888, Kansas's worst mining disaster struck Frontenac. Forty-four miners died in an explosion. Their bodies were buried in unmarked graves in the **Mt. Olive Cemetery** and **St. Mary's Catholic Cemetery** in

Pittsburg. An Eagle Scout project installed grave markers in the early 2000s. bit.ly/frontenacminedisaster

After World War I, mine production in the region slowed, and workers struggled to feed their families. The mines cut workers and decreased pay for those who were left. Miners enacted strikes, many led by Kansas union leader Alexander Howat, who opposed the Industrial Court's interference with the rights of miners. When the Kansas government pressured the national union to remove Howat, thousands of women—wives and relatives of the miners—marched in protest for three days in December 1921. To support justice and equality for miners, the women marched through coal camps. They blocked mine entrances and tossed red pepper flakes at workers who crossed picket lines, called scabs. Nicknamed the **Amazon Army**, they carried American flags and sang patriotic songs. Their actions were shocking for the time, but eventually, the protests bore fruit, leading to labor reforms. One marcher's son, Congressman Joe Skubitz, later was instrumental in passing mine safety legislation. amazonarmy.com

Union buster Andrew Carnegie donated funds for many libraries across the nation, including Pittsburg's. Because of the miners' outrage, Carnegie's name was not included on the **Pittsburg Public Library** exterior. The building's Prairie School style is unusual for Carnegie libraries. Inside the library, a mural entitled Solidarity depicts the Amazon Army's march. pplonline.org

Mining history can be a little bleak. Time for some fun! Delight your children at **Kiddieland Amusement Park** on Memorial Drive, and have a grand time riding the miniature train, roller coaster, Ferris wheel, and other rides. bit.ly/kiddielandpittsburg

Patriotic pride and love for American veterans will overwhelm you at the striking **Pittsburg State University Veterans Memorial Amphitheater**. The amphitheater features a half-size replica of the Vietnam Memorial Wall in Washington, DC. It includes bronze sculptures, an arch with an eternal flame and reflecting pool, plus a fifty-state flag display. psuvetmemorial.org

Pittsburg is famous for fried chicken. Eight miles outside of Pittsburg, neighboring restaurants **Chicken Annie's** and **Chicken Mary's** started for the same reasons. The restaurants' namesakes both had husbands who could no longer work in the mines. To support their families, the women began selling fried chicken. Eventually, Chicken Mary's granddaughter married Chicken Annie's grandson. Of course, they opened another chicken restaurant on the other side of town, **Pichler's Chicken Annie's**. Which is best? You make that call. bit.ly/crawfordcountyfriedchicken

Escape the chicken coop at **Typhoon**, Thai food at its best. The pineapple curry and the basil duck are top-notch. typhoonthai.com

You might have to wait at **Bob's Grill**, but the classic burger joint food is worth waiting for. bit.ly/bobsgrill

Three miles north of Pittsburg's center, hike through diverse ecosystems in **Frontenac's Wilderness Park**. Parts of the trails are accessible. Other trails climb former open-pit mines. Four fishing pits are available. bit.ly/wildernesspark

For hiking fuel, pick up a loaf of famous Frontenac Bread and other delicious food from **Pallucca's Italian Market**. palluccas.square.site

Keep heading north on Highway 69, to **Franklin**. The Amazon Army started its march from the Miners Union Hall here; the **Miners Hall Museum** shares the history of coal mining in southeast Kansas. minershallmuseum.com

From Franklin to **Arma**, walk the 1.75-mile world-record **Longest Sidewalk Between Two Towns**. bit.ly/longestwalkway

Fort Scott is twenty-one miles from Arma, so we recommend jumping back in the car instead of walking. The fort was established in 1842, with the intention of keeping the peace between Native American tribes. In 1855, the Army sold the buildings, and Fort Scott incorporated as a city in 1860. During the "Bleeding Kansas" period, the Free State and Western (pro-slavery) hotels faced each other across the parade grounds. The proximity bred violence. The opposing camps often faced off, with predictable results.

During the Civil War, **Fort Scott** became a logistics center. The current fort preserves twenty historic structures. nps.gov/fosc

Tour the City of Fort Scott on **Dolly the Trolley**, starting at the visitor center. bit.ly/dollythetrolley

Fort Scott Downtown Historic District is within sight of the fort and the visitor center. Enjoy the beautiful "painted lady" buildings as you shop and dine. The street bricks came from a Fort Scott factory, whose products also paved the Indianapolis Speedway and the Panama Canal.

Honor those who supported oppressed people at the **Lowell Milken Center for Unsung Heroes** and the **Gordon Parks Museum**, both in Fort Scott.

At the Milken Center, get to know brave souls like Irena Sendler, who rescued more than 2,500 Jewish children during World War II. lowellmilkencenter.org

Gordon Parks broke racial barriers as a pioneering African American photographer, film director, musician, and other vocations. Parks' memorabilia and artworks are in the museum. gordonparkscenter.org

Visit Parks's grave at **Evergreen Cemetery**. bit.ly/gordonparksgrave

After a long day learning about history, raise a glass to Bourbon County at **Sharky's Pub & Grub**. facebook.com/sharkyspub

Viñedo del Alamo Winery's name means "popular vineyard." Find out why in their 1922 tasting room on Poplar Road as you head north out of town. bit.ly/vindeodelalamo

On the way to the winery, cross the Marmaton River on the 1933 **National Avenue Bridge** in **Riverfront Park**. bit.ly/marmatonriverpark

Off-roaders, mountain bikers, and hikers will love **Kansas Rocks Recreation Park**, to the northwest of Fort Scott on a short detour from Highway 69. It's a taste of riding the Ozarks—in Kansas. ksrockspark.com

Back on the route, **Mine Creek Civil War Battlefield** near Pleasanton was the site of one of the Civil War's most massive cavalry battles. At the end of Confederate General Sterling Price's raid, the Union had cleared Kansas and Missouri of Confederate forces. Follow the battle's course on two miles of interpretive trails. bit.ly/minecreekbattlefield

Learn more about the Civil war and area history at **Linn County Historical Museum** in **Pleasanton**. bit.ly/linnhistorical

Enjoy diner classics at **Cookee's Drive-In**, just around the corner from the museum. facebook.com/cookeesdrivein

Take a quick detour to **Mound City**, where Union soldiers once camped in **Mound City Historical Park**. Imagine pioneer life at the park's historic structures. moundcity.org/historical-park

Sugar maples are native to the area. See them burst into color during October's **Sugar Mound Arts & Crafts Festival** in Mound City. sugarmoundartscrafts.com

Established in 1825, the community of **Trading Post** nine miles north of Pleasanton is Kansas's oldest existing settlement. One of Bleeding Kansas' most notorious murders, the **Marais des Cygnes Massacre**, happened here. Pro-slavery men murdered five free-state men and wounded five others. At the site, twelve markers tell the massacre's story. bit.ly/mdcmassacre

A massacre memorial stands in the **Trading Post Cemetery** next to the **Trading Post Museum**. kansastravel.org/tradingpostmuseum.htm

The University of Nebraska Center for Great Plains Studies named **Marais des Cygnes National Wildlife Refuge** one of the Great Plains' Top 50 Ecotourism Sites. *Marais des Cygnes* means "marsh of the swans." Visit the refuge just outside Trading Post. bit.ly/maraisdescygnesrefuge

Although we've made a ton of great stops on the Frontier Military Historic Byway, don't deep-six this fantastic travel opportunity. There's more to mine on this travel route.

Explore the last tallgrass prairie on the Flint Hills and Native Stone Byways

No matter how hard farmers worked to plow Flint Hills' soil, the flint won. Soon, settlers learned to turn the rocky hills into pastures. The impervious rock saved the Flint Hills portion of the tallgrass prairie for future generations. The white and gray stone that peeps through the grass and shows on hillsides is called chert, and is made up of layers of limestone and flint. See one of the last remnants of untouched tallgrass prairie at the **Tallgrass Prairie National Preserve**, which is a centerpiece of the **Flint Hills National Scenic Byway**. travelks.com/ksbyways/flint-hills

In the spring, the Flint Hills streams sparkle with rapids and waterfalls. Wildflowers reign in the spring and summer. Later in the year, the tallgrass puts on its autumn finery, and the cottonwoods' yellow leaves twirl in the wind before falling to the ground. Winter brings stark whiteness that exposes the strong bones of the land.

Picturesque native stone fences surround fields and farmsteads on the nearby **Native Stone Scenic Byway**. travelks.com/ksbyways/native-stone

After the Civil War, Kansas Legislature closed the open range (grazing land without fences or other barriers). The state paid farmers forty cents a rod (approximately 16.5 feet) to build and maintain stone fences, which had to be at least four feet high. The settlers also used the stone for buildings.

First, get settled

For a home base to explore these byways, stay in one of the lovely accommodations in the area.

The restored **Grand Central Hotel** in Cottonwood Falls is a relaxing option. Every room door bears a local ranch brand. Downstairs, the **Grand Grill** serves tender, juicy steaks. grandcentralhotel.com

Fall asleep to the sound of Cottonwood Falls at the **Millstream Resort Motel**, which is renowned for its quirkiness. bit.ly/millstreamresort

Guests at **The Cottage House** in nearby Council Grove receive discounts at various local eateries. cottagehousecgks.com

You can also camp at Richey Cove by **Council Grove Lake**. bit.ly/richeycove

At the northern end of the Flint Hills Byway, Manhattan has numerous lodging options. manhattancvb.org/28/Lodging

Let's start driving

The Flint Hills excursion begins at **Teter Rock**. This sixteen-foot man-made monolith nearly twelve miles from Cassoday looks like a Stonehenge refugee. Wild horses often gather near the rock. bit.ly/teterrock

Nearby **Texaco Hill** offers some of the Flint Hills' best views and astrophotography opportunities. Drive across the unfenced pasture on an unimproved road. bit.ly/texacohill

The **Cassoday Bike Run** started in 1991. From March through October, bikers still gather in Cassoday on the first Sunday of each month. cassodaybikerun.org

Matfield Green is ten miles north. The bank here was the last remaining business on Main Street; now it's an art gallery, the **Bank Art Space**, offering four art exhibitions each year. matfieldgreen.org/thebank

Ranching comes alive at **Pioneer Bluffs Center for Flint Hills Ranching Heritage**, on Rogler Ranch just north of Matfield Green. Tour the 1859 ranch and enjoy concerts, dances, cowboy celebrations, and more. pioneerbluffs.org

As you approach the city of **Cottonwood Falls**, stop at **Schrumpf Hill Scenic Overlook** for a 360-degree view of the Flint Hills. Interpretive panels explain the overlook. bit.ly/schrumpfhill

Waterfalls and three ghost towns await visitors west of Cottonwood Falls. In the spring, **Chase Lake Falls** are some of Kansas's most beautiful—three waterfalls drop along Prather Creek. The walk to the falls can be treacherous; wear hiking shoes. bit.ly/chaselakefalls

At **Chase Lake**, anglers will find channel catfish, black bass, saugeye, white bass, and bluegill. bit.ly/chasefishinglake

Farther west is **Elmdale**, a town that flooded in 1951 and subsequent years. The ghost town retains several buildings (no longer operational), including Bummie's Grocery, shaped to fit an odd-sized lot, and the Peoples Exchange Bank. bit.ly/elmdaleks

A few houses mark **Clements**'s location. The two-span **Clements Stone Arch Bridge** is near the homes. Take a field road to a small parking area and walk the bridge. It provides a beautiful view of the Cottonwood River. bridgehunter.com/ks/chase/90480

Continue west on Highway 50 to the **Drinkwater & Schriver Mill**, in **Cedar Point**. This historic site was once one of the finest mills in Kansas, but is now in need of restoration. cedarpointmill.com

Head back to Cottonwood Falls, where the **Chase County Courthouse** dominates the skyline. The 1873 white Second Empire–style building is stunning. Inside, take a close look at the beautiful walnut staircase.

A short set of steps on the third floor leads to a window overlooking **Downtown Cottonwood Falls**. Inspect the courthouse's former county jail. cwfks.org/chase-county-courthouse

While downtown, browse the shops. You'll find beautiful art galleries and antique stores. Flags outside stores mean they're open. chasecountychamber/shopping

On Friday nights at about 7:30, enjoy music at **Prairie PastTimes** artists' cooperative. Pleasant weather brings the **Emma Chase Friday Night Music** program outdoors. Bring your lawn chairs. bit.ly/emmachasemusic

Can't get enough music? The **Symphony in the Flint Hills** is held annually in a Flint Hills pasture. The Kansas City Symphony plays at sunset after a day of fun. symphonyintheflinthills.org/signature-event

The symphony's gallery in Cottonwood Falls offers Kansas books and art. symphonyintheflinthills.org

At **Keller Feed and Wine Co.** on Broadway, eat a *bierock*: a round meat-and-cabbage handheld pie. For dessert, choose bourbon peach cobbler with buttermilk topping. facebook.com/KellerFeedAndWine

Walk north to the 1914 **Cottonwood River Bridge** from downtown. bit.ly/cfbridge

The bridge is the southern end of the **Community Connection Trail**. The two-mile sidewalk connects Cottonwood Falls with **Strong City**. bit.ly/ccctrail

From Strong City, the trail connects with the Tallgrass Prairie Preserve's **Bottomland Trail**. Don't miss the majestic tallgrass in the fall. In rainy years, the grass can reach six feet tall. The trail is wheelchair-friendly in dry weather. bit.ly/bottomlandtrail

Kansas's beloved state motto is "Ad Astra Per Aspera," which means "To the stars through difficulties." Kansans usually abbreviate it to "Ad Astra." Drink Ad Astra beer at **Ad Astra Food and Drink** in Strong City. Everything tastes terrific, but their macaroni and cheese and the Chase County quesadillas are outstanding. adastrafoodanddrink.com

In June, take in Strong City's **Flint Hills Rodeo**, where you'll see top professional rodeo contestants. flinthillsrodeo.org

Immerse yourself in nature at **Tallgrass Prairie National Preserve**. The sound of the wind rustling through the tall grass on the eleven-thousand-acre preserve will soothe your soul. The bison grazing in their natural habitat will ignite your sense of awe at God's creation. nps.gov/tapr

Start at the visitor center. The center's limestone façade and tallgrass prairie-covered roof blend into the landscape. Register for a must-do bus tour, which will take you to see the park's bison herd.

Tour the historic **Spring Hill Farm** buildings. On hot days, cool down in the limestone mansion. Enjoy a look at pioneer refrigeration techniques in the spring room and the icehouse. At 110 feet wide and 60 feet deep, the barn is vast. Ramps on the sides enabled horses to walk into the barn's upper floors.

The park offers forty miles of trails. Hike the beautiful **Southwind Nature Trail** from the ranch to the **Lower Fox Creek School**. Inside the one-room schoolhouse, experience rural education. Outside, enjoy prairie views. Download trail maps at bit.ly/tallgrasspreservetrailmaps.

After the preserve, leave the highway for two out-of-the-way destinations. In the spring, visit **Lake Kahola Waterfall**, about fifteen miles northeast of Strong City. Lake Kahola is private. The falls are beautiful—it's worth requesting permission to visit here: kansastravel.org/kaholalakewaterfall.htm.

Dunlap is farther northeast. When Reconstruction ended, Southern governments tightened controls on their Black populations. Benjamin "Pap" Singleton, who was born a slave but escaped to freedom, led formerly enslaved people—called Exodusters—to Kansas. In 1878, Singleton brought them to Dunlap, his final Exoduster colony.

At first, Dunlap's white settlers imposed segregation. But segregation had faded away by the 1930s. Only two remnants of Dunlap's Black history remain: the Baptist church and the **Exoduster Cemetery**. London A. Harness, who died in 1993, was Dunlap's last Black resident, and the last person buried in the Exoduster Cemetery. legendsofkansas.com/dunlap-kansas

Follow the Neosho River northwest to **Allegawaho Memorial Heritage Park**. In 1925, erosion exposed a Kaw warrior's remains here. Locals erected a thirty-five-foot-tall obelisk from native rock and reinterred the warrior, horse, and grave goods. In 2000, the Kaw Nation bought the park's property and built a self-guided two-mile trail. kawnation.com/?page_id=7508

The annual **Washunga Days Festival** is held at the park. washungadays.com

If you feel like hiking or biking to your next destination, the **Flint Hills Trail State Park** will lead you west from Allegawaho to Council Grove's **Neosho Riverwalk**. A Kaw warrior, *Guardian of the Grove*, guards the riverwalk. bit.ly/flinthillstrail

The **Santa Fe Trail** created **Council Grove**. The Great and Little Osage Nations signed a treaty allowing trail passage under the **Council Oak**, giving Council Grove its name. Follow the self-guided tour. Historic highlights include the **Hermit's Cave** on Belfry Hill, the *Madonna of the Trail* (one of twelve such pioneer monuments on the Old Trails Road), the **Kaw Mission State Historic Site**, the **Post Office Oak and Museum**, the **Farmers and Drovers Bank**, and the **Last Chance Store**. councilgrove.com/historicsites

Join the **Tin Man** in his search for the Wizard of Oz near **Ray's Apple Markets**. The sculpture stands near the road, axe and oil can in hand. Dress up as Dorothy, the Scarecrow, or the Cowardly Lion for the perfect selfie. raysapplemarkets.com

Daniel Boone's great-grandson Seth Hays established **Hays House Restaurant** in Council Grove in 1857. Eat the country-fried steak and explore the building—it's as much a museum as it is a restaurant. The basement bar is fascinating. hayshouse.com

Ride your bike or hike on the **Flint Hills Nature Trail** east to **Admire**, and then head north to the **Native Stone Scenic Byway**, which begins at **Eskridge**. Whichever transportation mode you choose, watch for stone fences. In Eskridge, check out the Moorish architecture at the **Waugh Law Office**.

Alma is your first stop on Native Stone. It's famous as "The City of Native Stone," and as the home of Alma Creamery. **Alma Creamery** has been crafting cheese for five decades. Every one of their numerous cheeses is handmade. The cheese curds are especially—and justifiably—famous. Save money at their store when you buy cheeses that look less than perfect. almacheese.com

Alma's **Downtown Historic District** contains twenty-one historically significant buildings, many of which were built with native Cottonwood Limestone. Pick up a tour brochure at the **Wabaunsee County Historical Society and Museum**. wabaunseecomuseum.org

Find a county map inlaid into the terrazzo flooring of **Wabaunsee County's Courthouse** second floor. bit.ly/wbcocourthouse

Within an hour's drive north from Alma, you can visit five wineries: **Prairie Fire Winery** and **Wyldewood Cellars Winery**, Paxico; **Oz Winery** and **456 Wineries**, Wamego; and **Liquid Art Winery and Estate**, Manhattan.

Paxico, a slight detour off Highway 99 on Interstate 70, is an antique-shopper's paradise. It's full of antique shops, including **Mill Creek Antiques**. millcreekantiques.com

Enjoy the free **Paxico Blues Festival** each September. paxicobluesfest.com

North of Interstate 70, **Wamego**'s **Oz Museum** joins with **Oz Winery** to make Highway 99 "The Road to Oz." The museum holds over a century of Oz-themed artifacts, from L. Frank Baum's original books to MGM's 1939 movie production notes, to more recent collectibles. ozmuseum.com

On your way from Alma to Wamego, take a short spur west to **Wabaunsee** for some pre–Civil War history. Famous abolitionist preacher Henry Ward Beecher sent rifles to Kansas free-state settlers in cases marked "Bibles," and parishioners dedicated the **Beecher Bible and Rifle Church** near Wabaunsee in 1862. The church still holds Sunday services. bit.ly/beecherbibleriflechurch

Farther west on K-18, then south on Tabor Valley Road, visit a famous waterfall at **Pillsbury Crossing**. Deep Creek flows over a four-foot drop. Upstream, the road goes through a low-water crossing. Catch some channel catfish. bit.ly/pillsburycrossing

In this region, keen paddlers can check out the **Kansas River Trail**, which runs from Junction City to Kansas City. Manhattan, St. George, and Wamego all have river access points. Check the website for maps and safety information. travelks.com/ksrivertrail

If you don't end up on the river to Kansas City, find spectacular views at **Konza Prairie**, a short drive west from Pillsbury Crossing. Hike through lowland forest, cross Kings Creek, and climb limestone ledges into tallgrass prairie. Trails range from 2.6 to 6.2 miles long. Exhilarating hikes include steep climbs, uneven footing, and narrow pathways. keep.konza.k-state.edu/visit

Manhattan is your final stop on this itinerary, situated between Pillsbury Crossing and Konza Prairie. For fishing, hunting, and watersports, visit **Tuttle Creek State Park**, five miles north of Manhattan. bit.ly/tuttlecreeklake

Off-roaders will love **Tuttle Creek ORV Area**. bit.ly/tuttlecreekorv

Manhattan is home to **Kansas State University**, and offers all the zest for living that a major-college town can provide. Check out the university's cultural arts program. k-state.edu

Devour everything dairy, fresh eggs, and meat, at K-State's **Call Hall Dairy Bar** on campus. bit.ly/callhalldairybar

Manhattan also goes wild for Wildcat athletics. kstatesports.com

Check the **Game Day Guide** for football Saturdays. manhattancvb.org/277/Gameday-Guide

If you've loved your Flint Hills trip and want to learn more about the area, visit Manhattan's **Flint Hills Discovery Center**—an impressive building that celebrates the geology, ecology, and cultural history of the Flint Hills. flinthillsdiscovery.org

The center opens onto **Blue Earth Plaza**, where a water feature puts on a colorful nightly light show. mhkprd.com/172/Blue-Earth-Plaza

During the winter holidays, the plaza hosts the **Manhattan Festival of Lights**. mhkfestivaloflights.com

In Downtown Manhattan, eat at **Bourbon & Baker** with its fabulous cocktails, comprehensive bourbon list, and small plates. bourbonandbaker-manhattan.com

Savor delicious certified Angus steaks, fresh beers and ales at **LABCo. Market and Restaurant** in the **West Loop Shopping Center**. littleapplebrewery.com

To truly experience Manhattan, visit **Aggieville**—the oldest shopping district in Kansas. It's hopping with shopping, dining, and entertainment. Aggieville turns from K-State purple to green every St. Patrick's Day. aggieville.org

While in Aggieville, celebrate the end of your road trip by toasting the Flint Hills at Manhattan's two breweries: **Manhattan Brewing Company**, and **Tallgrass Tap House**. mhkbeer.com; tallgrasstaphouse.com

The Flint Hills has much more to experience--great hunting, fishing, and shopping. Extend your trip and explore the region.

Kansas has more delightful byways. **Gypsum Hills Scenic Byway** features mesas and canyons. Wildflowers take center stage each spring on **Smoky Valley Scenic Byway**, home to **Cedar Bluff State Park**. Renowned for birding, the **Wetlands and Wildlife National Scenic Byway** includes **Quivira National Wildlife Refuge**. The **Garden of Eden** in Lucas helps turn **Post Rock Scenic Byway** into the quirkiest Kansas byway. **Prairie Trail Scenic Byway** includes Lindsborg, also known as Little Sweden USA **Kanopolis State Park**, and **Mushroom Rocks State Park**. travelks.com/ksbyways

Kansas byways
- **Flint Hills National Scenic Byway** 47.2 miles, Highway 177 from Cassoday north to Council Grove
- **Frontier Military Historic Byway** 168 miles, Highways 69 and 5 from the Oklahoma line north to Leavenworth
- **Glacial Hills Scenic Byway** 63 miles, Highways 73 and 7 from Leavenworth north to the Kansas-Nebraska line
- **Gypsum Hills Scenic Byway** 42 miles, Highway 160 east from Coldwater to Medicine Lodge
- **Land and Sky Scenic Byway** 88 miles, Highway 27 north from Sharon Springs to the Kansas-Nebraska line
- **Native Stone Scenic Byway** 75 miles, An S-shape including Highways 4, 99, 18, and 177 from near Dover to the Interstate 70-Highway 177 exit near Manhattan
- **Post Rock Scenic Byway** 18 miles, Highway 232 from Wilson to Lucas
- **Prairie Trail Scenic Byway** 80 miles, Highways 141, 4, and 156 from Canton to the I-70 and Highway 177 interchange near Ellsworth

- **Historic Route 66** 13.2 miles, Highways 66 and 69A from Galena to Baxter Springs
- **Smoky Valley Scenic Byway** 60 miles, Highways 283, 4, and 147 south from WaKeeney to Ness City and north to Ogallah
- **Western Vistas Historic Byway** 102 miles, Highways 40, 83, and 95 west from Sharon Springs to Oakley and south to Scott City
- **Wetlands and Wildlife National Scenic Byway** 77 miles, Highways 4, 156, and Barton, Stafford, and Reno county roads from Hoisington in the north to north of St. John in the south

Roxie Yonkey has been writing about Kansas for thirty years, and has won numerous awards. Currently, she is Chief Exploration Officer at RoxieontheRoad.com and a Contributing Writer for TravelAwaits.com. Yonkey is on Facebook, Twitter, Instagram, Pinterest, and LinkedIn as @RoxieontheRoad.

Always interested in a new adventure, she loves to travel and enjoys road-tripping most of all. Join us on a great Kansas road trip in this book. It will show you how to enjoy the Midwest's many fun travel opportunities.

Roxie and her husband Eric have two cats, Dalbie and Lola. She enjoys reading, photography, gardening, repurposing pallets, and scrapbooking.

MICHIGAN

Michigan is a great state, founded in 1837 and known to many as the Great Lakes State, as it touches four of the five Great Lakes. It is also known as the Winter Wonderland, and the Wolverine State. It houses roughly ten million people.

Basic Michigan Facts
- The state capital is Lansing.
- The state motto is, "If you seek a pleasant peninsula, look about you."
- The state bird is the robin.
- The state flower is the apple blossom.
- There are forty-eight highways and byways to explore.

Fun Michigan Facts
- Michigan has enough pavement in roadways to construct a one-lane road from the earth to the moon.
- With 124 lighthouses, Michigan has more lighthouses than any other state.
- Michigan is second only to California in agricultural diversity. Michigan delivers more than three hundred agricultural products in a combination of livestock and crops.

As a lifelong resident of Michigan, I can't wait to share with you four of my favorite Michigan road trips, and some of the extraordinary places they have to offer. Michigan has more than twenty byways, so I have chosen four that represent different aspects of the state.

With a view of the mighty Mackinac Bridge, US 2 **Top of the Lake Scenic Byway** starts in St. Ignace and follows the Lake Michigan shore to

Manistique. Whether you're a foodie who wants to sample your first pasty or an outdoor enthusiast who wants to explore state parks, you'll enjoy this scenic route.

Then follow the **Sunrise Coast** (US 23) from the Straits of Mackinac along Lake Huron to Standish, where you'll encounter an International Dark Sky Park, sixteen lighthouses, and Shipwreck Alley. Next, we'll explore **US 12 Heritage Trail**, an east–west corridor, from Detroit to New Buffalo, which leads history buffs and automotive enthusiasts on an adventure through time.

Finally, explore the **West Michigan Pike** (US 31), which features Michigan's Gold Coast. Charming small coastal towns that are not only a draw for boating enthusiasts, but also for art lovers.

One of these is sure to become a favorite for you, too!

US 2 Top of the Lake Scenic Byway

With a majestic view of the mighty Mackinac Bridge, US 2 Top of the Lake Scenic Byway starts in St. Ignace and embraces the Lake Michigan shoreline ninety-two miles west to Manistique. Whether you're a foodie who wants to sample your first pasty, or an outdoor enthusiast who wants to explore state parks, you'll enjoy this scenic route.

The best way to explore this scenic byway is to stay in St. Ignace for a night. Then drive to Manistique, stopping to explore some sites along the way. Then spend a night in Manistique before exploring the town and heading back to St. Ignace, taking in the places that you missed on your way out. If you want to take some additional time to enjoy northern Michigan's natural beauty, stay at one of Michigan's state park campgrounds.

Where to stay

After a busy day in northern Michigan's fresh air, I always sleep well. Need a place to rest your head? Here are some spots to consider.

Located in St. Ignace, on Lake Huron, **Kewadin Casino** is an eighty-one-room hotel offering Las Vegas–style table gaming and slots. The rooms have a log-cabin feel, keeping with the "Up North" theme. Amenities include free Wi-Fi, free valet parking, an indoor pool, and a gym. Be aware that pets aren't allowed at Kewadin Casinos; however, service animals are welcome with the proper documentation. kewadin.com/acommodations/st-ignace-hotel

The one-hundred-room seasonal **Breaker's Resort and Beach Bar** right on the beach is a good option for early risers. If you will be up in time to see the sunrise, choose one of the balcony rooms to watch the sunrise over Lake Huron. breakersmi.com

If camping is more your thing, **Fayette Historic State Park** may be thirty-three miles west of Manistique, but this well-preserved old mining town located in **Garden** is worth the detour. You'll enjoy the serenity of white cliffs overlooking a Lake Michigan harbor and lush forests. If you love living history but are not an avid camper, situated in the museum village is another accommodation option, **Fayette Furnace Hill Lodge**. Once the manager's residence, this cabin sleeps up to ten people, and has a remodeled kitchen and one bathroom that includes a shower, tub, sink, and flush toilet.

If you want to get in some fishing, the mouth of the Black River is a favored fishing hole with the locals. Head north from US 2 on Black River Road to **Black River State Forest Campground**, where you'll find twelve rustic campsites. The sites are on a first-come, first-serve basis without reservations. michigan.org/property/black-river-state-forest-campground

The Big Knob State Forest Campground, located fourteen miles southwest of Naubinway, has twenty-three rustic sites. The beautiful thing about this campground is its dunes on Lake Michigan's beachfront. Pathways make for great outdoor recreation fun. Be aware that the campground has vault toilets and potable water from a hand pump. These sites are on a first-come, first-serve basis without reservations. www2.dnr.state.mi.us/parksandtrails/Details.aspx?id=687&type=SFCG

On the road

Castle Rock, three miles north of **St. Ignace**, is a great place to start this journey. The rock rises 195 feet above the water and showcases Lake Huron, Mackinac Island, and downtown St. Ignace. From the lookout point, you can see up to fifteen miles on a clear day. Where else can you get a million-dollar view for a dollar? castlerockmi.com/#!the-rock

Head south through town to jump on US 2. On this route, you'll find lots of things to do that will afford you a break from the car. Just west of St. Ignace is the **Mystery Spot** and, at the risk of exposing the mystery, this attraction is a gravity hill that features tilt-induced visual illusions. The Mystery Spot is a family-fun place where optical illusions abound. An interactive guided tour typically takes twenty minutes, depending on visitor participation. It's the perfect place to stretch your legs and play an eighteen-hole round of mini-golf or try to find your way through the Fort maze. The zip lines are another family-fun activity. mysteryspotstignace.com

Don't leave an encounter with some of northern Michigan's native species to chance. **Deer Ranch** is the oldest live white-tailed deer exhibit in North America, where you'll find white-tailed deer, white white-tailed deer, and albino deer. You can purchase some appropriate deer feed for a nominal fee, then feed, pet, and photograph the deer in a natural setting while getting some exercise on the trail. Each year, the ranch bottle-feeds a few fawns—call ahead to find out when, and they just may let you help. The gift shop has a large selection of Minnetonka moccasins and deerskin products like gloves. deerranch.com

The beachy waterfront along the south side of Highway 2 just west of St. Ignace, referred to as the **Dunes**, is the perfect place to pull over on the shoulder of the road, stretch your legs and enjoy Lake Michigan. You can even stop and play in the water. stignace.com

About six miles from St. Ignace as you head west on US 2, be sure to stop at the **Gros Cap Roadside Park** on the south side of the road. Here, you'll have the perfect photo opportunity of the Mackinac Bridge and Lake Michigan. If you decide to have a picnic lunch here, watch out for seagulls— the little thieves would like nothing more than to snatch a bite of your lunch. bit.ly/groscaproadsidepark

If you're a snow bunny and you just can't get enough Michigan in the winter, but you're visiting in the summer, get your fix at the **Top of the Lake Snowmobile Museum** in **Naubinway**, about forty minutes from Gros Cap. The museum is dedicated to the history of snowmobiling and displays vintage and antique snowmobiles, and it's open all year round. snowmobilemuseum.com

Another forty-minute drive from Naubinway is **Seney National Wildlife Refuge**—a twelve-mile trip north of US 2—which offers the perfect place to get back to nature for a day. While there's no camping in these almost 96,000 acres, you'll find lots of other ways to enjoy the environment through the diverse ecosystem that supports a variety of wildlife. Start with the Marshland Wildlife Drive where, if you're a bird-watcher, you'll have the opportunity to see trumpeter swans, common loons, bald eagles, osprey, and sandhill cranes. If you prefer walking for your bird-watching, the Pine Ridge Nature Trail is a great option. Bird-watchers, go to the website for a checklist of the dozens of birds you might see.

Other ways to enjoy the refuge's outdoor activities include Northern Hardwoods cross-country ski trails, and snowshoeing, with miles and miles of unpaved roads for hiking and biking through the backcountry. Guided tours and exhibits provide learning experiences about the resident wildlife and their habitats. fws.gov/refuge/Seney/visit/plan_your_visit.html

Head back out to US 2, and when you get to **Gulliver**, turn left on MacDonald Lake Road to get to **Seul Choix Pointe Lighthouse** (locally pronounced sis-shwa, and meaning "only choice" in French). The lighthouse is a brick-tower building that still lights the small harbor on Lake Michigan. Centuries ago, French fur traders and Native Americans used canoes as transportation across the sometimes-turbulent waters of Lake Michigan. A group of Frenchmen was caught in a storm and had to find a haven on the rocky peninsula. During the storm, it was their "only choice," so they named the area Seul Choix.

Today, you can enjoy a lighthouse tour and experience the outdoors with a picnic area, walking paths, and a public boat launch. A gift shop, library, and museum complete the experience for history buffs. greatlakelighthouse.com/home.php

Manistique is only twenty-four miles from Gulliver, and it's your next stop. A walk on the **Manistique Boardwalk** is a pleasant place to enjoy a picnic, get in some pier fishing, and enjoy the local wildlife. The Boardwalk is a great place from which to view the square-pyramidal **Manistique East Breakwater Light**. visitmanistique.com/breakwaterlight.shtml

Michigan's largest spring, **Kitch-iti-kipi (The Big Springs)**, is one of those beautiful spots that you'll be sorry you missed if you don't head out there. You will find this treasure tucked away in **Palms Book State Park** about eleven miles past Manistique off US 2. The clear pool is two hundred feet across and forty feet deep, with a stunning emerald-green bottom. More than ten thousand gallons of crystal clear water gushes from the spring every minute, and the water temperature is forty-five degrees year-round. A self-propelled group raft allows a closer look at the trout at the bottom of the springs. The water is so clear that you might think you're viewing the fish in a swimming pool. bit.ly/kitchitikipi

The return: food

After all of the activities that this road trip offers, you will work up an appetite—and what's a road trip without sampling some of those local favorites? On the way back to St. Ignace, stop at as many eateries as you can for delicious treats. In Michigan's Upper Peninsula, that means you must try Lake Superior whitefish or a pasty (meat and vegetables wrapped in pastry).

You can be sure to have some of the best food in the area at one of these local favorites.

The **Mackinaw Trail Winery and Brewery** is a family-owned and-operated business founded in Manistique in 2004. Today, the main operation is in the Lower Peninsula's city of Petoskey; however, Manistique still offers a tasting room with a lovely view of the water and an outdoor seating area. On Manistique Harbor, enjoy the fresh air and a glass of Mackinaw Trail wine or a craft beer. The tasting room's Manistique Music Nights are an excellent time to go down to the harbor, take in the view, appreciate a glass of wine or artisan brew, and listen to music with friends. mackinawtrailwinery.com

There seems to be a theme in Manistique. **The Upper Crust Deli**, on Manistique's waterfront, also has a pretty view to eat lunch outside on the surrounding deck. If the weather isn't cooperating, you can still enjoy the view through the large, light-admitting windows. The Upper Crust Deli offers counter service with house-made soups, salads, and sandwiches. If the large sandwiches don't leave even enough room for a cookie, remember that baked goods to-go make the perfect afternoon snack on the road. uppercrustdeli.com

After you leave Manistique, head east on US 2 and then take a slight detour north when you reach US 33. **Goodale's Sweet Spot** in **Curtis** has red-and-white candy-striped walls that add to the vintage atmosphere. They serve Jilbert's ice cream locally made in Marquette. The variety of flavors ranges from the typical vanilla, chocolate, and strawberry to those featuring Michigan ingredients like cherries and Mackinac Island Fudge. A couple of favorites are the Amaretto Cherry and Mackinac Island Fudge flavors. It's challenging to get enough of this one! facebook.com/Goodalessweetspot

When you arrive back in St. Ignace, you're spoiled for choice, with plenty of great food options on offer.

Java Joe's Café is more than a place to have a great cuppa Joe. This café is a must-stop for breakfast or brunch—Joe makes both granola and yogurt in-house. I'm a foodie, so Joe taught me about his house-made kaymak—a yogurt cheese that he serves with fruit and honey for a healthy breakfast. For a more decadent option, try the pancakes and crepes. With over twenty types of pancakes and a half a dozen versions of crepes, it's difficult to decide, but the banana pancakes and Almond Joy pancakes are fantastic. My choice for crepes is the three fresh crepes stuffed with a homemade cream cheese mixture and then topped with Michigan cherries.

The *Detroit Free Press* named Java Joe's breakfasts in the Top Ten in Michigan and *USA Today* selected them as Top 20 in the nation. facebook.com/JavaJoesCafe

It's time for more than coffee and breakfast, so head to **Jose's Cantina**—a great eatery that takes Michigan ingredients like Traverse City cherries and Lake Superior whitefish and puts a Mexican spin on them, creating standout dishes. Ranked the number one fish taco in Michigan, Jose's award-winning Lake Superior whitefish tacos are a must-try. Pair that with a cherry margarita on the deck for alfresco dining with stunning views of the lake for a fiesta of sorts. The sundeck looks directly onto the beach.

Jose's Cantina is a seasonal restaurant, open April through October, and it's an excellent choice for vegetarians and vegans. Their flexible chef can turn almost any dish into a vegan version. joses-cantina.business.site

Also in St. Ignace, **The Gangplank Pub & Grub** is a seasonal outdoor-dining restaurant with a view of Lake Michigan. The beef burgers are never frozen, and the fries are fresh-cut in house. If you want to try some Lake Superior whitefish, try the boat-to-table whitefish fingers as an appetizer. The fish is dusted with seasonings and deep-fried. The whitefish sandwich, which is lightly breaded, deep-fried to a golden brown, and served on a toasted brioche bun, is another great choice. bit.ly/thegangplank

If you still haven't had enough of road-tripping Michigan, you can extend your adventure by linking your US 2 Top of the Lake Scenic Byway trip with Michigan's Sunrise Coast (US 23). History buffs will love exploring Mackinaw City and Colonial Michilimackinac. Just head over the five-mile Mackinac Bridge from St. Ignace into Mackinaw City, and start your adventure down Michigan's Sunrise Coast.

Michigan's Sunrise Coast (US 23)

Continue your road trip from St. Ignace, which is on Michigan's US 2 Top of the Lake Scenic Byway, across the **Mackinac Bridge**, which spans the **Straits of Mackinac** connecting Michigan's Upper and Lower Peninsulas. At five miles long, the Mighty Mac is the largest suspension bridge in the Western Hemisphere.

Since the Sunrise Coast is a two-hundred-mile road trip, stretching south from Mackinaw City to Standish, you'll want to select your activities and plan to stay at various stops along the way. Overnighting in Mackinaw City and Mackinac Island for at least one night each is a great start. Then you can choose some campgrounds along the way, depending on how much time you have to explore the area.

You won't want to start down the Sunrise Coast without a side trip to **Mackinac Island**.

My favorite way to get to the island is with **Shepler's Mackinac Island Ferry**. If you take the right departure, you'll have a detour under the Mackinac

Bridge. Shepler's docks are in both Mackinaw City and St. Ignace. See their website for the current schedule. sheplersferry.com

The **Grand Hotel** located on Mackinac Island is a four-star resort and a National Historic Landmark that sits on a cliff overlooking the Straits of Mackinac. It was once a summer retreat for visitors taking lake steamers from Detroit, Chicago, and Montreal, and the railways also brought travelers from across the country. Today, of Mackinac Island's million-plus annual visitors, 130,000 stay at the Grand Hotel.

The hotel, furnished with antiques and chandeliers, is truly grand. All 390 guest rooms are unique, wallpapered in a variety of designs and carpeted in a wide array of styles. The hotel's red geranium logo is ubiquitous. It's even woven into the carpeting in the parlor. While the typical Victorian-era beds are high, the staff quickly provide step stools upon request. The staff's stellar service comes with a no-tipping policy.

Enjoy relaxing in the white rocking chairs on the world's longest front porch (660 feet) and gazing out over the Straits of Mackinac and a spectacular view of the Mackinac Bridge. The fresh air and the view release the stress from life on the mainland.

A meal plan is usually included with your stay. The Grand Hotel has a dress code that requires dressing for dinner, but if that's not really your thing, the modified American meal plan affords opportunities for dining in a more casual environment. grandhotel.com

Make a visit to **Surrey Hills Carriage Museum**, which displays some early horse-drawn carriages. I also enjoyed a carriage tour of the island, and I stopped for a peek at Lake Huron through **Arch Rock**, 146 feet above the shoreline. mict.com

No motorized vehicles are allowed on Mackinac Island, so rent a bike and go for a ride around the island's perimeter or take a horse and buggy carriage tour to see the island's highlights.

If you're a history buff, be sure to explore **Fort Mackinac** on Mackinac Island. With reenactments and demonstrations, history comes alive in Fort Mackinac. The fort is a military compound with significant history from the Revolutionary War, the War of 1812, and the Civil War. The fort contains fourteen restored buildings, including the oldest building in Michigan. Each building comes furnished in period settings and exhibits that highlight the building's purpose.

Throughout the day, interpreters dressed in period costumes provide tours and demonstrations, including an exciting Drill, Tactics, and Firearms program. Find out what the daily life of a soldier was like living at Fort Mackinac. bit.ly/fortmackinac

The Richard and Jane Manoogian Mackinac Art Museum, on Main Street in Mackinac Island, is a collection of Mackinac-related art. The curators present the pieces in four long-term displays featuring early nineteenth- to late twentieth-century maps, Native American art, and photography. Audio-visual demonstrations allow visitors to get a deeper understanding of some of the main pieces. bit.ly/manoogianmuseum

After the museum, take a walk on Main Street; when I was there, my walk was complete with free samples from several specialty fudge shops. I had to keep sampling until I found my favorite. I'm still undecided, so I guess a return trip to the island is required to complete my research!

Back on the mainland, whether your idea of camping is a simple tent or pulling in your luxury RV, the Sunrise Coast offers several state parks with a variety of camping options, including rustic cabins within the state parks. Be aware that camping isn't allowed on Mackinac Island.

The closest to Mackinaw City, and one of Michigan's oldest state parks, **Onaway State Park** is 158 acres inland from the coast, with the campground beautifully situated among white pines. If you can't wait to get out on the water, the park has rowboats, canoes, and kayaks for rent to take out on Black Lake. Or if you're interested in some fishing, Onaway is known as the "Sturgeon Capital of Michigan." bit.ly/onawaystatepark

A little farther south, and back out on the coast, **Thompson's Harbor State Park** features two rustic cabins for those who prefer a little more shelter than a tent can provide. Cedar Haven Cabin and Stone Path Cabin each sleep up to six people, with a pull-out couch and two sets of bunk beds. Each cabin includes a gas stove and lanterns, outdoor hand pumps, and vault toilets. While you're still roughing it, it's a step up from a tent. The perfect conclusion to your day's activities is viewing the sunset over Lake Huron. bit.ly/thompsonsharborsp

You'll also find several other state parks along Michigan's Sunrise Coast with a variety of accommodations. **Cheboygan State Park**, **Hoeft State Park**, and **Tawas Point State Parks** are all state parks where you can camp and enjoy an overnight with nature.

Once you've figured out your lodging, it's time to explore. The focus of this area is twofold: history and nature, and this road trip has several interactive experiences that bring history alive.

Colonial Michilimackinac, located in downtown **Mackinaw City** right as you come off the bridge, is the site of one of the most extended continuous archaeological digs in North America. You can see archaeology in action daily. bit.ly/colonialmichilimackinac

Headlands International Dark Sky Park, a short drive from Mackinaw City, boasts a different group of dazzling stars on display each season. So even if you've been there before, you're bound to get a whole new show each time you stop by. Who knows, you might also get lucky and catch a glimpse of the Northern Lights! midarkskypark.org

Time to eat! At **Mama Mia's** in Mackinaw City, you'll find a tasty variety of specialty pizzas, pasta, salads, and sandwiches. Vegetarian selections are well-represented. While you are waiting for your food, take advantage of the free Mackinac Bridge Museum, which contains bridge memorabilia that tells the story of the Mighty Mac. facebook.com/MamaMiasMackinaw

Since 1887, **Murdick's Famous Fudge** has been a family-owned business. Starting with real butter, fresh cream, and 100 percent Belgian chocolate, they transform the ingredients into Pure Michigan fudge. In my book, it's a must-have road-trip snack. MurdicksFamousFudge.com

Just a fifteen-minute drive south of downtown Mackinaw City on US 23, **Historic Mill Creek Discovery Park** is a Michigan State Park and historic site. The park, once home to an eighteenth-century water-powered sawmill, sits on more than six hundred acres that incorporate more than three miles of trails. See what life was like through Mill Creek at Work: Sawpit and Sawmill Demonstrations. Take a guided Beyond the Sawmill walking tour to learn more about the history of the Park. Costumed interpreters provide historical demonstrations and tours to bring history alive. bit.ly/historicmillcreek

Continuing south, the **40 Mile Point Lighthouse**, located on County Park Road in **Rogers City**, received its name due to its position forty miles northwest of Thunder Bay and forty miles southeast of Old Mackinac Point. This lighthouse features a stunning 1896 white tower.

In 1905, the *Joseph S. Fay* freighter wrecked on the beach in the shallow waters below the tower. You can still see it there today. You can also go for a swim, have a picnic, or climb the light tower. It's a great place to stretch your legs and explore during your road trip. michigan.org/property/forty-mile-point-lighthouse

From Rogers City, go west on M 68 to **Ocqueoc Falls**, the largest waterfall in Michigan's Lower Peninsula. From the main falls, take a short walk down the river, and you'll discover another smaller waterfall. bit.ly/ocqueocfallsmlp

After all of that fresh air, address your appetite! **Up North 23 Restaurant and Lounge**, located in Rogers City on the Lake Huron shore, is the perfect place to take in a stunning view of the lake while enjoying a meal on the deck. The chef sources ingredients from local farmers, including the components for the restaurant's famous house-made BBQ chips. Since the restaurant's owners are potato farmers, the chips couldn't get much fresher. upnorth23.com

Stomach full, head back out on US 23. **Rockport State Recreation Area** is east of the highway as you approach **Alpena**, thirty miles south of Rogers City, and it is *the* destination for amateur archaeologists and dinosaur-loving kids. The abandoned limestone quarry has fossils that are more than four hundred million years old. The kids will love the fact that each visitor is allowed to remove up to twenty-five pounds of fossils from the park each year. This park is Michigan's one hundredth state park, and is mostly undeveloped. bit.ly/rockportsra

Off the coast from Alpena is the **Thunder Bay National Marine Sanctuary**, a 4,300-square-mile area that serves to protect one of America's most nationally significant groups of shipwrecks. This area is called "Shipwreck Alley" because fog and other unpredictable weather coupled with a rocky shoreline have claimed about two hundred ships in the Thunder

Bay area. More than the number of shipwrecks, which makes this site nationally important, is the wide variety of vessel types found here. The wrecks include a five-hundred-foot-long German freighter and an 1844 sidewheel steamer.

The **Great Lakes Maritime Heritage Center** in Alpena is the visitor center for Thunder Bay. Learn about Northwestern Lake Huron, which is one of the most dangerous sections of water on the Great Lakes. Immersive exhibits, including replicas of the sunken ships, give great insight into the plight of mariners in the region. Another great thing about this attraction? It's FREE! thunderbay.noaa.gov

Negwegon State Park, twenty miles south of Alpena, is another perfect destination for stargazers. The park is under dark sky protection, and it's a great place to view stars at night with the naked eye. Take note of the Milky Way as it swirls around the earth. bit.ly/negwegonsp

Tuttle Marsh National Wildlife Area is four hundred acres surrounded by five thousand acres of wetlands, making it the perfect off-the-beaten-path environment for bird-watchers. The wildlife area is an excellent place for those who like watching local creatures. The site has various viewing areas where you might encounter white-tailed deer, beavers, otters, foxes, and even coyotes. michigan.org/property/tuttle-marsh-wildlife-area

On Tawas Point, often referred to as the "Cape Cod of the Midwest," sits the **Tawas Point Lighthouse** located at 686 Tawas Beach Road in East Tawas. It's the only authentic Victorian-era style lighthouse on the Great Lakes. If you dream of experiencing the life of a lighthouse keeper, there's a two-week program available to participate in at this lighthouse. bit.ly/tawaspointlighthouse

There is so much more to Michigan's Sunrise Coast—we've just scratched the surface of what it offers. Note that if you're starting your exploration of the Sunrise Coast in Standish, you can extend your Michigan adventure by linking Michigan's Sunrise Coast road trip with the US 2 Top of the Lake Scenic Byway.

If you jump on Interstate 75, you can continue road-tripping across the state from Detroit to New Buffalo on US 12 Heritage Trail.

Michigan's US 12 Heritage Trail

Next, we'll explore US 12 Heritage Trail, a 208-mile east–west corridor from Detroit to New Buffalo. This was once the main route connecting Detroit and Chicago. Today, the road leads history buffs on an adventure through time. For this driving route, Michigan's automotive heritage is the cornerstone.

If you're a die-hard road-tripper, start this journey in the Detroit area, where you'll discover everything automotive. Stay in Detroit for a couple of nights, then meander down the US 12 Heritage Trail, where you'll find plenty more to pique the interest of automotive enthusiasts, not to mention history buffs and nature lovers. Of course, on a road trip this long, you'll need some vital sustenance, and US 12 Heritage Trail has plenty of that, too.

Because the route is around 250 miles, I'd suggest staying at least one night somewhere along the way, to make sure you don't rush the trip.

Start your adventure in **Detroit**, waking up in an impressive hotel. Once the Detroit Fire Department headquarters, **The Detroit Foundation Hotel** still sports the architectural details of a fire station. With the fire pole in the dining room and the red arched doors, you can still imagine firefighters dashing out to go on a fire run. Today, this industrial-chic hotel focuses on all things Detroit-made. You'll find Bon Bon Bon candy and Germack nuts in the minibar. The wall art features local artists, and the hotel restaurant bartenders wear Detroit Denim vests.

The rooms feature exposed brick, earth tones, and bright white linens that together offer a respite from the city's hustle and bustle. The one-hundred-room hotel offers many complimentary amenities, including Wi-Fi, a bike rental service, car service within a three-mile radius, and newspapers. detroitfoundationhotel.com

After checking out, take some time to explore Detroit. Art lovers won't want to miss the **Detroit Institute of Arts** in Midtown Detroit; the museum has one of the largest art collections in the United States. With more than one hundred galleries covering 658,000 square feet, the selection is significant. It features works like Vincent van Gogh's *Self-Portrait*, and Diego Rivera's twenty-seven panel *Detroit Industry* mural, which captures Detroit workers during the Great Depression. dia.org

What's a Coney dog? It's an American classic hot dog, topped with chili sauce and often onions and mustard. You'll find these Detroit specialties throughout Michigan. While you're in Detroit, you'll want to take a minute and compare **American Coney Island** to **Lafayette Coney Island**, which is right next door. Locals have an ongoing argument as to which is the best. Stop and decide which is your favorite. americanconeyisland.com/home.htm; bit.ly/lafayetteconey

Buddy's is the birthplace of the Detroit-style pizza that originated in 1946 when Gus Guerra took an auto steel pan and created a square pizza. What makes it unique is the house-made crust that is double-stretched to make it light. The seasoned forged-steel square pans give you a crispy, crunchy bite every time. On top of the crust are Wisconsin brick cheese and other ingredients of your choice, then sauce tops the cheese. Food Network named Buddy's one of the "Best Five Pizzas in the Nation." There are several locations throughout the Detroit area. buddyspizza.com

No trip along the US 12 Heritage Route would be complete without a visit to **The Henry Ford** in Dearborn on the western side of Detroit—after all, we owe the need for highways and byways to Henry Ford. The Henry Ford includes a combination of four experiences, including the Henry Ford Museum of American Innovation, Greenfield Village, Ford Rouge Factory Tour, and the Giant Screen Experience.

The **Henry Ford Museum** is chock-full of history. Not all of the automobiles here are Fords; the museum contains a car collection that represents cars from around the world. Some must-see exhibits include the limousine that President John F. Kennedy's Presidential was riding in when he was assassinated, the Rosa Parks bus, and the rocking chair that Abrabam Lincoln was sitting in when killed.

Greenfield Village is a two-hundred-acre site created from a collection of about one hundred historic buildings that Henry Ford relocated from all over the United States and reconstructed in Dearborn. At Greenfield Village, you can see Thomas Edison's Menlo Park Laboratory and the Wright Brothers' Cycle Shop. You can also ride in a Model T, a Model AA Bus and various horse-drawn carriages, as well as taking the Weiser Railroad, and riding the Herschell-Spillman Carousel.

The **Ford Rouge Factory Tour** takes visitors through an actual working factory that today manufactures Ford F-150 trucks. thehenryford.org

Heading west, make a stop at **Hidden Lake Gardens** in **Tipton**, just over an hour past Dearborn, which is owned and operated as part of Michigan State University. The garden has 755 acres to explore in both indoor and outdoor spaces. The indoor Plant Conservatory features exotic plants and tropical settings. Outdoors, you can enjoy five miles of hiking trails to trek. You can also see one of the most extensive Bonsai collections in the Midwest at Hidden Lake Gardens. canr.msu.edu/hiddenlakegardens

If you're itching to get back to the automotive theme, stop at **Brooklyn** in the Irish Hills area, where you'll find **Michigan International Speedway**. With a fifty-year history, this two-mile moderate-banked D-shaped speedway on more than fourteen hundred acres is one of NASCAR's most entertaining tracks. mispeedway.com

Cambridge Junction Historic State Park and Walker Tavern Historic Site, also located in Brooklyn, sits at the intersection of the Old Chicago Road (US 12) and La Plaisance Pike (M 50). Here, you'll find a humble story-and-a-half farmhouse. The Walker Tavern, built circa 1832, was once a place for travelers to rest or dine as they took the exhausting five-day road trip from Detroit to Chicago. Today, the tavern and two other historic structures make up the eighty-acre state park. A reconstructed barn and the tavern contain exhibits about travel and work in the 1840s and '50s. The Visitor Center, housed in the 1929 colonial revival Hewitt House, plays storyteller, with tales of early automobile tourism in the Irish Hills. Learn about the quirky twentieth-century roadside tourist attractions, including Frontier City, the Prehistoric Forest, and Mystery Hill. bit.ly/cambridgejunctionhsp

After exploring Cambridge Junction Historic State Park, take a break for lunch and a wine tasting at **Cherry Creek Cellars**. Housed in an 1870s schoolhouse at 11500 Silver Lake Highway in Brooklyn, Cherry Creek Cellars is a boutique winery that uses old-world handcrafting based on the owners' European roots.

The Double Gold Medal winner, the Raspberry Beret, is particularly good. It features sweet Seyval Blanc wine blended with raspberries for a fruity, sweet, and refreshing treat. cherrycreekwine.com

The **Rooms at Grayfield**, in **Jonesville**, about halfway along your route, is a five-star luxury Bed and Breakfast housed in the restored 1890s Michigan Southern Passenger train depot. The inn offers six unique ensuite guest rooms, three with king beds and three with queens. While many bed and breakfasts have a frilly, fussy atmosphere, the decor at the Rooms at Grayfield is a great mix of classic and understated. You'll particularly enjoy the outdoor grounds that are arranged like outdoor rooms. My favorite area is around the koi pond. Freight trains or an occasional old-fashioned steam train still roll past the former train station to remind you of what train travel once was. roomsatgrayfield.com

Olivia's Chophouse, also in Jonesville, serves upscale gourmet meals that include steak and seafood specialties. That said, you'll find more casual daily specials like Taco Tuesday and Pizza Thursdays as well. Be sure to ask about daily specials. I had house-made red skin potato chips with a house-made ranch dip, which were added to the menu due to an over-purchase of red skin potatoes. I almost ordered a second helping; they were just that good! oliviaschophouse.com

Antique hunters will want to stop in **Allen**, five miles west of Jonesville. The tiny town stakes its claim as "The Antique Capital of Michigan"—and with more than five hundred antique dealers, it's no wonder. Treasure hunters come from all over the Midwest to rummage through the village's many antique booths. bit.ly/michiganantiques

If you seek out nature and wildlife venues, **Fernwood Botanical Garden and Nature Preserve** in **Niles**, 111 miles west of Allen, is a must-see. When I visited, a young deer wandered into the garden area for a surprise visit and made my time there even more special. The garden gets its name from the vast assortment of ferns curated there. Fernwood is also an excellent place for those who enjoy bird-watching.

Paul Busse of Applied Imagination in Kentucky brought another unique feature to Fernwood: the railway garden, which comprises model trains and mini replicas of local historic buildings with beautiful plants. Busse is a landscape architect and naturalist, who created both outdoor and indoor railway gardens that combine garden design, art, and history—each a key element at Fernwood. fernwoodbotanical.org

Only a few miles from Fernwood, in Buchanan, is **Bear Cave**—the Great Lakes area's only cavern, located in the Bear Cave RV Resort campground. Formed from tufa rock that's secondary limestone, this rock bed is about twenty-five thousand years old, and lies on a glacial drift that was deposited during the last ice age. A forty-foot stairway winds through the cave, which is full of stalactites and petrified leaves. Metal oxides color the entire cave.

Bear Cave's relatively small size holds significant history—thieves left their booty from an Ohio bank robbery in the cave. The robbery was the inspiration for the 1903 classic silent film *The Great Train Robbery*. The cave also played a significant role in the Underground Railroad.

If camping is your style, you can stay at **Bear Cave RV Resort**. Campsites including five tent sites, ten park model rentals, and seventy hookups. rvonthego.com/michigan/bear-cave-rv-campground

Finish up your adventure in **New Buffalo**. **Oink's Dutch Treat** screams fun on so many levels! With more than fifty-five flavors of ice cream, choosing gets the fun started. Then the building's décor adds so much interest that, while you might have to wait for your order, you'll have plenty of pigs to browse in all forms—the store is completely covered in pig and ice cream memorabilia. I'm not sure if the Oink name is to remind you not to be a pig and overeat ice cream, or if it's encouragement to go all in. More than likely, it's also a play on owner Roger Vink's name. In any case, you'll have fun at Oink's. oinksdutchtreat.com

All this fun just scratches the surface of what Michigan's US 12 Heritage Trail offers.

Your Michigan road-tripping doesn't need to stop here. You can see more of the Great Lakes state by continuing your journey north from New Buffalo up the West Michigan Pike, US 31, to Ludington. That route provides plenty of opportunities to be a beach bum.

Remember, you can link your US 12 trip to Ohio on the east end—check out the chapter on **Ohio**—with the **Lake Erie Coastal Ohio Trail**—they connect off US 75. On the west end, you can extend your road trip south into Indiana (check out the Indiana chapter)—the **US 12 Heritage Trail** continues into **Michigan City**, **Indiana**, where there's even more fun in the sun on Great Lakes beaches.

West Michigan Pike (US 31)

Finally, explore the West Michigan Pike (US 31), which features 184 miles along Michigan's Gold Coast from near the state line at New Buffalo all the way north to Ludington. The coast is full of charming small towns that are a draw not only for boating enthusiasts and nature lovers, but also for art aficionados and history buffs.

Crews completed the paved West Michigan Pike in 1922, making it the first road in Michigan built for tourists. Advertised as "Lake Shore All the Way: Chicago to Mackinaw," it drew travelers from Chicago to Michigan, seeking relief from summer's sweltering temperatures. The West Michigan Pike gave visitors greater access to the coastal communities from the Indiana state line up through the Straits of Mackinac. In 1929, they widened the road and rerouted it as a superhighway. Since then, lodging, activities, and restaurants have flourished along the byway, and today Michigan's US 31 has many "best of" designations along the way.

I like to set up a base camp near the middle of the route, somewhere near Holland, which allows me to take day trips in either direction, or just appreciate all that Holland has to offer. There are great places to stay all along the route, though, so take your pick!

Here are some unique accommodations you should consider for an overnight stay that becomes an experience in itself.

Set in a restored Tudor mansion, the **Hawkshead Inn** in South Haven is a country-chic inn overlooking Hawkshead Golf Course. The nine charming, exclusively decorated rooms, some with sitting areas, fireplaces, or golf course views, make this inn a great retreat. A free in-room continental breakfast is an excellent way to get the morning started. hawksheadlinks.com

The Wickwood Inn is a Bed & Breakfast in Saugatuck. It has eleven guest rooms with elegant touches like fresh flowers and designer décor. The owner of the Wickwood Inn, Julee Rosso, wrote five cookbooks, including the Silver Palate Cookbook, so needless to say this venue is a foodie's delight. wickwoodinn.com

For basic accommodations, but an experience unlike any other, you might decide to spend the night in Muskegon on the submarine *USS Silversides* as part of an "overnight encampment." Overnights are open to those who are five years old or older, and the *USS Silversides* can sleep up to seventy-two overnight participants. There's a minimum of twenty overnight guests, but smaller groups can be joined with larger groups to create a full house.

Not just a place to sleep, the USS Silversides Submarine Museum's historic vessels bring history to life. You can walk the deck and investigate the submarine before you sleep in the berths. While you're on board, be sure to check out the museum exhibits. For reservations and more information on how your family can experience history, check out the website. silversidesmuseum.org

If you're an outdoor lover and camping is more your style, the Lake Michigan shore has some beautiful campgrounds to try. **Warren Dunes State Park**, right at the southern end of the route, has 1,952 acres of fun and three miles of Lake Michigan shoreline, delivering a load of things to do. There are stunning views from the top of the 260-foot, dunes, and this is also an excellent place to give hang gliding a try. If you're in for milder adventures, the park has six miles of hiking trails. You'll unwind to the sounds of Lake Michigan's waves if you opt for lakefront camping. Whether you prefer modern with hot water, bathrooms, and electricity or a more rustic campsite, you can have it all in Warren Dunes State Park. You'll find it in Sawyer, about a ten-minute drive north of New Buffalo. bit.ly/warrendunessp

Don't confuse Silver Lake State Park and Silver Beach, as they are at opposite ends of the byway. Silver Lake State Park is in Mears, just half an hour from your northernmost point of Ludington, while Silver Beach is in St. Joseph, just north of Warren Dunes. **Silver Lake State Park** is another park that allows tent camping near the lakeshore. This park is popular, so be sure to reserve early. bit.ly/silverlakesp

Holland State Park sits between Silver Lake and Silver Beach, halfway along the West Michigan Pike, and offers two great campgrounds, each with distinctive elements. Snuggled between the dunes on Lake Michigan, the Beach Campground maintains ninety-eight paved campsites, thirty-one with full hookups. The Lake Macatawa Campground features 211 campsites, eleven with paved lots.

If cabins are your preference, you'll love the new camper cabin, The Whitetail. It sports stunning views of both "Big Red"—a beloved local lighthouse painted a vibrant shade of red—and the Holland Channel. The Beach Campground opens the first weekend in May and closes the last weekend in September. Wooded sites open in April and close in October. A full hookup is $45. Reserve your campground up to six months in advance by calling 1-800-44-PARKS or reserve online at MiDNRReservations.com.

Whether you're a nature enthusiast, art lover, wine aficionado or foodie, you will find plenty to capture attention along West Michigan's Pike. Each of these coastal towns has something unique to offer.

Beginning in New Buffalo, hit US 31 and head north. A star attraction at **Silver Beach** in **St. Joseph** is the carousel, with its forty-eight unique figures and two chariots. Choose your favorite horse and ride beneath one thousand twinkle lights. Explore some of the local shops downtown, and take a walk on the pier. silverbeachcarousel.com

Sitting about two hundred yards off Lake Michigan's beach, **Silver Beach Pizza** in St. Joseph offers pizza fashioned from dough that's made from scratch daily. The most popular pizzas are the Carousel, which is a nod to the carousel across the tracks, and the Garlic Greek. You won't need to save room for dessert here, as they don't serve it. Kids will enjoy the fact that a train stops at the adjoining train station twice a day. silverbeachpizza.com

About half an hour north of St. Joseph, make a stop in **South Haven** for a bite to eat. Built in 1896, the structure that houses **Clementine's** was once the Citizens State Bank. The stately building sits with a golden copula crown on the corner of Phoenix and Center Streets. Inside, you'll find exposed brick, a tin ceiling, and a variety of dishes made with Michigan ingredients. One fan favorite is the classic "Mess of Lake Perch"—yellow lake perch that is pan-fried. In 2019, Clemetine's sold fourteen tons of perch. Not only that—they also served eight miles of golden-brown onion rings, which they serve stacked on a wooden peg. Just imagine how delicious the food is here! ohmydarling.com

On your way north to Saugatuck, take a quick detour to one of my favorite vineyards: Fenn Valley Vineyards in **Fennville**. Visit during the fall months, and you can tour the vineyards to see how the grapes go from vine to glass. The tour includes an all-important tasting. Another option is to have a picnic in the vineyard, where they have options for private vineyard meals. My favorite drop is the 2016 Michigan Wine Competition Double Gold medal award winner, the Edelzwicker 2015. To receive a Double Gold medal, two panels of judges have to award a Gold medal to the wine unanimously.

Wine lovers have plenty more to see; West Michigan Pike boasts a variety of wineries, including those on the **Lake Michigan Shore Wine Trail**, where you can experience award-winning wines and wineries. The Lake Michigan Shore American Viticultural Area (AVA) possesses ninety percent of Michigan's vineyards, as Lake Michigan's "lake effect" softens the extreme climate of the north. The abundance of wineries, along with sunsets over Lake Michigan, will make for an enjoyable experience for wine lovers. miwinetrail.com

From Fenn Valley, it's just fifteen minutes to **Saugatuck**, back on the coast. **Saugatuck Dune Rides** provides a forty-minute ride where you'll learn about the town of Singapore that was lost to the sand, and perhaps see some wildlife along the way. When I took this ride, deer were out for a cold drink by the water. saugatuckduneride.com

If you're an art lover, Saugatuck is the perfect destination for your explorations. In fact, this region is known as "the art coast of Michigan." You'll find DIY opportunities and have the chance to see what local artists are doing in their studios, or you can check out local art galleries. The town is often paired with nearby Douglas for the attractions that the two offer in combination. Check out the website for information on the arts and more. saugatuck.com

The **Star of Saugatuck Boat Cruises** is another family-fun adventure. While they offer cruises throughout the day, my favorite is the sunset cruise, which allows you to enjoy the stunning sunsets over Lake Michigan while you're on the water. saugatuckboatcruises.com

Just ten minutes north is Holland where, with its Dutch Heritage, you can enjoy what *Forbes* called one of the "Prettiest Towns in America" all year round. In spring is the annual Tulip Festival, where you can enjoy the blossoms of more than six million tulips; in summer, take a beach day with "Big Red," Michigan's most photographed lighthouse in the background; fall brings appreciation of Michigan's spectacular foliage along South Shore Drive; and winter amps up the European flavor with Holland's outdoor Christmas market, the *Kerstmarkt.*

deBoer Bakkerij Restaurant, which has two locations in Holland, offers authentic Dutch food. DeBoer Bakkerij is a fourth-generation family-run bakery that added dining options in 2008. At the northern location, you can pick up bread and baked goods, and grab breakfast from Tuesday to Sunday. On the south side, breakfast, lunch, and dinner are available Tuesday to Sunday.

They offer scratch-made soups from fresh ingredients that rotate seasonally. For a traditional Dutch lunch, you'll find Dutch pea soup on the menu year-round, and it's great paired with the pigs in the blanket.

At the bakery, buy some house-made bread for sandwiches to enjoy a picnic lunch at one of Michigan's roadside parks, or grab some pastries to enjoy a taste of Holland snack later in the day. A cup of coffee to go made from the beans that they roast in house, paired with those pastries, gives you some of the best Dutch cuisine this side of the pond. deboerbakery.com

Located on the shores of Lake Macatawa—the inland Lake on which Holland sits, and which connects to Lake Michigan at the coast—**Boatwerks Waterfront Restaurant** offers a waterfront outdoor seating area where you can enjoy Michigan's amazing sunsets over dinner. If the weather permits, plan to eat on the deck where it's fun to watch the boats on the lake. Boating types dock their boats in the deep-water port or at the pier.

Boatwerks has a casual boating theme with an industrial-style ceiling and lights. The bar top reminds me of handmade wooden boats from a bygone era, with alternating dark mahogany boards and light wood inlays.

The menu includes Michigan favorites like Lake Superior whitefish, either served as an appetizer dip with fresh vegetables and pita chips or as an entrée with an herb- and panko-crusted coating and topped with citrus dill cream sauce. The restaurant also offers other Michigan fish, like salmon, walleye, and perch. boatwerksrestaurant.com

An hour-long drive from Holland, you'll find **Michigan's Adventure** in **Muskegon**—it's a great place to get some roller-coaster thrills! This 250-acre amusement park is the largest in Michigan, and has fifty-two rides—more than any other park in the state. In addition to roller coasters, Michigan's Adventure offers lots of family rides that are good for all ages. The water park portion, WildWater Adventure, is a great way to cool down on a hot day. miadventure.com

Your last stop on this itinerary is **Silver Lake State Park**, thirty miles north of Muskegon in **Mears**. If you find riding the dunes in an off-road vehicle (ORV) exciting, you have two options in Silver Lake State Park: You can rent an ORV at a business in Mears, or you can bring your own dune buggy or four-wheeler. You can also take a dune tour and just relax and enjoy the ride.

This itinerary just scratches the surface of what the West Michigan Pike (US 31) offers. Remember, you can link your trip to Michigan's US 12 Heritage Route and extend your fun in Michigan by exploring Michigan east to west, ending in Detroit.

Amy Piper publishes the popular Midwest Travel Blog FollowThePiper.com, and is a valuable member of the Midwest Travel Network. In addition to her love of all things travel, Piper also enjoys making images, trying restaurants in unusual buildings, and reading about far-off lands. You may have also come across her work in print magazines like Collectible Automobile, Savvy Retiree, *or* Shop

Local Lansing; *when she has been featured on Great Escape Radio; or across mutual travels. Above all, Piper hopes that travel expands your horizons and quenches your thirst for adventure, and that this book helps you do just that.*

Learn more about Piper at AmyPiper.com.

Twitter: twitter.com/amythepiper

FB: facebook.com/followthepiper

IG: instagram.com/amythepipertravels

MINNESOTA

M innesota was settled by the Ojibwe and the Dakota Native People in 1849, and entered the union in 1858. Known for being the "Land of Ten Thousand Lakes," Minnesota actually has nearly eleven thousand lakes. Lake Superior, the world's largest freshwater lake, borders Minnesota on the North Shore. The Headwaters of the Mighty Mississippi begin at Lake Itasca in Bemidji, MN and flow some 2,350 miles to the Gulf of Mexico.

Basic Minnesota Facts:
- The state capital is St. Paul.
- The state motto is "L'Etoile du Nord," which translates to "Star of the North."
- The state bird is the common loon, though some would say the mosquito is the state bird.
- The state flower is the showy lady's slipper.
- There are twenty-two highways and byways to explore, which are listed in the index in the back of this book.

Fun Minnesota Facts:
- The Mall of America, located in Bloomington, is the nation's largest shopping mall.
- Minnesota gets its name from the Minnesota River and is a Sioux word which means "sky tinted" or "cloudy water."
- Minnesota has more bike trails than any other state.

Minnesota River Valley Byway

The Minnesota River Valley National Scenic Byway is 287 miles long, beginning at the southern tip of Big Stone Lake on the Minnesota/South

Dakota border and continuing to Belle Plaine, Minnesota. This scenic byway travels multiple roads, so look for signs indicating the Minnesota River Valley National Scenic Byway as you're driving.

Throughout this scenic drive are multiple historic sites that are related to the **Dakota people** and the **Dakota War of 1862**. There are many opportunities to learn more about both the Dakota People and the conflict along this scenic drive. Some landmarks will be mentioned here.

Let's begin this scenic drive in **Browns Valley**, a town that lies along the **Laurentian Divide**. This is where a small rise in the land influences which way the water flows.

At the southern tip of **Big Stone Lake** in **Ortonville**, along the South Dakota border, is where you'll find the headwaters of the Minnesota River.

Big Stone Lake's **Bonanza Education Center** hosts year-round activities, teaching people of all ages about the native prairie, the natural springs and the bur oak and basswood forests that are in the area. Check out their online calendar for events. bonanzaeducationcent.wixsite.com/bonanza

You can see **Paul Bunyan's anchor** in Ortonville at the **Big Stone County Museum**, where you can learn more history about the area. exploreminnesota.com/profile/big-stone-county-historical-museum/2162

You'll want to check out **Big Stone National Wildlife Refuge** in **Odessa**, which is just east of Ortonville. This refuge is over eleven thousand acres of tallgrass prairie, wetlands, granite outcrops and river woodlands. Eleven miles of the Minnesota River flow through this refuge, which provides habitat for migratory birds and is also used for fish and wildlife conservation and recreation. Visitors are welcome to fish, take hikes and just enjoy the wildlife. bit.ly/bigstonenwr

As you meander down the scenic byway, you'll pass **Marsh Lake**, which has the largest pelican rookery in Minnesota. It's one of only two nesting colonies of the white pelican in the state. As many as ten thousand pelicans, tundra swans, snow geese, and sandhill cranes come to migrate here.

The upper portion of the Minnesota River flows through a chain of lakes from Big Stone Lake to **Lac qui Parle Reservoir** near Montevideo. There are so many wildlife viewing opportunities along the way! This area is very popular with bird-watchers, so you may want to bring your binoculars with you. There are thousands of different bird species known to be in the area.

Take in the **Lac qui Parle Mission** in **Montevideo**—a historical site where missionaries helped create the first written Dakota alphabet. Visit a recreated chapel that is filled with artifacts about the Dakota, as well as information about how the alphabet was used to translate the Bible into the Dakota language. mnhs.org/lacquiparle

Take a self-guided tour at the twenty-four-building village at **Chippewa City Historical Park**, which features a pioneer church, school, and historical homes. The buildings once inspired famous artist Terry Redlin, and if you're familiar with his work, you will recognize the buildings in this village from his Country Doctor series. Strolling through the village, you can easily imagine what life would have been like decades ago.

Visit **Swensson Farm Museum** outside of Montevideo. This is a seventeen-acre farmstead with a twenty-two-room brick farmhouse resting on a foundation of local granite. This site is included on the National Register of Historic Places. bit.ly/swenssonfarm

Twenty minutes southeast from Montevideo, outside of **Granite Falls**, a great place to stop is the **Fagen Fighters WWII Museum**. On display is some of the most significant aircraft and vehicle equipment that was used during World War II. It would be easy to spend hours solely in the library, leafing through aircraft operating manuals and leaflets. You'll find thoroughly restored airplanes and ground vehicles at the Museum, and all of the vehicles are restored to running condition. You could spend several hours here if this topic is of interest to you. fagenfighterswwiimuseum.org

There are plenty of places to grab a bite to eat in Granite Falls, from fast food to local restaurants. Head downtown to see the **Granite Falls Suspension Bridge**, built under license from the same company that designed the Brooklyn Bridge.

South of Granite Falls is the **Upper Sioux Agency State Park**, which is on the Minnesota River. This state park preserves the land that was destroyed during the Dakota War of 1862. You'll find all kinds of terrain here, replete with native plants. Camping is available, including the unique opportunity to stay overnight in a tepee. There are three eighteen-foot tipis available for rent. You're likely to see golden and bald eagles in the area, as well.

The Minnesota River is generally calm. You'll have a chance to see **Patterson's Rapids** twenty miles downstream from Granite Falls. There are also some smaller waterfalls that trickle into this part of the Minnesota River.

Now on to Redwood Falls. Check out **Ramsey Park**, which is the largest municipal park in the state of Minnesota. It's been coined the "Little Yellowstone of Minnesota," and includes a trout stream, scenic overlooks, the picturesque Ramsey Falls and the **Ramsey Park Zoo**, where you'll find buffalo, elk deer, prairie dogs, game, and waterfowl. bit.ly/ramseyparkzoo

The next town along the Minnesota River is **New Ulm**, about an hour southeast. New Ulm is very proud of its German heritage, making this interesting town a place that you could easily plan to spend an entire day exploring.

No trip to New Ulm would be complete without a tour of **Schell's Brewery**—the second oldest brewery in the United States, which is still operating and thriving. Stop in for a tour of the historic grounds and beer samples. In town, the **Hermann Heights Monument** (known by locals as Hermann the German) is a 102-foot statue that you can climb, offering beautiful views of New Ulm and the **Minnesota River Valley**. The **Glockenspiel**, also downtown, is a forty-five-foot clock with thirty-seven bells that can be heard daily at noon, 3 p.m. and 5 p.m. schellsbrewery.com

People travel from all around to eat at **Veigel's Kaiserhoff**, a tavern serving traditional German specialities. You'll find ribs, schnitzel, and bratwurst on the menu. Another great place to eat is **New Ulm Turner Hall**, which claims to be the oldest bar in Minnesota. Murals of German castles decorate the walls. kaiserhoff.org; newulmturnerhall.org

Take a guided tour of the **Wanda Gág House**. Gag was an American artist, author, translator and illustrator. She might be best-known for her children's book, ***Millions of Cats***, which is the oldest book still in print. Her childhood home in New Ulm has been restored and is on the National Register of Historic Places. wandagaghouse.org

The **Brown County Historical Society** is a beautiful building with rotating exhibits. There are three floors (wheelchair accessible), and the

Society maintains an award-winning display about the US–Dakota War of 1862. browncountyhistorymn.org

Step back in time with a trip to the **Harkin Store**. This authentic 1871 general store features costumed interpreters that enhance the experience, and you'll have views of the Minnesota River from the porch. mnhs.org/harkinstore

Another German experience is a trip to **Domeier's German Store**. It's eclectic and filled from wall to wall with treats and goodies from Germany. You'll find gnomes, antiques, knickknacks and lots of cuckoo clocks.

On your way out of town, visit **Morgan Creek Vineyard**, a beautiful winery with a lovely setting. There's lovely outdoor seating with a fireplace, a view of the grapes growing and a bubbling creek. It is a lovely place to enjoy the serene setting and a glass of wine while you nosh on something from the kitchen. morgancreekvineyards.com

Heading toward Mankato. you'll have a chance to visit the reintroduced Bison at **Minneopa State Park**. There are just over twenty bison that are free to roam the 331 acres of land. These bison have genetics that show they're descendents of the type of bison that Lewis and Clark would have seen in the 1830s. Drive your car along the designated road and, if you're lucky, you will see the bison. They might be in the distance, or they might walk directly in front of your vehicle. Set your radio to a channel indicated in the park, and learn about the bison as you meander through. Drive up the hill to the historic **Seppman Mill** for a great vantage point.

Also in **Minneopa State Park**, hike down behind the thirty-nine-foot **Minneopa Falls**, or admire them from the top. It's a beautiful waterfall in every season. There are paved walking paths, picnic areas and restrooms.

Heading into **Mankato**, stop for close-up views of the **Minnesota River** at **Sibley Park**. The **Blue Earth River** and **Minnesota River** join near the park, which is beautiful, with lovely flowers, ponds, water fountains, a petting zoo, and a playground.

Heading down Riverfront Drive in Mankato, you'll come to **Reconciliation Park**, right along the Minnesota River. Here sits a sixty-seven-ton bison carved from Kasota limestone, which is found in the area, honoring the thirty-eight Dakota Indians that were hanged near **Reconciliation Park**. Just north of Reconciliation Park, you can't miss the mural that covers eight silos that are 135 feet tall. For the best vantage point, head to the other side of the Minnesota River along Highway 169 on your way out of town. The mural is a beautiful depiction of reconciliation and a community coming together.

You're now in Historic **Old Town Mankato**—a lovely few blocks that can easily be walked. Enjoy local shopping, a bakery, the **Hub Food Park** and more. Stop in for some ice cream at **Mom & Pop's**, then head over to **Riverfront Park**, where you'll have a great view of the Minnesota River. It's a lovely park, and has an amphitheater that hosts local and national music acts. hubfoodpark.com; momandpopsicecream.com

While you're in downtown Mankato, consider a self-guided **Walking Sculpture Tour**. There are twenty-four sculptures throughout downtown, and the tour is a great way to see more of this vibrant neighborhood. There are many great options for lunch or dinner in the area. Visit the **Betsy-Tacy House**, which is the preserved and restored childhood home of author Maud Hart Lovelace. Also make a stop at the historic **Hubbard House** to tour the beautiful gardens. cityartmankato.com; betsy-tacysociety.org/visits-tours; blueearthcountyhistory.com/hubbard-house

Next along the road is **St. Peter**, which is another small, charming town along the banks of the Minnesota. Take a tour of the **Linnaeus Arboretum** on the beautiful campus of **Gustavus Adolphus College**. Set on 130 acres, the Arboretum has more than three miles of trails to walk, as well as botanical gardens and a, naturally, a lot of trees. gustavus.edu/arboretum

Take a right at the stoplight at Broadway and Highway 169 to drive over the historic **Broadway Bridge** that takes you over the Minnesota. This bridge was built in 1931, and is on the **National Register of Historic Places**. Once you've taken in the rushing river, you'll need to go back to the highway to continue along the scenic drive.

On your way out of town, stop at the site where the **Treaty of Traverse de Sioux** was signed between the Dakota people and the US Government. The **Treaty Site History Center** contains exhibits, and you can take a self-guided tour of the Minnesota River Valley trails and learn about Dakota culture in this area that's along the Minnesota River Valley in the north of town. nchsmn.org

North of St. Peter is the **W. W. Mayo House** in **Le Sueur**. Part of the National Register of Historic Places, this is the home that was built by Dr. William W. Mayo, and where his first medical practice stood. Dr. Mayo volunteered to go to New Ulm to help with the wounded during the height of the US–Dakota War of 1862. Two years later, he moved to Rochester, Minnesota and established what is now known as the **Mayo Clinic**. The W. W. Mayo House eventually served as the home for the family who built the **Green Giant Company**, which originated in Le Sueur. mnhs.org/mayohouse

Ten minutes north of Le Sueur is **Henderson**, known to Prince fans as one of the locations where the movie *Purple Rain* was filmed. A statue downtown and a mural memorialize the musician. Speaking of downtown, an entire block is listed on the National Register of Historic Places, and there are plenty of small-town shops to visit and meander through.

If you're feeling adventurous in Henderson, take a short trip off your route for a zip-line tour or high ropes course at **Kerfoot Canopy Tour**. This is an opportunity to see the Minnesota River Valley from high above the ground! kerfootcanopytour.com

Next, visit **Ney Nature Center** just outside Henderson, a 446-acre nature center that overlooks the Minnesota River Valley. This brings you about ten miles south of Belle Plaine, where the Scenic Drive ends. neycenter.org

We'd be remiss if we didn't tell you to drive about thirteen miles north of Belle Plaine to **Jordan**, home of **Minnesota's Largest Candy Store**. Stop there for sure! You'll be shocked that so much candy exists—and it's all under one roof! The store has locally made pies, sodas you've likely never heard of as well, as those that bring back fond memories, and puzzles—lots of puzzles! Shop to your heart's content to satisfy the sweet tooth that may be riding in your car.

North Shore All-American Scenic Drive

Some argue that the scenic drive that starts in Duluth and ends at Grand Portage is the prettiest stretch of road in Minnesota. As you drive along the shores of Lake Superior, it won't take you long to fall in love with this scenic byway. The 145-mile stretch of road *could* be driven in under five hours, but the minute you hit the road, you'll know that one day is not possibly enough to see everything. You'll see for yourself why the area draws so many people back year after year.

The area is popular for hiking, mountain biking, kayaking, fishing, and . . . just driving. The landscape is absolutely the main attraction on this drive. If you love waterfalls, you'll be delighted—you can find them everywhere on this scenic byway. Superior National Forest protects the maples, pines, and aspens. The ocean-like Lake Superior casts different shades of blues, which contrast nicely with the rich greens of the trees. Small motels, camping, state parks, and cabin rentals are abundant in the area.

It's unlikely that you'll ever stop discovering new things along this drive. It's so scenic that it's a photographer's dream; and it's full of hiking and biking trails, streams, creeks and waterfalls, making it the outdoorsy traveler's dream. Each season brings its own unique beauty. Summer and fall are peak seasons for visitors. Due to harsh winter lake conditions, you'll find that most restaurants and shopping are open from May until October. If you go off-season, there are still food options along the way.

There are eight state parks on the North Shore, as well as national and state forests, community parks, wayside rests, and trails that can be used year-round. There are simply too many parks, falls and sites to mention here; this drive will leave you wanting to learn and see more in the area.

Pro tip: Wear clothes and shoes that are good for hiking. You'll want to walk everywhere on this route—over rivers and streams, or along the lake, so you'll want to be dressed appropriately. Depending on the time of year, it can be quite cool, so bring layers of clothing. Of course, you can make the drive without getting out and doing any hiking—but hitting the trails will certainly enhance your experience!

This scenic drive begins in Canal Park in **Duluth**, and extends to Grand Portage near the Canadian border. Duluth is an attraction in itself, and you'll want to devote at least a day to discovering this great town, in addition to the time you've allocated for the scenic drive. The North Shore All-American Scenic Drive is peppered with must-eat restaurants, but you can always fuel up with delicious food before leaving Duluth. canalpark.com

Canal Park is where the famous **Lift Bridge** is located; you can get close-up views of the ships coming in and out of port. Canal Park is lined with hotels, restaurants, art galleries, quaint shops, breweries, a distillery, and so much more. We recommend eating wild rice soup at **Grandma's**, or having one of the best sandwiches of your life at **Northern Waters Smokehaus** where they specialize in smoked fish gourmet sandwiches. Grab a cup of coffee at **Amazing Grace Cafe & Grocery** to bring some java and a treat along on your drive. grandmasrestaurants.com; northernwaterssmokehaus.com; amazinggracebakeryandcafe.com

Before you are even out of town, you'll come across a museum tour that cannot be missed at **Glensheen Mansion**. Tours are throughout the day and last several hours. You'll also want to allow time to roam the grounds of this stunning property, which was constructed as the family home of lawyer and capitalist Chester Adgate Congdon. The building was designed by Minnesota architect Clarence H. Johnston Sr., and was built between 1905 and 1908. glensheen.org

When you're heading north on Hwy 61 to leave Duluth, make sure to stay right onto Highway 61—don't take the four-lane highway.

And so it begins! We recommend allowing time for a leisurely drive, as you're going to want to spend the day stopping whenever you see a cool river or stream or waterfall that you just spotted—and there are a lot of them. It's common to encounter drivers going very slowly, or even pulling over to the side of the road to let others pass. Ideally, travel midweek to encounter fewer people.

As you drive, to your right is the largest freshwater lake of all of the Great Lakes: stunning **Lake Superior**.

Just north of Duluth is an eatery you'll definitely want to try: **New Scenic Cafe**. This restaurant has lovely views of the lake, a garden out front, and incredibly inviting Adirondack chairs. Prepare yourself for a delightful and unique menu, packed with seasonal goodness! On your way out, grab something from the cafe's Mise en place Marketplace to take something yummy home with you. newsceniccafe.com

There are many smokehouses in the area, but make a stop at **Russ Kendall's Smoke House** in Knife River—it will not disappoint. Leave with some smoked fish to enjoy somewhere along your drive. facebook.com/RussKendalls

Two Harbors is one of the next towns you'll encounter, and it's packed with things to do. Head to **Agate Bay Beach** to climb on the rocks or stroll the beach. If you're lucky, you'll find an agate to take home with you. Next, enjoy some craft beer at **Castle Danger Brewery**—note that while the town of Castle Danger is farther up the coast, the brewery is in Two Harbors. If you didn't grab enough smoked fish, check out **Lou's Fish House**, which is also known for its ice cream (no fish flavors, thankfully)! There is also lodging in the Two Harbors area, including hotels, resorts, and camping options. As you head north out of Two Harbors, **Betty's Pies** is a must—grab a slice of pie (or two), and maybe even a burger or hot dog and fries, if you're super hungry. Just make sure you save room for that pie—you'll thank us later! castledangerbrewery.com; lousfishhouse.com; bettyspies.com

On this route, you also get to experience driving through Silver Creek Cliff Tunnel. It is so neat to emerge from the darkness to views of Lake Superior. There's a beautiful overlook hidden there, as well as access to a lakeside trail. It's a great spot to have a quick lunch or snack on some of the smoked fish you've picked up along the way.

Gooseberry Falls State Park, one of the most popular places in all of Minnesota, is the next stop. The park has trails that will take you through forests, and you'll be treated to more views of Lake Superior. Gooseberry Falls is an incredible sight to see, and you can climb into the water at various spots. The falls are gorgeous; no matter the time of year you visit, you won't be disappointed. bit.ly/gooseberryfalls

Just up the coast, visit a beach with pink pebbles at **Iona Beach**. Dip your toes in the water and listen to the tiny rocks as they move against each other with the tides. You must also visit **Split Rock Lighthouse**, where you can walk around the grounds and up the lighthouse for incredible views of Lake Superior. There is an entry fee, but it is so worth the price of admission. mnhs.org/splitrock

Keep going north and you'll run into Silver Bay, where you should check out **Palisade Head**, a scenic overlook above Lake Superior. There are plenty of camping sites near Palisade Head, as it is located inside **Tettegouche State Park**. bit.ly/palisadehead

Next stop is **Tofte** and its interesting **North Shore Commercial Fishing Museum**. The museum is small, but it is a great place to stop to learn about the north shore and the benefits of commercial fishing in the area. Tofte is also where **Temperance River State Park** has two footbridges high above a rolling stream running through a ravine. Hiking trails follow the river and the area is popular with rock climbers. bit.ly/temperanceriversp; commercialfishingmuseum.org

Lutsen, which is made up of a handful of resorts, is close by. There's a cool mountain tram, as well as alpine slides and a stunning golf course: the **Superior National at Lutsen**. If you find yourself here in the winter months, **Lutsen Mountains** is a great destination for downhill skiing or a winter getaway at the resort. We highly recommend **North Shore Winery**, tucked into the area with beautiful views of Lake Superior, where you can relax, sip some wine and reflect on the beauty and wonderment of the North Shore Scenic Drive. superiornational.com; lutsen.com; northshorewinery.us

Twenty minutes farther north, **Grand Marais** is a historic fishing and trading town. You'll want to park and walk to take in the eclectic mix of cute shops, galleries and restaurants. Walk along the waterfront for wonderful vistas. Take a half-mile hike out on the spur of land called **Artist Point**, on the trail that leads to the lighthouse. It's truly a dreamy setting, and you have to remind yourself that you're in Minnesota.

North House Folk School is open year-round, and offers the teaching of traditional northern crafts. There are more than four hundred courses available, including boat building, wood-fired baking, northern ecology, and timber framing. Tours are also available. northhouse.org

While you're in Grand Marais, you must stop at **Sven and Ole's**. This pizza shop will quickly become your favorite. Then, walk on over Broadway to **World's Best Donuts** for some dessert. Be sure to double-check their hours ahead of time. They're open seasonally and may close earlier in the afternoon on certain days. It's part of the charm of a small-town bakery! After the real food, grab some brain food at **Drury Lane Books**—the cutest store, right on the shoreline. svenandoles.com; worldsbestdonutsmn.com; drurylanebooks.indielite.org

You'll want to take a detour after Grand Marais, and drive nearly fifteen miles to **Naniboujou Lodge & Restaurant**. This lodge dates back to 1927, when an exclusive club was built amid a dense forest that offered endless hunting opportunities.

Naniboujou was built as a private membership club, and its charter members included New York Yankee Babe Ruth and former heavyweight boxing champion Jack Dempsey. A French artist painted the dining room with psychedelic and brightly colored Native American designs; the room has been called the "Sistine Chapel of the North Woods." The Lodge has a colorful past, and still operates today—albeit in a very different way! Guests now come to enjoy the peacefulness and natural environment.

There is lodging available in the summer and winter, and the restaurant has fine dining in a casual and relaxed atmosphere. There is even an afternoon tea menu. Check the website for hours of operation. naniboujou.com

Another impressive activity in this area is **Devil's Kettle Falls**, located in the **Judge CR Magney State Park**, twenty minutes from Grand Marais. Devil's Kettle is legendary in these parts of Minnesota; once featured on the Discovery Channel, it's famous for being a waterfall that goes nowhere. We suggest doing a little online research before or after you hike to this fascinating waterfall, to learn more about what's happening geologically. Hikers should be warned that it is considered a difficult hike—it's 2.5 miles that includes more than two hundred steps to climb on the way back. It's not easy, but you're treated to a bonus waterfall along the way, and it'll give you a good excuse to eat some more of that great Minnesota food that you encounter along the Scenic Drive. And if you haven't had quite enough hiking, the **Superior Hiking Trail** also runs directly through the park.

After all that hiking, you might want to head back to Grand Marais and **Voyageur Brewing Company**, for a rest, a cool view of Lake Superior, and some tasty craft beer. voyageurbrewing.com

On a side note, another scenic Byway starts at Grand Marais and travels fifty-seven miles inland; the route is called the **Gunflint Trail Scenic Byway**.

Continuing on Hwy 61 and nearing the end of the North Shore Scenic Drive, you'll reach **Grand Portage State Park**. Here, you'll be treated to Minnesota's highest waterfall. A one-mile loop trail to the falls is easily accessible, even for those with a wheelchair or mobility issues. There are three viewing decks at **High Falls**. There are also interpretive displays that introduce the culture and traditions of the Grand Portage Ojibwe community, members of which directed the development of the displays. This is the only state park that is located within an Native American Reservation on land owned by the tribe.

As well as the one-mile loop to High Falls, there is also a five-mile round-trip hike to **Middle Falls**—this one is more difficult and rugged, should you be up for that.

Haven't had enough of waterfalls? **Pigeon Falls** are just a short stroll from **Grand Portage State Park** or the **Pigeon River Provincial Park**—this cascade separates the United States and Canada.

Right off of Highway 61 in Grand Portage, check out **Hollow Rock Beach**. It's named after the hollow rock formation that you can spot in the water near the beach. There happen to be cozy little cabins available to rent here, or there are lodge rooms and suites at **Grand Portage Lodge & Casino**. grandportage.com

By this time, you're likely joyfully exhausted by all that you've seen—and excited to see more. If and when you make a return trip down the **North Shore Scenic Drive**, you'll discover things that you didn't see on the way up because, as we've mentioned, there is just so much to see and do on this single stretch of scenic byway.

Historic Bluff Country National Scenic Byway

The **Historic Bluff Country National Scenic Byway** is an absolutely beautiful drive stretching eighty-eight miles from Dexter to La Crescent when traveling west to east. You'll be traveling on Minnesota Highway 16 for the most part, but there is a small loop that can be taken between Wykoff and Fountain where you'll be on Highway 80 and US Highway 52.

Whether you are looking for bluffs to hike, trails to bike, rivers and streams to fish or caves to explore, this part of Southeast Minnesota truly has it all, including an Amish community. Expect to see wooded bluffs, charming villages, and lush, rolling hills, fields and pastures. The terrain is very unique to this part of the state. If you love the outdoors, the **Historic Bluff Country National Scenic Byway** will be one you'll want to get familiar with. The route is beautiful in the warmer months, with greenery and wildflowers lining the roadway. Winter is also a beautiful time to visit, and the trails are perfect for cross-country skiing. Be aware that not much will be open in the winter, but it can be a nice winter getaway.

An interesting geographical fact about this byway is that it's part of the **Driftless Area**. This means that glaciers bypassed this region, leaving steep hills and deep river valleys, making the conditions perfect for spring-fed trout streams and rivers.

At the heart of this scenic byway is the **Root River**, which is very lush and can be explored by bike, canoe, tube, or kayak! The river has a gentle flow that can change with a rainfall. There are quaint, artsy communities along the way to explore.

The **Root River State Trail** is a forty-two mile hiking and biking trail beginning in Fountain and running through many of the picturesque communities on this byway, including Lanesboro, Whalan, Peterson, Rushford, and Houston. It is built on an abandoned railroad, and much of the route is level, making it wheelchair accessible.

If you're planning to spend a few days in the area, you can find lodging all along the byway. Camping, cabins, a horse ranch, and bed and breakfasts are all in the area, so the type of experience you have is totally up to you.

We'll start this scenic byway in **La Crescent** and head west. La Crescent is a beautiful city to explore in itself. It's the largest city on this scenic byway, and it's nestled right along the Mississippi River. Another scenic byway mentioned in this book, the **Great River Road Scenic Byway** in La Crosse, Wisconsin, begins across the Mississippi from La Crescent.

If you're traveling with children, they'll enjoy the **La Crescent Aquatic Center**—a swimming pool with water slides. La Crescent also has a Best Western if you'd like one last chain-hotel stay before spending time on this byway. bit.ly/lacrescent

If you're traveling in the fall, check out **Van Lin Orchards** on your way out of town, and grab some apples to snack on during your trip. If you have the time, stay for the corn maze and wagon rides. bit.ly/vanlinorchards

Twenty minutes from the orchards is **Houston**, home of the **International Owl Center**—the only all-owl education center in the entire United States. Displays give insight into these fascinating feathered creatures. There is also a small gift shop with plenty on offer for the owl lover. The center also rehabilitates owls that have been injured, and offers education on how to help injured owls should you happen upon one. Check the website to learn about the Festival of Owls and other events that happen throughout the year. internationalowlcenter.org

If you're traveling with little ones, the **Natural Playground** at **Houston Nature Center**, located at Houston's Trailhead Park, is a great place for kids to get active with nature. They can look for buried fossils, use a hand water pump, climb through tunnels and caves or sit at a fire ring. houstonnaturecenter.com

Trailhead Park is a great resource for the entire area. It's an educational information center for the trailhead of the Root River Trail, and some argue that it's one of the best trailheads of the entire state.

You'll find an adorable destination farm in Houston called **Sweet 16 Farm**. Here, you can shop for bouquets of flowers that are cut fresh from the farm. They also have a small hop garden, grown with one hundred percent sustainable methods, and they host a Hop Harvest Fest every year. Events are planned throughout the year to visit the farm. Check the website before planning a visit to ensure that they're open. sweet16farm.com

Next up is the **Rushford Peterson Valley**. There are multiple lodging opportunities here, with inns, bed and breakfasts, and campgrounds. You'll run right through Rushford Village, which actually encompasses the towns of both Peterson and Rushford, on this Scenic Byway.

Peterson is a cute town to stop for ice cream or rent canoes, tubes, and kayaks.

Visit the **Peterson Station Museum**, where you can learn about the former railroad in an old rail station that also serves as a genealogy center. petersonmn.com/peterson-museum

Rushford is home to one of Minnesota's culinary delicacies: *lefse*— a Norwegian flatbread made with potatoes. Head to **Norsland Lefse** for traditional *lefse* and other Norwegian treats. norslandlefse.com

When you head back out on the byway, you'll definitely want to stop and get a slice of "world-famous pie" at the **Aroma Pie Shoppe** in **Whalan**. The pies are hugely popular in the area; one bite of these pastries, and you'll understand the draw. Here too is another small-town bakery that closes seasonally during the winter. facebook.com/aromapieshoppe

Next up is **Lanesboro**, likely one of the most popular towns on the Historic Bluff byway. Lanesboro is the heart of Bluff Country, and it's also known as **Minnesota's bed and breakfast capital**. If you plan to stay in Lanesboro, you'll want to research before you go to check out the huge range of options.

In addition to bed and breakfasts, there's a unique lodging opportunity in Lanesboro at **Stone Mill Hotel & Suites**. You can stay in one of the whirlpool bathtub suites or enjoy an in-room iron-claw fireplace. The hotel offers on-site dining, as well, and you can even get a massage. Ask about the packages that include tours around town. stonemillsuites.com

Because of the popularity of the area, you'll want to decide ahead of time if you plan to stay in Lanesboro. Summer and fall are the busiest seasons for travelers—be sure to book ahead!

You're not going to find any chain stores or fast-food franchises in Lanesboro. There's not even a stoplight in town! What you will find is a wonderful cultural experience with locally grown foods, great wine and dining, a thriving local arts scene and quaint, unique shops. Ice cream parlors and bakeries are strewn around town for when that sugar craving hits.

Outside the **Lanesboro Museum**, you'll find a telephone booth. It's not operational in the traditional sense, but is instead used as an art installation, having been repurposed as a storytelling portal. Down the road is the Lanesboro Arts Juried Sales Gallery, where you'll find paintings, sculptures, photos, jewelry and more from more than ninety artists, all for sale after they've been selected by a jury. The Exhibition Gallery here shows works from local artists. facebook.com/lanesborohistoricalmuseum; lanesboroarts.org

Catch a theatre production by professional artists at the **Commonweal Theatre Company**, which has been in operation since 1989. commonwealtheatre.org

There are bikes propped up all over town, because this is such a great area for cycling. If you don't have a bike, join others walking—or maybe even rollerblading, if that floats your boat! Bikes are also available for rent at several places throughout town.

Make your way on foot or wheels to check out the **Stone Dam** and its beautiful waterfall near downtown Lanesboro. The dam was built in 1868 and is registered as a National Historic Place. The Root River runs right through town, so you can expect to hear the water throughout your time in Lanesboro.

You won't find any breweries in Lanesboro, but you'll find plenty of locally brewed beer at any of the restaurants scattered throughout the town.

There's a ton of trout fishing on the Root River; consider a guided fly-fishing trip with the **Root River Rod Co**. The company also offers lodging in Lanesboro and has fishing gear for sale, whether you book a guided fly-fishing tour or not. rootriverrodco.com

A ten-minute drive north of Lanesboro is **Eagle Bluff Environmental Learning Center**—a campus that hosts people of all ages to learn about life outdoors and wildlife. There are more than nine miles of public hiking trails that can be enjoyed seven days a week. If you're feeling adventurous, try the rock-climbing wall! The center is also a wonderful spot for birding and scenic overlooks. Eagle Bluff has one of the most stunning overlooks of the Root River. eaglebluffmn.org

Head back out along the byway from Lanesboro. We mentioned that there is an Amish community along this byway; you're very likely to see a buggy driving down the road, or even stopping at the sites you're also taking in. There are a number of Amish businesses along the route, so you'll likely buy some of their wares on your travels. Lanesboro is the heart of Amish Country, but if you want to see more of the Amish community, you can veer south off the byway just west of Lanesboro, and head to **Harmony** and **Canton**. Here, you'll see beautiful farmland, horse-drawn buggies, and Amish churches.

Your next stop is **Preston**, which is also known as "Minnesota's Trout Capital," so it's only fitting to learn more about trout fishing at the **National Trout Center (NTC)**. The Center hosts events throughout the year, and you can also pick up information for a self-guided nine-hole trout-fishing course. nationaltroutcenter.org

If you're thirsty, head to **Trout City Brewing**—a popular spot in Preston. In addition to locally crafted beer, they also offer wine and hard ciders (and soda pop), as well as coffee and a range of sandwiches. troutcitybrewing.com

Preston is also home to the **Southeastern Minnesota State Veterans Cemetery**—a beautiful cemetery that honors area veterans and overlooks the area.

Take a **self-guided walking tour** of Preston. You'll see a historic grain elevator and other historical buildings in the beautiful downtown.

North of Preston, a quick detour off of the byway, is **Fountain**, which is known as the Sinkhole Capital of the United States. There are more than ten thousand sinkholes of various sizes near Fountain and in the surrounding region. There are underground caverns and waterways, making for unique landscapes.

Located to the southwest of Preston, you'll find **Forestville/Mystery Cave State Park**. You could easily spend hours or even the day exploring this interesting place.

The state park is located within the karst region of Minnesota. Karst occurs in areas of soluble rocks—usually limestone or dolomite. **Mystery Cave** is a maze of corridors with more than twelve miles of passages. Learn about stalactites and stalagmites, along with the underground pools at the site. It's interesting to note that the cave is forty-eight degrees year-round, even though it's located in the frozen tundra of Minnesota!

In nearby **Forestville**, there's a neat place to learn about history, called **Historic Forestville**. You can take a guided tour with costumed historical figures of the town, who explain what life was like in the nineteenth century. Travel from the visitor center to a garden, kitchen, and a family house, then continue on to a general store filled with nineteenth-century merchandise. mnhs.org/forestville

As you approach the end of your route, you'll find a **Laura Ingalls Wilder Site** that's on the National Register of Historical Places in Spring Valley: the **Spring Valley Methodist Church Museum**. Laura's husband, Almanzo Wilder, grew up on a farm near Spring Valley, and his family attended the Spring Valley Methodist Church. Records indicate that Laura and Almanzo attended church here in 1890–91. The church is built in the Victorian–Gothic style of architecture, and has twenty-one stained-glass windows. Almanzo Wilder's family barn still stands today in rural Spring Valley, but you can only catch a glimpse from the road. springvalleymnmuseum.org

The Historic Bluff Country National Scenic Byway continues on to **Dexter**, where the route connects with Highway 90.

King of Highways Scenic Byway—Hwy 75

America's Highway 75 is also known as The King of Trails—it runs from the Gulf of Mexico to Canada, including 414 miles through Western Minnesota known as the King of Highways Scenic Byway. This route is the longest of the byways in the state.

Western Minnesota might not be top of mind when it comes to road trips, and perhaps that's what is most attractive about the King of Highway Scenic Byway. Travelers can enjoy historical sites, rivers, lakes, farm land, grasslands, and state parks on this quiet stretch of highway.

Steeped in Native American history, this trail was first used by Native Americans seeking food and shelter during their travels. As the train brought more people and settlers to the area, it was finally paved and became part of the history of Highway 75.

This scenic drive will allow you to slow down and enjoy small, agricultural towns with endless views of the native prairie, natural grasslands, rivers, and glacial ridges, and there are lots of opportunities for water activities, fishing, and bird-watching. The **Red River** meanders northward 550 miles from Breckenridge to Lake Winnipeg in Canada, and plays a very big part in the area.

We'll pick up the King of Highways Scenic Byway just south of Winnipeg in **Hallock**, northwestern Minnesota.

Movie buffs might know Hallock as the main filming site of the movie *Fargo*. Visit **Far North Spirits** outside of Hallock for locally grown, distilled, and distributed spirits. This is the northernmost distillery in the country. farnorthspirits.com

Southeast of Hallock is **Lake Bronson State Park**, which has more than fourteen miles of hiking trails where you can see a diverse wildlife habitat. Kayak and canoe rentals, as well as campsites, are all available, and there's a popular swimming pond and beach for you to enjoy.

If you're not up for camping, opt for a unique overnight stay at Hallock's **Scandinavia** Airbnb—an entire second-floor apartment above a coffee shop, in a historic building that was once a bank. facebook.com/hallockmn

Another state park, the tidy and well-kept **Old Mill State Park**, is tucked away on the prairie. A log cabin and steam-powered flour mill are on display, reminding visitors of times past. If you're lucky, maybe you'll see the grist mill fired up to grind flour. Check the events calendar for special events and interpretive programs. Bird-watchers will especially love this state park, as there are about one hundred species of birds residing here. Red-tailed hawks, owls, warblers, and even magpies and scarlet tanagers are just some of the birds that can be observed. The hiking trails are not too strenuous, and there is a man-made pool that is fed by spring water.

Get nostalgic with a night at the drive-in movie theater in Warren at **Sky-Vu Drive In**. For more than fifty years, movies have been shown here, rain or shine! Watch the movie from your car, or whatever chair (or couch) you choose to bring along. About the only change in fifty years is that you can now tune in to an FM radio station for the movie's sound. The on-site snack bar has everything from popcorn and candy to BBQ sandwiches and pizza, all at very reasonable prices. Sky-Vu Drive In theater runs from May to October, and the movie schedule can be found online. skyvumovies.com

While you're in the area, cruise two miles west to see a car that was smashed by a UFO in 1977. The car is on display at the **Marshall County Historical Society**, and has been untouched since the encounter. While you're there, you can learn more about what happened on that strange night.

The Red Lake River is popular for tubing in the region; head forty miles southwest, over to Red Lake Falls, and spend the afternoon or day tubing at **Voyageur's View Campground**. Shuttles are offered to the launch spot, where you can also set up camp if you want an immersive experience. Enjoy the beautiful scenery from the water on your leisurely four-mile river float, which takes you past islands in the river where you can stop and play. Tubes and coolers are available for rent at the campground; check their website for hours and rates. voyageursview.com/river-tubing

Farther south, and located on the banks of the Red River, **Crookston** is home to the University of Minnesota-Crookston, and is one of the larger cities along the King of Highways. Whether you are in town to visit the university or need a place to take a travel break, Crookston has plenty of places to dine and sleep. Stop for a bite at **Wonderful Life Foods**, where those with diet restrictions will appreciate the gluten-free options. You can find organic healthy foods and snacks, including everything from scones to wild rice soup. Reflect on your travels over a good cup of coffee or kombucha. The back half of the restaurant is a natural foods store—the perfect place to pick some road food that's not Twizzlers for the rest of your drive down the King of Highways. facebook.com/WonderfulLifeFoods

Take a short detour down to the **Pembina Trail Scientific and Natural Area (SNA)**, twenty minutes southeast of Crookston, for a unique experience of the glacial Lake Agassiz. Here you will have the unique opportunity to see three types of topography, and if you're lucky, you might spot a moose or an eagle in the area. Stop and smell the prairie wildflowers that are unique to the area. bit.ly/pembinatrail

The Red River typically floods most every spring, so make sure to research if you plan to travel during spring flooding. Back on the byway, learn more about the Red River in **Shelly**, at the **Red River History Museum**. The Red River Valley creates a border between Minnesota and North Dakota, and was a key trade route for the Hudson's Bay Company. bit.ly/redrivermonument

While you have the river on your mind, consider spending some time catfishing in the towns of **Halstad** and **Hendrum**. This whole region of the Red River is a favorite for boaters and anglers, and locals celebrate Catfish days in June.

About forty minutes south of Halstad, Moorhead is the largest city you'll encounter along the MN stretch of the King of Highways. Moorhead is directly across the river from **Fargo**, North Dakota. Between the two cities, there is plenty to see and do, including the **Red River Zoo**, **Fargo Air Museum**, **Plains Art Museum**, the **Children's Museum at Yunker Farm**, and endless options for local restaurants, breweries, bars, theaters, and hotels. If you want to break up the King of Highways drive a bit, you could easily spend a few nights exploring these cities. redriverzoo.org; fargoairmuseum. org; plainsart.org; bit.ly/childrensmuseumatyunker

The **Red River** creates lots of water recreation in the Moorhead/Fargo Area. For outdoor activities in the summer, you'll find pontoon riverboat rides, canoeing, kayaking, and bike rentals in the area.

Moorhead has a great Scandanavian museum called the **Hjemkomst Center**. Learn about the fascinating history of the Norse people who traded in the area centuries ago, and check out the stunning Hjemkomst Viking Ship on display that was built by a local high-school counselor, who then sailed it from Duluth to Norway. hcscconline.org/the-hjemkomst.html

While driving on the KOH, don't miss the opportunity to see the headwaters of the Red River in Breckenridge. **Red River Monument** marks the headwaters—it's a great photo opportunity for the family. bit.ly/redrivermonument

If you want another photo opportunity—this time with the world's largest catfish— you'll have to take a quick exit off of the KOH and head to **Wahpeton**, North Dakota, which is just west of Breckenridge. This "Wahpper" of a catfish, as referred by the locals, is forty feet long and weighs five thousand pounds!

Back in Minnesota, thirty-five miles south of Breckenridge, **Wheaton** offers architecture and history lovers a chance to see the **Wheaton Depot**, built in 1906 by the Chicago, Milwaukee, and St. Paul and Pacific Railroad. This site was listed on the National Historic Register of Historic Places in 1985, and is now a museum.

Half an hour south of Wheaton, near **Clinton**, is the continental divide known as the Laurentian Divide, where the water flow of the region's watersheds splits, flowing north to Hudson Bay and south to the Gulf of Mexico. There is a roadside marker that points out where you can see the Divide.

Just down the road, near **Ortonville**, visit **Big Stone Lake**, which is about twenty-six miles long and borders South Dakota. The lake is great for fishing—particularly walleye—with public access points and docks for public use. There are numerous resorts and camping spots dotted around the lake, as well as fine dining. The area offers small shops and antiquing, and for lodging, there are a couple of motels, cabin rentals, resorts, and unique VRBO and Airbnb options.

Make a stop at the **Big Stone County Museum** where you can see **Paul Bunyan's Anchor**, which is made from a huge slab of granite. Legend has it that Big Stone Lake was one of Paul Bunyan's favorite lakes to fish. bit.ly/bigstonecountymuseum

You simply must make a stop in **Madison**, thirty miles south of Ortonville—it's the **Lutefisk Capital of the USA**. To commemorate the Nordic delicacy that is especially popular in Minnesota at Christmas time, the town has on a display a twenty-five-foot Lutefisk named Lou. Lou is a great photo opportunity for those who like to visit oddities while traveling. For those who are curious, Lutefisk is whitefish—typically cod, but it can also be haddock or pollock—that's been air-dried, salted, and then pickled in lye until it flakes. It's rather gelatinous, and is a Scandinavian delicacy.

Madison is also home to a **Speedway Track** with races on Saturdays during the summer. bit.ly/madisonspeedway

Minnesota's first poet laureate, Robert Bly, had a farm south of Madison, which now serves as a museum with his books and furniture intact. The **Robert Bly Study** is where he wrote the book of poetry, *Silence in the Snowy Fields*. lqphc.org/robert-bly-studio

Dawson is fifteen minutes from Madison, and is known as **Gnometown, USA.** Tales of gnomes in this town have been passed down from generation to generation, and there are carved wooden gnomes all over town. Locals who exemplify goodness and positivity in the community are awarded "gnome status," and celebrated with their own gnome statue in Gnome Park. gnomedaws.com

Leaving the gnomes behind, visit the beautiful walking trail at the **Lac qui Parle River**, slightly northeast of Dawson. The trail is adjacent to the river, and you'll see beautiful flowers, trees and native vegetation before taking an adorable walking bridge across the river.

Next on your adventure, visit the **Historic Lund-Hoel House and the Carriage House Interpretive Center**, home to a historically accurate Victorian house that has been restored to its original glory. Learn about the banker—a self-made millionaire—who built the home at the turn of the century. Check the website for tour schedules. canbymuseums.org

South of Canby, **Ivanhoe** is known as "Little Europe," and has a strong Polish Heritage. You'll find cute English gardens throughout town, which is also home to 450 wind turbines. The US 14 Laura Ingalls Wilder Highway intersects with the King of Highways in Ivanhoe.

Lake Benton is known as the "Original Wind Power Capital of the Midwest." There are more than six hundred turbines in the area, and you can learn more about them at the **Heritage and Windpower Learning Center** in town. Tours are available by appointment. bit.ly/lakebenton

The historic **Lake Benton Opera House** is home to a popular regional performing arts center that showcases local actors performing popular musicals. lakebentonoperahouse.org

Visit downtown **Pipestone**, twenty miles south of Lake Benton, to see around twenty Sioux quartzite buildings that are on the National Register of

Historic Places. The majority of these buildings were built in the 1890s, and the quartzite has a unique, red tone.

The **Historic Calumet Inn** in Pipestone is a beautiful and historic hotel that was built in 1888. The hotel is also made of Sioux quartzite, and has survived fires and age. There are thirty-six rooms available for lodging, as well as restaurant dining and a lounge. Some say the hotel is haunted by ghosts. calumetinn1888.com

Pipestone National Monument is a must-see attraction, with its natural rock formations and beautiful waterfall. It's a wonderful place to hike; take the beautiful scenic paved path that is dotted with informative mile markers teaching the history of the Native Americans in the area. Pipestone has a rich Native American history, and you can learn about the quarrying and history of pipe-making here. nps.gov/pipe

Luverne is the southernmost Minnesota town along the KOH. **Blue Mounds State Park** here is home to prairie grasses, Sioux quartzite and bison grazing on the prairie. On-site camping is available. bit.ly/bluemoundsstatepark

There is so much to do and see on the King of Highways in Minnesota—there truly is something for everyone!

Minnesota Byways
- Apple Blossom Drive Scenic Byway
- Avenue of Pines Scenic Byway
- Edge of the Wilderness National Scenic Byway
- Glacial Ridge Trail Scenic Byway
- Grand Rounds National Scenic Byway
- Great River Road National Scenic Byway
- Gunflint Trail National Scenic Byway
- Historic Bluff Country National Scenic Byway
- Historic Highway 75 "King of Trails"
- Lady Slipper Scenic Byway
- Lake Country Scenic Byway
- Lake Mille Lacs Scenic Byway

- Minnesota River Valley National Scenic Byway
- North Shore All-American Scenic Drive
- Otter Trail Scenic Byway
- Paul Bunyan National Scenic Byway
- Saint Croix Scenic Byway
- Shooting Star Scenic Byway
- Skyline Drive
- Superior National Forest Scenic Byway
- Veterans Evergreen Memorial Drive
- Waters of the Dancing Sky Scenic Byway

Kelly and Dustin Ratcliff are the writers behind a Midwest Travel Blog, diningduster.com. *They love to dine, drink, and discover new things in the Midwest. Mostly, their travels take them through their home state of Minnesota and into neighboring states. They love trying new, plant-based foods at local restaurants, and try to visit as many breweries and wineries as possible. They love touring a good botanical garden.*

Learn more at:
diningduster.com
facebook.com/diningduster
instagram.com/diningduster
twitter.com/diningduster

MISSOURI

M issouri is an amazing state, founded in 1821. Commonly known as the "Show-Me State," it is home to roughly six million people.

Basic Missouri Facts:
- The state capital is Jefferson City.
- Its state motto is *Salus populi suprema lex esto* (which means "Let the welfare of the people be the supreme law").
- The state bird is the eastern bluebird.
- Its state flower is the white hawthorn blossom.
- There are ten Scenic Highways and Byways to explore.

Fun Missouri facts
- Missouri has more than six thousand caves.
- Four of the largest earthquakes in North America have occurred in or near New Madrid, Missouri.
- Missouri is bordered by a whopping eight other states!

Missouri is commonly called the "Show-Me State" by residents and visitors alike. Missourians are known to be welcoming to tourists visiting their state's many beautiful and fun landmarks, and they're more than likely going to be right there enjoying the sights along with you.

Since Missouri falls smack dab in the middle of the United States, it's often regarded as a "fly over" state for people trying to get from one coast to the other. But if you stick to that opinion, you're missing out on some of our country's most beautiful places. In fact, it's safe to say that with a short visit to Missouri, you just might fall in love with the hospitality, the open land, the cool breeze, and the miles upon miles of parks and exciting outdoor areas to explore.

For many, one of the biggest draws to Missouri is the historic highway, Route 66. Not only does this storied road draw tourists from all over, it brings life and excitement to numerous small towns along the way. And since the section of Route 66 that runs through Missouri is just 313 miles long, it really is the perfect road trip for a fun weekend getaway, or a week-long vacation.

Due to the popularity of Route 66, we're all finding ways to reconnect on the roadway once again. What was once intended to be a "quicker route" to get from coast to coast is now a roadway that people use to slow down and go back in time. As for our family, we love to straddle the past and the present; taking a tour of Route 66 in Missouri allows us to do just that.

The next time you're craving a road trip on Route 66, load up the family, turn on some tunes, and let the Missouri sunshine lead you down the highway with tons of historic and fun places to stop along the way.

Just be ready . . . you're going to see numerous types of terrain in Missouri, some of which include flatlands, high hills, and even some of those "Missouri Mountains" that we all love to travel on. And the attractions listed below aren't even all you might find! Route 66 is one of those trips that will have you making pit stops every so often so you can get out of your car and snap that picture to keep in your memory bank forever.

Enjoy your time in Missouri, because it truly offers some of the best road trips and pit stops to explore. Pair that up with all the outdoor fun, and you can rest easy knowing that your visit to the "Show-Me State" will be anything but dull.

This section of the book is a little snippet of how Missouri has captured our hearts. We're so happy to "show you" a suggested list of places to stop and see along your Route 66 journey.

Starting Your Journey on Route 66 in Missouri

Depending upon from which direction you want to start your journey, you'll either be going on this trip forward or backward, relative to how I've described it here. For my sanity, and the purpose of keeping it all straight, we're going to start by hopping on Route 66 in Saint Louis, MO, and going west from there, highlighting the most famous places that are a must for you to stop and take in.

When in the St. Louis area, Route 66 will have you exploring all the variations in Brentwood, Maplewood, Kirkwood, Des Peres, and Ballwin. With all the fun that you can have in the St. Louis area, you could easily plan a weekend adventure there and still not get through all of the sights.

St. Louis & Eureka Route 66 Attractions

Regardless of whether you're a foodie, a history buff, or just taking the family looking for fun, St. Louis has something for everyone to love.

Chain of Rocks Bridge—St. Louis

Located on the north edge of **St. Louis**, you'll find the **Chain of Rocks Bridge**. And if you're thinking that a stop at a bridge might not be anything worth seeing, you couldn't be more wrong. This mile-long bridge is set sixty feet above the Mississippi River and was planned to be a regular bridge, spanning forty feet across the water. But all that changed once there was a bit of an issue with dangerous rock ledges under the water, which would make it unsafe for boats and barges to pass. Due to this, there is now a twenty-two-degree bend in the middle of the bridge that was created to help divert watercraft away from the dangerous parts of the water. Cars haven't been able to cross this for many years, but the bridge is currently open to foot and bike traffic. This unusual span makes for a great afternoon walk across the water. If planning a stop, call (314) 416-9930 for current information and make sure there aren't any expected closures, etc. during that day.

St. Louis Gateway Arch—St. Louis

Standing proud at 630 feet, this historic landmark can't be missed. Known as the "Gateway to the West," there's a reason why it brings people from all over the world to take a tram ride straight to the top. The museum portion of the arch has recently gone through renovations as well (2018–2019), and it's quite impressive and packed full of history. Not only is the **St. Louis Arch** the tallest man-made monument in the Western Hemisphere, it's also the tallest building in Missouri that is open to the public. (And if you visit on a windy day and take the tram to the top, you just might feel it swaying a bit in the wind!) gatewayarch.com

Donut Drive-In—St. Louis

There's always time and room for donuts! This adorable bakeshop was actually voted as having the best donuts on Route 66, and after one bite, you're going to know why. From glazed donuts to old-fashioned treats, there's a reason that they've been around for as long as they have. Get there early to get them hot and fresh! (314) 645-7714

Ted Drewes Frozen Custard—St. Louis

You know the custard is good when they've been in business for more than eighty years. People come from ALL OVER to have their custard and will wait in line without complaint to get a taste. While their menu is loaded with sundaes, malts, and shakes, the one thing that Ted Drewes is known most for is their "concretes," so solid they're served to you upside down. Talk about faith in their product, right?!

When you're looking for a place that will deliver with taste and sweetness every single time, a stop at Ted Drewes will have you happy and full in no time at all. They do have multiple locations, so check their website for the latest hours and times. teddrewes.com

National Museum of Transportation—St. Louis

If you're a fan of planes, trains, and cars, the **Museum of Transportation** will be such a fun stop for you. This museum does a great job of focusing on transportation history and how automobiles, planes, and trains have changed over time. There are many trains located right in the museum; it's just a fantastic overall experience to see how things evolved in the transportation industry. Call ahead at (314) 965-6212 to make sure they're open on the day you plan to visit.

Route 66 State Park—Eureka

It just makes sense to visit **Route 66 State Park** when you're traveling along Route 66, right? Located on the Meramec River, this state park has over 400 acres to stretch your legs and explore. Make sure to make a pitstop at the Route 66 State Park Visitor Center to learn a bit of history about Route 66 and that area.

Although camping isn't allowed in this park, you can easily spend the day fishing, hiking, canoeing, or just having a wonderful picnic. Bird-watching is also popular here, and there have been said to be more than forty different types of birds located in and around the area. mostateparks.com/park/route-66-state-park

Once you're done with these areas in and around St. Louis, it's time to mosey into Franklin County, Missouri and explore some of the attractions in **Sullivan** and **Stanton**.

Sullivan & Stanton Route 66 Attractions

After spending some time in the city, you'll find a change of pace a pleasant surprise as you explore these fun sights.

Meramec Caverns—Sullivan

Since Missouri is also known as the cave state, taking a cave tour has to be on your Route 66 radar. Make sure that you wear good shoes and are prepared to do a bit of walking. It is a guided tour, but the terrain can be slick at times. It's also a good idea to bring along a coat or a jacket because inside the cave, the temperature stays at 60 degrees all year long.

The tour is about 1.25 miles in length, and it will take about an hour and a half to complete. Again, it is guided, but you will be expected to walk and stay with your party during this time. If you are traveling with a large group, they do have a shortened tour that might be a good option as well.

Make sure to pay attention to all the fantastic formations that you're going to see in the cave. This is the largest commercial cave that you're going to find in the state of Missouri, and that's saying a lot, because the state boasts more than 6,000 caves! You can call ahead to reserve your spot at (573) 468-CAVE.

Meramec State Park—Sullivan

This is another beautiful Missouri State Park located on the Meramec River. Situated about an hour outside of St. Louis, this park offers ample space to explore and enjoy nature. There are more than thirteen miles of hiking trails, and the river is great to float on with a kayak or a canoe.

Plus, this state park does have a campground, so you could easily set up a tent or rent a cabin there to extend your stay and enjoy more of the area. Keep your eyes peeled while you're there because there are more than forty caves scattered throughout the park. mostateparks.com/park/meramec-state-park

Jesse James Wax Museum—Stanton

Are you interested in learning more about Jesse James? Do you believe the stories of how he died, or did he fake his own death? Depending on who you talk to, you're going to get a different opinion or story.

But if you're curious to know more about the life of this famous bandit, a stop at the **Jesse James Wax Museum** is a good idea. Not only will you be able to see film footage that showcases interviews with Jesse James and others, you'll also see some really cool wax figures. The place is loaded with artifacts, and you'll be surprised to learn the true story of Jesse James that you're sure to remember. jessejameswaxmuseum.com

Moving on down the road will lead you into Crawford County to continue your exploration along Route 66.

Cuba & Leasburg Route 66 Attractions

This county in Missouri is packed with an array of artistic creativity that adds a fun appeal to the sight-seeing of Route 66.

The Wagon Wheel Motel—Cuba

Located in **Cuba**, booking a night at this motel will have you sleeping in an area that has been a thriving business since the early 1900s. The original neon sign will lure you in, and the coziness of the stone cabins and other buildings will have you resting peacefully as well. It's a great place to stay for a night or two so that you can explore all the other fun sights in the town. wagonwheel66cuba.com

Cuba Murals—Cuba

Cuba is actually known as the Route 66 Mural City; that's because fourteen murals are located at various spots all over town. Each mural has a story or significant meaning. You can find a guide at the I-44 Visitor Center (Exit 208) or at many local businesses. Not only are these murals beautifully maintained, but they're located in the town's most beautiful places. If you have a group, there are also tour-guided bus tours that are available. (573) 885-2627

Route 66 Rocker and Fanning 66 Outpost—Cuba

Talk about a big rocker! While the **Route 66 Rocker** no longer holds the "World's Largest Rocking Chair" title in the Guinness Book of World Records, it's still quite the sight to see. Standing just over forty-two feet tall, this steel rocker that's painted bright orange is undoubtedly enough to catch your attention and have you pull over to take another look. Fun fact? The Route 66 Rocker weighs more than 27,000 pounds!

It's a picture-perfect chance to stand next to the rocking chair to keep a record of all the unique and fun things that you see along the way. The rocker is also right outside a wonderful store, **Fanning 66 Outpost**, with more than 75 flavors of fudge, more than 300 flavors of popcorn, and other delightful treats and souvenirs. They also have 250-plus glass-bottle soda choices! Going in for a snack and a keepsake is such a fun way to round out the day. 573-885-1474

19 Drive-In Theater—Cuba

Just off a stretch of Interstate 44 (exit 208), this sizable drive-in screen is sure to draw in a crowd. Pull in with a car full of people and buckle down for a show. Movies are announced online, and there is sure to be a feeling of nostalgia as you're tuning to the FM station to hear the audio. (573) 885-7752

Onondaga Cave State Park—Leasburg

Even though you might have to get off Route 66 a bit for this one, it's worth it. We go back to the fact that Missouri is just loaded with caves, and you'll have the option to explore a few of them here. Take a guided tour under the park and let your eyes be amazed by all the beautiful formations that are waiting underground.

The state park also offers a flashlight cave tour. Explore the museums that are there and to learn about the history of the area. And while you're waiting for your cave tour, go out and explore the campgrounds and hiking trails.

This is just another fantastic state park that offers overnight camping, great kayaking and canoeing options, hiking, cave exploration, etc. mostateparks. com/park/onondaga-cave-state-park

As you can tell, each county that we're covering has something unique and fun to explore.

St. James & Rolla Route 66 Attractions

The largest town in this county is Rolla, but other towns are close by that offer some really great Route 66 experiences.

St. James Winery—St. James

Opened in 1970, this is currently Missouri's largest winery. Known for its delicious wines and juices, it features a tasting room, where you can sample some of the establishment's favored options. They have more than forty different types of wines that can be purchased there, or at many stores located all over the state.

On the weekends, there are wine cellar tours. The popularity of the wine that is produced at **St. James Winery** has grown so much, it now produces more than 500,000 gallons of wine each and every year. The distribution area of their wine has expanded as well, and they now have their wine located all over the USA, in sixteen different states.

While they have many glass bottles of wine available for purchase, they also have great options to take along on a river floating trip. Since glass isn't allowed on the rivers in Missouri, St. James has plastic bottling options, so that no one has to be without. stjameswinery.com

Maramec Spring Park—St. James

Located in the vicinity of your Route 66 tour, this park is another beautiful wonder that you need to see and explore. The spring water is gorgeous and clear, and there are actually more than 100 million gallons of water flowing from this spring each and every day. People from all over come to this park because of the trout fishing.

This isn't a state park, it's actually privately owned. Just shy of 2,000 acres, it has playgrounds, tons of fishing, camping, a store, a cafe, fish-feeding, picnic areas, hiking areas, and more. There is a fee to get into the park, but once you're in it, you'll find that you'll easily spend several hours there without even realizing that the time is passing by. If you're a history buff, there is a lot of great information here to explore and learn about during your visit. (573) 265-7124

Rolla's Stonehenge—Rolla

Taking in the sights of this stonehenge has some pretty cool history that goes along with it. It's in **Rolla**, which is also the location of the Missouri University of Science and Technology College. The "stonehenge" was created by students who used a form of water-jet technology to make a replica of England's iconic landmark. What took them one month to do would have taken years with the old stone carving methods used by ancient peoples. This stonehenge is the winner of several awards as well, and it's a fun stop and another really cool photo opp, too. (573) 341-4111

Veterans Memorial Park—Rolla

While in Rolla, stopping at the eleven-acre **Veterans Memorial Park** is a great way to pay tribute to our military. There are places to walk and also picnic areas, too, so stretch out and relax. scrvg.org

Once your time in Rolla is done, it's time to move on down the road and continue on with your sightseeing adventures.

Uranus & Waynesville Route 66 Attractions

This county has thirty-three of the original miles of Route 66, so there are plenty of things to see and do here.

Funk Yard on Route 66—Uranus

Have you always wanted to see the World's Largest Belt Buckle? The **Funk Yard** has you covered. It might look like a lot of "stuff" as you approach, but once you start processing through it all, you'll find that it's full of some pretty cool treasures. Make sure to check out the double-decker bus that was actually used in London for many years, and is now equipped with tables and chairs to serve ordered food. Unique and fun, and an exciting stop full of many exciting things. 573-844-4241

Uranus Fudge Factory and general store—Uranus

The town of **Uranus** is quite the attention grabber for those traveling down Route 66. Not only does the name draw in the attention, so do many of the cute and quirky stores that they have in their town. A stop at the **fudge factory** is always a good idea because you'll get to taste some delicious samples of fresh fudge before deciding on what flavor you want to purchase for yourself.

Along with fudge, there are novelties and souvenirs and a lot of other quirky trinkets and gifts. You'll see a lot of Uranus jokes plastered all over cups, t-shirts, and more, and you might even notice a "Thanks for picking Uranus" sign or two along the way.

Make sure that you check out their enormous variety of taffy, too. bit.ly/uranusfudgefactory

Frog Rock—Waynesville

How many times will you get the chance to take a selfie with a giant rock painted like a frog? Only on Route 66 do opportunities like this occur! Charge up your phone and be ready to get up close and personal with this giant frog. Considering it's just a giant rock that someone painted to look just like a giant frog, it's really cool to see up close and get your picture taken with. It's only one of those things that will add a little fun and flair to your travels. "Hop" to it and check it out! (573) 336-6355

Trail of Tears Memorial Trail -Waynesville

Learn all about the Cherokee Nation that was in this area along a one-mile paved walking trail. All along the route are storyboards that detail the times and the life of the Cherokee Nation. You can take a quick peek into the history of the area and the Trail of Tears by walking along the path and reading the boards.

And while you're in the area, take the time to explore the rest of the park, too. There are great fishing spots and even an underwater cave. (The cave does have an option for scuba diving, but you must have clearance and assistance from the local sheriff's office for that adventure.) You can easily make this a stop a great place to have a picnic and just enjoy some activity outside of the car. (573) 774-6171

Route 66 Pulaski County Courthouse Museum—Waynesville

A stop at this courthouse museum will give you a quick peek at how an original courtroom looked back in the early 1900s. Many other displays are set up to enjoy. While there is no fee to get in, donations are appreciated. (573) 774-6566

Hard to believe that you've seen so many cool attractions on your Route 66 travels thus far. But there are still others to see and explore!

Lebanon Route 66 Attractions

Home to many great Route 66 attractions, this county was established in 1849.

Laclede County Route 66 Museum—Lebanon

The great part about this museum is that you can enter, take your own tour, and enjoy the sights. Since this museum shares a building with the local library, the **Lebanon-Laclede County Library**, it boasts many fun finds and artifacts about Route 66. Some old signs, displays and collections will have you taking a trip down memory lane. (417) 532-2148

Lebanon I-44 Speedway—Lebanon

Do you have a need for speed? This speedway is the only oval asphalt track in Missouri, and they offer races every first and third Saturday night

(April–September) that are open and available to the public. It's a local attraction and also draws in big tourist crowds. (417) 532-2060

Lake of the Ozarks—Lake of the Ozarks

While the **Lake of the Ozarks** isn't technically part of Route 66, this is one of those areas in Missouri that can't be left out. The Lake of the Ozarks is a place that people travel to from all over the US to come and have fun. With over 1,100 miles of shoreline, there is plenty of water and space for everyone to have fun in the sun.

The town is made up of delightful eateries, shopping, and family-fun activities like go-karts, skeeball, mini golf, jet skiing, boating, and more. It's literally one of the busiest places in the entire state during the summer months.

There are thousands of options for hotel rentals, camping, cabin rentals, Airbnbs, and more for families to be able to go to the lake and have a nice weekend or week away. Boat rentals are a massive aspect of lake life, too. And don't forget your swimming suits!

If you're looking for a fine place to stay overnight on your Route 66 trip, you really can't go wrong with finding a place at the Lake of the Ozarks. It's a great area for tourists that has practically anything and everything possible to do. funlake.com

Marshfield & Strafford Route 66 Attractions

Located in the southern portion of Missouri, this county was established in 1855 and is full of many adorable and fun towns and attractions.

Webster County History Museum—Marshfield

If you're a fan of history, this is the place for you. Loaded full of local facts and history, you can easily spend a few hours researching and reading up on tons of fascinating subjects. (417) 468-7407

Hubble Space Telescope Replica—Marshfield

Famous astronomer Edwin Hubble was born in **Marshfield**. For this reason, there is a Hubble Space Telescope replica that can be viewed, and it's located on the west side of the square in the town. It's just another cool piece of history that offers a great selfie opportunity. (417) 859-3925

Route 66 Mural in Marshfield—Marshfield
Located in **Boswell Park**, this giant Route 66 mural was actually painted by a high school graduate of Marshfield. Over the course of about one hundred hours, the painting was added and is a great addition to the town.

Wild Animal Safari—Strafford
Taking a break and enjoying the animals is a splendid experience while traveling on Route 66. funlake.comoffers a great time that is unique compared to other options, such as zoos. This location has more than 300 animals and offers a 250-acre park that is a drive-thru and walk-thru in specific portions, so that you can get up close and personal with some of the critters. You can take a guided tour bus tour as well.

You'll see camels, tigers, giraffes, zebras, monkeys, and more. Make certain that you call ahead to verify times that they're open and secure a spot. animalsafari.com

Springfield Route 66 Attractions
For this portion of your Route 66 trip, you will find yourself in an area with a larger city, **Springfield**. This will give you plenty of other options for a lot of fun activities, too.

Fantastic Caverns—Springfield
Looking to explore a cave but give your feet a rest? **Fantastic Caverns** is your choice! This guided tour lasts less than an hour, and you'll get to sit in comfort and see the sites of the cave. It's hard to believe that you see formations that have taken literally thousands of years to form. The cave was discovered in 1862 by a local farmer, because his dog noticed an opening on the side of a hill. Five years later, twelve women from Springfield answered an ad to explore, and they were the first to go inside the cave.

One highlight of the tour is getting to see the names of the twelve women who initially explored the cave still written on the inside walls. fantasticcaverns.com

Route 66 Car Museum—Springfield
With more than seventy-five cars spanning many model years, you can easily pass the time walking around this museum. Most of these cars are going to be unique and well-worth checking out. If you're a car fan and love to see how automotive history evolved, this will be a wonderful stop for you on your Route 66 journey. (417) 861-8004

Pythian Castle—Springfield
Do you believe in ghosts? This haunted castle located in Springfield might be a tad bit off course, but it's an exciting adventure to take. What used to be an orphanage turned military-owned, this castle gives history tours, ghost tours, and more. Are you curious and brave enough to step foot inside? Who says you can't add a little spooky fun to your Route 66 road trip? (417) 865-1464

Springfield/Route 66 KOA Campground
Parking your rig at this KOA is a great way to extend your time in this area. Since it's located in such a significant part of town, it's an excellent way to rest and get up early to explore the rest of the city. There are a few lakes nearby and a golf course as well. You'll be secluded enough to feel like you're really camping, but close enough to get out and explore the city and surrounding areas. (417) 831-3645

Keep in mind that Springfield is one of the largest towns in the state of Missouri, so while you're touring the area and checking out some of the sights of Route 66, there are plenty of other interesting activities that you can easily partake in.

Spencer & Everton Route 66 Attractions
There are actually quite a few abandoned towns and homes in this county because of traffic routes shifting once the interstates were built. This county

in Missouri also has the longest stretch of Route 66, at just over twenty-five miles, all of which is straight.

Ghost Town of Spencer—Spencer

While Spencer's town was never large or bustling per se, it was a stop for many while they were traveling in Route 66. In fact, it used to be quite the place. But in 1912, that all stopped when the road could no longer be traveled, and the traffic just went away. Twenty years later, there was chatter about Route 66 being built in the area so that town was purchased for four hundred dollars by a man who built up and reopened it. It was booming once again, and **Spencer**, was back on the map.

But like all good things, it came to an end when Route 66 was realigned in 1961, and Spencer became a ghost town for the second time. It still sits that way today. A quick drive through the small area is a throwback to what it used to be. A few buildings have been updated and are nice to see, but it's also just an excellent example of how quickly this town changed once the focus of the road and highways changed as well.

Gay Parita Sinclair Station—Everton

When you think about the past days, visions of what gas stations looked like may be part of your reminiscing. A stop at this Sinclair station that was opened originally in 1930 will show you just how they looked. You'll notice the vintage neon signs, and will just have to stop and imagine all the old cars stopping in and fueling up before getting back on the road.

Carthage, Webb City & Joplin Route 66 Attractions

This portion of Route 66 will have you exploring the southern portion of Missouri. It's known for Missouri hills and mountains, so the driving experience here will give you some fantastic scenic views.

Boots Court Motel—Carthage

This motel is located in **Carthage**, and was originally built in 1939. While it doesn't offer up a ton of rooms available for rent, there are a handful that are open for overnight stays. A total of thirteen rooms were built upon this property, but there are currently five open to the public. This motel still has the same look and feel of when it was thriving back in the day, and it was actually purchased and saved from demolition for restoration. Over the years, it's changed hands a few times, and there have been some "modern" upgrades, such as better roofing that requires less upkeep.

While the motel rooms don't have TVs in them, there is Wi-Fi available, and you can pull right up to the front door and unload your overnight bags with ease. For reservations, please call (417) 310-2989.

Carthage Disc Golf Course—Carthage

Disc golf is trendy in Missouri, and Carthage is home to an eighteen-hole disc golf course that is located right off Route 66. Bring along your discs and take a break from the car. The course is a great way to see the beauty of the area and explore a bit outdoors, too. (417) 359-8181

Precious Moments Chapel and Gardens—Carthage

More than likely, you might have a Precious Moment figurine or two sitting on a shelf at home. The creator of those beautiful figurines also has a chapel located in Missouri. This chapel, created by Sam Butcher, was one of his many visions that he brought to life.

In the **Precious Moments Chapel**, you'll see beautiful artwork, thirty different stained-glass windows, and more. There are more than eighty various hand-painted murals that line the walls, all telling a life story. People gather here from all over the world to appreciate Butcher's creativity and find peace in his religious references as well. Most, if not all, of the murals, have some sort of Biblical reference.

One of the most famous parts of the chapel is known as the "Hallelujah Square." This painting is in the center and is meant to represent what heaven looks like, through the eyes of a child. One of the most interesting things about the painted murals is that they tend to pay tribute to his faith in God and his love for others.

Many of the murals will have hidden clues in them that are about things that happened in his life and others' lives, and are just another way to have them remain in his memory and artwork.

The chapel is a place where people come to enjoy the artwork and see the views of someone who had a dream that they wanted to share. There is a visitor center and a gift shop on location as well. preciousmomentschapel.org

66 Drive-In Theater—Carthage
When's the last time that you've been at a drive-in theater? Spots are limited to a first-come, first-serve basis, and there isn't a bad seat in the house. Park the car for a double-feature outdoor showing that everyone in the family will love. Located in Carthage's town, this really is a treat and a throwback to the good ol' days.

During its prime, it had spots for four hundred cars to line up. The theater did shut down between the years 1985–1997, but reopened and has been going strong since. This is one of the last true drive-in theaters that are located on Route 66.

It's suggested to arrive at least an hour in advance, as it's a popular attraction for tourists and locals. During every showing, you'll get two movies for the price of one. Don't forget to pack your own portable radio so that you can easily tune in to hear the film if you're sitting outside of your car in a lawn chair or on your blanket. There is a full concession stand available. (417) 359-5959

Praying Hands Monument—Webb City
Thirty-two feet tall and weighing in at more than 110 tons, these praying hands are truly a breathtaking sight. They're meant to grab attention as they sit atop a massive hill. Created by a local artist (J.E. Dawson) in 1972, it's another great stop along Route 66 that is worth viewing and snapping a few photos. (417) 673-1154

Route 66 Mural Park—Joplin
Joplin was a hopping spot for Route 66 back in the day, and this is why they've dedicated a space in their town for Route 66 Mural Park. You'll have

the chance to get up close and personal with two murals, *Cruisin' into Joplin* and *The American Ribbon*. Make sure to take the time to get a selfie of you standing in front of the red 1964 Corvette. bit.ly/joplinmuralpark

Now that you've had the chance to get a quick idea of some really great places to visit along your Route 66 trek through Missouri, why not learn some other cool and interesting facts as well?

Missouri Route 66 Events

The state of Missouri knows how to have fun. With all the beautiful outdoor space, it just makes sense to use the areas and towns to host events celebrating Route 66. Below you'll find a variety of fun activities that are listed by months, to help you better plan out your Route 66 road trip.

Please keep in mind that dates and times might change year-to-year, so always verify the information online before setting off.

April
Missouri Cherry Blossom Festival—Marshfield

Join in on the fun of this beautiful festival. Spend several days walking around, attending concerts, shopping local vendors, and taking in the sight of blooming cherry blossom trees. This event draws in a lovely crowd and it's a pleasant experience to be a part of. With Missouri weather being good during the month of April, it's splendid to be outdoors and exploring the town and nearby area. There are many great restaurants and places to stay as well, so you could easily book a fun trip for the weekend. cherryblossomfest.com/WordPress

May
Route 66 Summer Fest—Rolla

Downtown **Rolla** is hopping for their annual summer fest activities. Locals and tourists gather to celebrate the history of Route 66. Not only is there a Miss Route 66 pageant, there are also street dancers, a great Route 66 cruise, motorcycle show, pony rides, kids' activities, drummer's competition, and so many food options in the always tasty food court. route66summerfest.com

June
Pulaski County Regional Fair—St. Robert
This regional fair is always a good time, and it's packed full of activities each and every day. There's bull-riding, a pie contest, craft vendors, and more. pulaskicountyregionalfair.com

July
Route 66 Cruise-A-Palooza—Webb City
Enjoy the fun of a carnival, food trucks, fireworks, car show, petting zoo, and more. This has been a tradition for several years and is always a hit for the locals and those who want to come and join in on the festivities.
Route 66 Yard Sale: 100 Miles of Treasures
Who wouldn't want to travel along Route 66 and seek out treasures for bargain prices? It's true what they say—one person's trash really can be someone else's treasure, and this Route 66 yard sale will have you exploring the towns all along the way. Put on your walking shoes, bring your cash, and get ready to load up the trunk of your car with deals. This is typically held at the end of July, and early August, so make sure to plan ahead so you don't miss out. This event has been happening for more than 30 years! bit.ly/route66yardsale

August
Birthplace of Route 66 Festival—Springfield
Are you ready to see where it all started? This birthplace festival will have you loving all the history and fantastic events celebrating Route 66. A car show, parade, and even a 6.6k run are just a few of the fun events that you can partake in. route66festivalsgf.com

September
Bourbon BBQ & Car Show—Bourbon
This event is just like it sounds. Good BBQ and a car show. There's nothing better than enjoying the weather of Missouri during the fall months and eating some delicious food, too.

October
Gearhead Invasion—Cuba

Do you love cars, trucks, motorcycles, and basically anything on wheels? If so, you don't want to miss out on this high-octane event. There are some rules regarding the cars and other vehicles that can be entered for show, which can be an interesting way to know what's going to be there to see. It's open for registration for pre-'67 cars, pre-'72 trucks, pre-'87 custom vans, and all different years for custom motorcycles. There are also movies shown in the drive-in theater, and the days are packed full of other activities and events. carshowsnow.com/event/gearhead-invasion/

Route 66 Cuba Fest—Cuba

Homemade apple butter, trolley rides, live music, family-fun activities, a 5k race, and more are just all part of this festival. Tour the town, see the sights and have a great time enjoying the ambiance.

November
Route 66 Birthday

Don't forget to celebrate the birthday of Route 66! This isn't a singular event to a come to in Missouri, but it's one that you can celebrate wherever you are! The exact date to celebrate is November 11th, since Route 66 opened officially on November 11th, 1926.

Taking a journey on Route 66 in Missouri is a simple way to plan a fantastic road trip. While there are many more stops than the ones mentioned in this chapter, you should plan on at least seeing these. If you're genuinely interested in exploring everything that Route 66 has to offer, dive deeper into the options and plan your trip.

One thing is for sure. Visiting Missouri and traveling the Route 66 route will allow you to explore small towns, cool attractions, underground adventures, and more.

Thena and Matthew are the brains behind the popular Midwest Travel Blog: hodgepodgehippie.com *and are valuable members of the Midwest Travel Network. In addition to their love of all things travel, Thena and Matthew enjoy reading, camping, and tandem-biking together all over towns in the Midwest. You may have witnessed them pedaling all over your town at one point in time or another! Above all, Thena and Matthew hope that travel gives you hope, happiness, and excitement and that this book helps you find and explore towns, events, and activities that are waiting right outside your door.*

Learn more about Thena and Matthew (and their fun family travels) at HodgePodgeHippie.com

NEBRASKA

Nebraska is an amazing state, founded in 1867. "The Cornhusker State" is home to roughly 1.9 million people.

Basic Facts:
- The state capital is Lincoln.
- The state motto is "Equality before the law."
- The state bird is the western meadowlark.
- Its state flower is the solidago.
- There are nine highways and byways to explore; they are listed in the index in the back of this book

Fun facts
- Nebraska is the popcorn capital of the world.
- Kool-Aid was invented in Nebraska.
- Gerald Ford, the only person to serve as Vice President and President of the United States without being elected, was born in Omaha.

Many people view Nebraska as a flat state with little to offer visitors. If you drive through the state along Interstate 80, it might seem that way—nothing but cornfields and cow pastures. But the view from that particular stretch of asphalt doesn't even begin to tell the full story. Nebraska is home to nine scenic byways and highways that beckon you to get off the interstate and travel the backroads—over rolling hills, deep gorges, amazing river valleys, and something you'll find nowhere else in the United States—the Sandhills of central Nebraska. Formed as part of a prehistoric sea, the Sandhills echo those ancient days when giant mammals and fish called this land home. From the plesiosaurus to a half bear/half bison, the prehistoric side of Nebraska has some stories to tell.

The state has been home to several Native American tribes, who roamed the state, as well as set up permanent communities along the major rivers and creeks. From the Ponca in the north to the Otoe in the south, Indigenous people called Nebraska—which the Omaha tribe called Flat Water—home long before European settlers traveled cross country along the Mormon, California, and Oregon Trails. Key Nebraska landmarks—including Chimney Rock and Scotts Bluff—played a role as nineteenth-century GPS apps for the pioneers on their westward adventures. Today, those monuments stand as reminders of the state's past as a key player in the country's westward expansion.

Each of Nebraska's scenic highways and byways has a story to tell. From the days of Jesse James and other outlaws using the state's northern border as hideouts, to the Lewis and Clark expedition exploring the Missouri River en route to their destination where the Columbia River meets the Pacific Ocean in Oregon, Nebraska's byways have their compelling tales, told by attractions, unique shops, and restaurants preparing delicious food.

Lewis and Clark Scenic Byway

Captain Meriwether Lewis and Second Lieutenant William Clark led a team of soldiers and civilians—known as the Corps of Discovery—on an expedition of the northern half of the Louisiana Purchase, from St. Charles, Missouri, to the Oregon coastline where the Columbia River meets the Pacific Ocean. Beginning in 1804, the thirty-three-member team traveled up the Missouri River, eventually arriving in Nebraska. The explorers' accomplishments have been recognized through the years, but Nebraska honors them even more with their own scenic byway. Covering nearly one hundred miles from Omaha to South Sioux City, Highway 75 follows the expedition's travels along the mighty river. lewisandclarkscenicbyway.com

Your **Omaha** stop includes a bevy of attractions to explore. Focusing on the downtown area, the **Old Market** invites you to visit its unique shops and restaurants. It's always Christmas at the **Tannenbaum Christmas Shop**.

With ornaments and other decorations, you can find the perfect Christmas item for your home or as a gift. While there, check out **Old Market Sundries**, which is a great spot to pick up an Omaha souvenir or remembrance. As you peruse the Old Market, you'll want to stop in at **Hollywood Candy**, home to dozens of candies and full of nostalgia. You'll find one of the world's largest collections of Pez dispensers, as well as classic lunch boxes, and vinyl albums. Hollywood Candy is home to a small theater, where you can put in a DVD, grab some popcorn, and watch a movie while you relax. The store is also home to a vintage arcade, with pinball machines from the 1970s. oldmarket.com

While in the Old Market, you can enjoy almost any type of dinner you can think of, from classic steak and potatoes to Mexican, French, Italian, and burgers and fries. **M's Pub**, the oldest restaurant in the Old Market, opened in the mid-1970s and features a casual menu. It's known for its *lahvosh*, an Armenian cracker with Havarti cheese and topped with a variety of meats and vegetables. **Le Bouillon** brings a taste of Paris to your palate, with interesting appetizers, such as seasoned olives and almonds, or French onion soup, and entrees, including duck frites and cassoulet (white beans, garlic sausage, rabbit confit, and pork belly). Offering a Mexican menu, **Trini's** is the oldest restaurant in the Old Market Passageway, with one of the most attractive views in the city. Upscale diners will enjoy dinner and wine at **V. Mertz** in the Passageway or at **Omaha Prime**, where you can find amazing steaks. mspubomaha.com; lebouillonomaha.com; trinisoldmarket.com; vmertz.com; omaha-prime.com

South of the Old Market, the **Durham Museum** offers a glimpse into Omaha's history. At the height of its heyday as the city's Union Station, the depot saw about 10,000 people come through its doors each day. However, as people moved to driving autos on their travels, rail passenger numbers quickly faded. After several years of sitting, the building was purchased by a local entrepreneur and donated to the city as a museum. The Durham is one of Omaha's most popular attractions, where visitors can learn all about its rail background, as well as local and regional history. Omaha's Business Hall of Fame is located at Durham, and among its notable members is

Warren Buffett, one of the world's richest people. The museum is also home to special exhibits, including Smithsonian Museum traveling projects. The museum's top floor resembles life during its day as Union Station, with sculptures representing travelers, such as a woman traveling to a new city, a business executive on his way home, and two military personnel visiting while awaiting trains for their next destinations. durhammuseum.org

While in Omaha, enjoy a walk through the **Gene Leahy Mall**, heading toward the **Missouri Riverfront** through **Heartland of America Park**. A walk along the riverfront takes you to **Lewis and Clark Landing**, which pays homage to the unions that helped build the city's grand buildings. *A Salute to Labor*, the second-largest sculpture recognizing union workers, is located along the north end of the landing. Continue your walk and cross the Bob Kerrey Pedestrian Bridge, the nation's longest pedestrian bridge connecting two states. Running 3,000 feet long, "The Bob," as it is known locally, connects Nebraska and Iowa, with the state line in the center of the bridge. You'll want to take your picture at the state line. You can continue with a longer walk on the Iowa side, with trails going north and south. During the summer, reserve a spot on the **River City Star**, a paddleboat that takes you on an hour-long tour of the river. Lewis and Clark could only dream of such a venture. rivercitystar.com

Omaha has a plethora of hotel choices for overnight stays. However, consider reserving a room at the **Magnolia**, a boutique hotel that dates back to the early twentieth century. The **Hilton** and **Marriott** hotels near the Omaha arena offer upscale quality accommodations.

Heading north out of Omaha, **Fort Atkinson State Historical Park** honors the nation's first military fort west of the Missouri River. Located in **Fort Calhoun**, Fort Atkinson is a replica of the original fort, which served the country 1819–27. The living history attraction often hosts reenactors, who share what life was like during the fort's operation. Fort Atkinson is located near a spot where Lewis and Clark met with the area's Native American leaders. A monument marks the location of the council. Enjoy a walk around the fort and its exterior, where you'll find older buildings and a statue honoring the expedition leaders. fortatkinsononline.com

Your next stop will be **Blair**, the seat of Washington County. Take a stroll along downtown's Washington Street, where you can see buildings dating back to the late 1800s. With mom-and-pop stores dotting the cityscape, you can help the local economy with stops at stores. Take a stroll through **Black Elk-Neihardt Park**, with a nearly forty-five-foot tall mosaic monument honoring Native American spirituality and culture, as well as a paved path providing a comfortable stroll alongside trees that are colorful during the fall. Enjoy a meal from south of the border at **Fernando's**, with delicious nachos as an appetizer, and entrée combinations featuring burritos, tacos, and enchiladas. Reserve a table at **Our Specialtea**, where you can relish old-fashioned British tea and biscuits or enjoy a sandwich with your drink. blairnebraska. org; fernandos-cafe-cantina.business.site; facebook.com/ourspecialteashop

Located about forty-five minutes north of Omaha, you may choose to spend a full afternoon in **Tekamah**. You can spend hours browsing the home décor accessories and handmade candles at **Master's Hand**. The boutique store also offers lunch, for which you need to make reservations. Before leaving, grab some handmade chocolates, such as fudge bars, as well as a variety of milk- and dark-chocolate treats. Wine aficionados will enjoy a stop at not one, but two vineyards and wineries. **Silver Hills Winery** and **Big Cottonwood Vineyard and Winery** each grow their own grapes to create a variety of white and red wines. The seasonal wineries are open from spring through December, depending upon weather. You can also enjoy a bite to eat and a cold drink at **Chatterbox** tap room. Downtown Tekamah features a few restaurants to choose from when planning a meal. Before leaving town, you'll want to learn about area history at the **Burt County Museum**. Featuring artifacts and memorabilia donated by locals, the museum, located in the former Houston House, offers an interesting look into the history of the community, including being the hometown of black-and-white Western star Hoot Gibson, considered a top box office draw in the early 1900s. mastershandcandles.com; silverhillswinery.com; bigcottonwoodwinery.com; chatterboxbrews.com; burtcountymuseum.org

Travel fourteen miles west along Highway 32 to **Oakland**, the "Swedish Capital" of Nebraska. The hometown of a United States ambassador to Sweden,

Oakland is proud of its Scandinavian history, showcased at the **Swedish Heritage Center**. Located inside the former First Covenant Church along Highway 77, the heritage center explores the town's history through a series of exhibits, including items such as wedding dresses, furniture, dinnerware, and folk costumes. Flags from each Swedish province are also displayed. Enjoy a walk along Oakland Avenue, taking in the beauty of buildings refurbished to resemble Swedish storefronts, as well as dala horses on light poles. Grab a meal at any of the local eateries. swedishheritagecenter.org

Staying on Highway 77, you can travel the Byway of the Art. **Lyons**, about seven miles north of Oakland, is home to a storefront theater. Park your car and take a walk along the main street, taking in the architecture of the early and mid-1900s. During your walk, next door to Cosmic Studio, is the theater. While it looks like a storefront, it can actually be lowered and a bleacher set rolled out, so people can sit and watch parades or the occasional public movie showing.

Continue north to **Bancroft**, home of Nebraska poet laureate John G. Neihardt. The author is best known for his book *Black Elk Speaks*, based on a series of interviews with the Lakota chief. The **Neihardt Center** features a look into the poet's life, as well as Lakota and other Native American tribes' cultures. The one-room studio in which he worked is also located onsite. neihardtcenter.org

Decatur offers beautiful views of the Mighty Mo. Locals believed that the town once had a trolley, so it placed a trolley in the city park as part of the Byway of the Art. A short walk away is the Decatur Museum, which offers special exhibits highlighting the town's history. facebook.com/DecaturMuseum

Toward the northern edge of the scenic byway, you'll enter the **Omaha (Umonhon)** and **Winnebago (Ho-Chunk)** reservations. Macy, home of the Omaha, celebrates the harvest season with a powwow each August. The **Winnebago Powwow**, the oldest in North America, is held over four days on the last weekend of July. Featuring statues and information about each group, the community also honors its history with the **Clans Sculpture Garden and Cultural Plaza**. The Ho-Chunk history and culture is shared at the **Angel DeCora Memorial Museum and Research Center**. facebook.com/omahatribeofnebraska; winnebagotribe.com

The final stop on the Lewis and Clark Scenic Byway, **South Sioux City** is home to Siouxland's **Freedom Park**. With a half-sized replica of the Vietnam War Memorial, the park recognizes the service of American military personnel and veterans through a series of events, as well as flag displays along the entrance's drive. For a unique overnight stay, consider sleeping in a treehouse. **Kottage Knechtion Treehouse Bed and Breakfast** caters to one couple at a time, with a room eighteen feet above the ground. The treehouse includes a deck, where you can relax and enjoy an impressive view of five acres of scenery. In the morning, breakfast is served at nearby the **Koffie Knechtion** coffee shop. siouxlandfreedompark.org; facebook.com/TheKoffieKnechtion; facebook.com/KottageKnechtion

Lincoln Highway Historical Scenic Byway

Running the length of the state from Blair to the east and Sidney on the western edge, US Highway 30—aka Lincoln Highway—covers about 450 miles of prime Nebraska landscape. The first transcontinental highway starts in New York City and ends in San Francisco. Spanning thirteen states, the highway opened in 1913. From the Missouri River to the plains of the Wyoming border, you have an opportunity to take in some of the most beautiful views in the country, with cornfields and beanfields dotting the rural areas in between communities offering looks at Nebraska's history and unique attractions. The highway's original design had US Highway 30 running through downtown Omaha, crossing the river over the Douglas Street Bridge and running along Dodge Street, the city's busiest avenue, to suburban Elkhorn. In 1929, a new bridge was built in Blair, north of Omaha, so after sixteen years of running through Nebraska's largest city, the highway was rerouted through the Washington County community. lincolnhighwaynebraskabyway.com

While Omaha is home to outstanding attractions, such as the **Durham Museum**, **Henry Doorly Zoo and Aquarium**, and **Great Plains Black History Museum**, Lincoln Highway's history continues to live along a mile-long tract of brick road in Elkhorn. The city preserves this stretch of the old Highway 30, so visitors can experience what travel was like during the early days of the highway.

Kicking off your drive in **Blair**, visit the **DeSoto National Wildlife Refuge**, about three miles east of the city. With a lake offering fishing, boating, and swimming, as well as impressive waterfowl views during migration season, the wildlife park also features hiking trails. DeSoto was the site of the 1865 sinking of the riverboat Bertrand. The river boat's 250,000 artifacts were saved and several are displayed at the visitor center. Blair is home to excellent dining options, including several downtown spots. fws.gov/refuge/Desoto

Fremont, named after Civil War General John C. Fremont, is home to an impressive collection of downtown antique stores. As you browse the collectibles, such as books, home furnishings, and vintage clothing, you'll likely work up an appetite that can be satisfied at restaurants, including Asian, Mexican, and traditional American fare. Before leaving, grab a cup of your favorite coffee at **MiLady Coffeehouse** in the historical May Brothers Building. The coffee shop features an eclectic seating area, as well as a stage where local musicians perform. **Bryson's Airboat Tours** offers hour-long tours of the Platte River. The company got its start in 2004 when owner Tim Bryson offered airboat rides for people with medical issues. The business grew from there, and has become one of Nebraska's most popular outdoor attractions. visitfremont.com; maybrothersbuilding.com/coffeehouse; brysonairboattours.com

Who knew that the 1944 D-Day Invasion during World War II had its beginnings in **Columbus**? Andrew Jackson Higgins, who spent his childhood in the Platte County city, designed the amphibious boat—nicknamed the Higgins Boat—that carried troops from ships to Normandy Beach. Higgins based his design of the landing craft on the shallow rivers near Columbus. The **Andrew Jackson Higgins Memorial**, a life-sized replica of the Higgins boat with soldiers exiting to the beach, honors the local hero at Pawnee Park. The park includes other monuments, such as those honoring Iraqi war veterans and heroes, and victims of the New York terrorist attacks on Sept. 11, 2001. **Pawnee Park** is also home to picnic areas, walking trails, tennis courts, and horseshoe courts. Take a break and enjoy a drink and burger at **Glur's Tavern**, the oldest continually running tavern west of the Mississippi River. The tavern has entertained numerous politicians and celebrities through the years, including Buffalo Bill Cody. Columbus is also home to Nebraska's original salad dressing—**Dorothy Lynch**. While it was invented in a nearby town, the company that produces the tangy treat is located at **Dusters Restaurant** in downtown Columbus. Enjoy lunch at Dusters, with its grain bin ceiling, but don't even consider putting anything on your salad, but Dorothy Lynch. columbusne.us; bit.ly/glurstavernne; dustersrestaurant.com; dorothylynch.com

Site of the second **"Seedling mile"** for the Lincoln Highway, **Grand Island** has grown to become one of Nebraska's five largest cities. Signs promoting Burma Shave still line the stretch of road that's closed to traffic, but is open for tourists to walk along and explore. Originally built by Leo Stuhr in 1936, today the nearly nine-decade-old gas station is better known as **Kensinger Service and Supply**. It resembles the look it had when Studebakers and other classic cars made their way along the Lincoln Highway in the old days, and you can still stop and fill up your car's tank at the service station. bit.ly/kensingerservice

The **Stuhr Museum of the Prairie Pioneer** is a must-see when visiting Grand Island. The museum complex includes so much to see and do that it's easy to spend a few hours exploring the region's history. Designed by the same architect who created the Kennedy Center for Performing Arts, the Stuhr Building is impressive itself, with its square design representing the plains and located in the middle of a pond, accessible by a walkway. Once inside, you'll be astounded by the dual staircases, highlighting an open space with minimal exhibits. The second floor features a look at plains history, including special exhibits. Across the complex is Fonner Rotunda, which includes Native American and western artifacts and memorabilia. A sculpture of a Native American family is located in the center of the lobby.

More than 200 pieces of farm equipment, including an 1880 thresher and several horse-drawn vehicles, highlight the attractions at the

Antique Farm Machinery Building. Open May 1 through Labor Day, the museum also includes a collection of antique cars, such as a 1909 Model T. Also located on the museum's grounds are a traditional Pawnee earth lodge and log cabin settlements. After a walk around the arbor area, which includes a pond, surrounded by flower gardens, a windmill, shrubs, and trees, head to the living history town. It's based on a railroad town in the late nineteenth century; you'll often find reenactors working as a shopkeeper, blacksmith, and even a hat maker at the millinery. Several houses are located at the railroad town, including the childhood home of Nebraska native and Academy Award–winning actor Henry Fonda. stuhrmuseum.org

Grand Island's downtown district—nicknamed **Railside**—not only recognizes its railroad history, but is home to boutiques and unique stores, including a bevy of antique shops. While downtown, consider catching a movie at the classic Grand Theater, followed by dessert at the **Chocolate Bar**, which also serves as a coffeehouse. With an eclectic décor, the Chocolate Bar attracts guests of all ages. For a fun dining experience, check out **Sin City Grill**, which names burgers and drinks after classic Las Vegas performers. You'll crave both pizza and the beach with a visit to **Wave Pizza Company and Bonzai Beach Club**. The décor screams out Key West, while the food is simply amazing. arriverailside.com; thechocolatebargi.com; sincitygrillgi. wordpress.com; wavepizzaco.com

Each year, thousands of people flock to the area for major events, such as the **Nebraska State Fair** and the seasonal migration of the Sandhill cranes. The state fair attracts more than 300,000 people over an 11-day period in late August. With carnival rides, animal exhibits, concerts, great food, and more, there's something for everyone. In early spring, more than 500,000 sandhill cranes converge in a one-hundred-mile-wide area, from Grand Island to North Platte, as part of their northerly migration, taking them to places such as Wisconsin, Alaska, Canada, and even Siberia. With people from around the world flocking to the area to watch the birds, the **Crane Trust Nature and Visitors Center** offers crane-watching tours, as well as information. Open year-round, the nature center also has hiking trails along the Platte River, as well as a herd of bison that visitors can view. statefair.org; cranetrust.org

How many cities can say they have a museum that stretches across an interstate? As home to the **Great Platte River Road Archway Monument**, Kearney celebrates the westward expansion of not just the pioneers, but also the cars and trucks that followed the great cross-country migration of the Lincoln Highway. The museum traces the history of pioneers who crossed the state along the California, Oregon, and Mormon Trails. Exhibits detail the challenges people faced as they sought a better life out west. A nice touch is the bolts of lightning you'll see as you traverse the plains as the pioneers did. A second section of the Archway features life on the open highway, from watching a movie at the drive-in to camping along the way. Of course, every highway museum needs a 1950s diner. Speaking of cars, the **Classic Car Collection** beckons you to come and explore about 150 vintage autos on display. Conveniently located on the Lincoln Highway, the museum showcases vehicles in classic displays, including a gas station, drive-in theater, and in front of downtown storefronts. The museum rotates vehicles, since the collection has more than 200 cars in its collection. archway.org; classic-carcollection.org

Nebraska's art collection calls **Kearney** home. The **Museum of Nebraska Art (MONA)** displays art from Nebraska artists, or people who have Nebraska connections. With paintings, sculptures, and other pieces on exhibit in open galleries, you can browse art on three floors inside a former post office. The outdoor sculpture garden—named in honor of CliffsNotes founder Cliff Hillegass—includes a statue of its namesake reading one of his study guides. The garden includes a variety of statues, including basketball players living their dream of playing. mona.unk.edu

Kearney is the center of the annual Sandhill crane migration. The area gets the bulk of the cranes, which spend the day eating in cornfields before heading to the sandbars on the Platte River to roost for the night. **Rowe Sanctuary** sponsors guided bird blind tours, where you can watch the birds arrive for their nightly roost or morning launches. You can also visit Rowe for information as you patrol the area's cornfields to watch the cranes on self-guided tours. **Fort Kearny State Park** is an excellent spot for crane watching, as well as a nice area to tour and learn about the fort's role in the mid-1800s. outdoornebraska.gov/fortkearny; rowe.audubon.org

Buffalo Bill Cody called **North Platte** home. And, as he loved the city, the city continues to love him back. Several city attractions have a connection to the Wild West Show founder and entertainer. His ranch—known as Scout Ranch—became part of the state park system. Today, you can tour the house and ranch grounds as part of the **Buffalo Bill Historical State Park**. His ranch includes a barn with old wagons and equipment used to operate it, as well as his cabin, once used during his hunting expeditions. **Cody Park** features a carousel, a children's play area, railroad museum, and a small zoo, as well as ball fields and picnic areas. You can also enjoy an ice cream treat at the park's ice cream stand. While in town, **Fort Cody Trading Post** is a great spot to pick up souvenirs, as well as see oddities, such as a two-headed calf and a miniature version of Buffalo Bill's wild west show. outdoornebraska.gov/buffalobillranch; ci.north-platte.ne.us/parks/cody-park

Lincoln County Historical Museum showcases the area's history, including the time it welcomed more than six million military members during World War II. Since North Platte was along a major train route, the soldiers, sailors, marines and airmen would often spend a short time in North Platte. Several local women staffed the Canteen as volunteers, providing coffee, fruit, and other treats to the troops, as well as lending a friendly ear. Some people established personal relationships, writing letters to each other, and a few even married. The museum's Canteen exhibit features a replica of the coffee area, as well as World War II artifacts, including military uniforms, a weathered American flag, and a captured Nazi flag. The museum also offers a look at life in North Platte during the early twentieth century, such as old television sets, cameras, and clothes. The Lincoln County Historical Museum is also home to a living history town, where you can tour sixteen buildings dating back to the 1800s, including a log cabin and one-room schoolhouse. lincolncountymuseum.org

With an impressive monument, North Platte honors veterans at the **Twentieth Century Veterans Memorial**. With life-size sculptures representing all five military branches, the memorial includes a fifteen-foot-tall wall that depicts each of the armed conflicts during the twentieth century, from World War I to the first Middle Eastern campaign. The memorial also honors the women who volunteered at the North Platte Canteen during World War II. About twenty-five minutes east of the city, **Fort McPherson National Cemetery**, near Maxwell, deserves a visit. Veterans from the Indian wars to the Middle East are interred here. An entire aircrew from World War II was buried together. Located a short distance from the original Fort McPherson, the cemetery is also home to the remains of fifty Buffalo Soldiers, who were reinterred there in 1907, when Fort Robinson closed in northwest Nebraska. bit.ly/20thcveteransmemorial; bit.ly/fortmcpherson

Antiquing enthusiasts will love visiting **Grain Bin Antique Town**, about a twenty-minute drive south of town. The antique shops are located in fourteen wooden grain bins from the Great Depression. The idea for the marketplace grew from a couple's enjoyment of the original grain bin as an extra room on their farm. They'd enjoy a nice evening in the bin, taking in the views of the valley surrounding them. Finding the extra bins on another farm, they bought them and then decided to create Grain Bin Antique Town. Each bin houses a variety of antiques, including books, dishes, clothes, and trunks. grainbinantiquetown.com

As you continue to cruise along Highway 30, make sure you're hungry for your next stop at **Ole's Big Game Steakhouse and Lounge** in **Paxton**. Open since 1933, Ole's quickly became a bar following the end of Prohibition. Ole was an avid hunter, killing a buck and putting the mount in the bar. That, as they say, started it all. For more than thirty years, Ole would go on hunting trips, bringing home animals that he had bagged. From a black bear to a polar bear, and almost everything in-between, they found their spot in the restaurant and bar. The animal collection—plus, the great steaks and burgers—brought visitors from around the country, including celebrities, such as Robert Duvall and boxer Jack Dempsey. Today, Ole's is in the hands of different owners, but the tradition of showcasing the animals and offering delicious food continues to attract people from around the globe. olesbiggame.com

Enjoy a walk along the beach or maybe a dip in the water at **Lake McConaughy**, about twenty minutes north of Ogallala. The man-made lake is the largest in Nebraska and attracts thousands of visitors annually. Home to boating, skiing, and fishing, "Lake Mac," as locals call it, reaches a depth of 140 feet. It's also a great spot for camping. Travel back to the days of yesteryear at **Ogallala's Front Street**. With a replica of a Western storefront, Front Street celebrates the town's history as the end of the trail for Texas cattle drives. Nebraska's "Cowboy Capital" is home to the **Front Street Steakhouse** and **Crystal Palace Saloon**, where you can enjoy an amazing steak dinner followed by a step into the saloon for a cold sarsaparilla. Front Street is also home to a museum highlighting the city's Western history, as well as the seasonal Crystal Palace Revue, a Western song and dance show. ilovelakemac.com; ogallalafrontstreet.com; crystalpalacesaloon.com

Near the western edge of the Lincoln Highway, Western enthusiasts will enjoy a stop in **Sidney**. With the **Fort Sidney Complex** and **Boot Hill Cemetery**, you can trace the Army's presence in the area in the late 1860s, as well as visit a historical graveyard, which got its name because cowboys were buried with their boots on. Cityofsidney.org/192/Attractions

Heritage Highway 136

Covering nearly 240 miles over ten counties in southern Nebraska, Heritage Highway 136 was created in 1999 as a way of celebrating the region's history and social contributions. Running from Brownville in the east to the village of Edison on the western edge, Heritage Highway includes historical attractions, such as the Homestead National Monument, Willa Cather's childhood home, and the childhood home of Clarence Mitchell, famous for his "spitball" pitches in Major League Baseball. heritagehighway136.com

If you're up for another adventure, check out the Glacial Hills Scenic Byway, about an hour south of Brownville. You can learn more about the byway in the Kansas chapter.

Brownville is a unique village, in that the entire town was named to the National Register of Historical Places. With buildings dating back to the turn of the twentieth century, the small town is best enjoyed by parking your vehicle and walking the main street. With shops and boutiques, as well as a few restaurants, you'll find it's an interesting place to spend a few hours. Stroll along the Missouri River in the town's park, as well as the **Gov. Robert W. Furnas Arboretum** and **Whiskey Run Creek Nature Trail**, before stopping by **Whiskey Run Creek Vineyard and Winery**, which is located inside a century-old barn. brownville-ne.com; whiskeyruncreek.com

As you pass through **Auburn**, stop and visit the **Nemaha County Veterans Memorial**. Saluting area men and women who have served in the military's five branches, the memorial is well-designed and invites you to explore the park. About thirteen minutes north of Auburn lies **Peru**, home to Peru State College. The college and downtown Peru offer a pretty area to enjoy a walk, among vintage college buildings, as well as the downtown architecture. peru.edu

It seems appropriate that the first homestead in America was located in Gage County, where the Oregon Trail first crossed into Nebraska. The **National Homestead Monument of America** in **Beatrice** is located on the land where Daniel Freeman established the first homestead in the United States. Supported by President Abraham Lincoln, Congress passed a homestead bill that went into effect Jan. 1, 1862. After allegedly bribing the county clerk to open his office at midnight, Freeman filed the first claim to 160 acres of land outside Beatrice. Homesteaders had five years to improve the land by building a home and making the soil farmable. Freeman succeeded while most people failed. Homesteading—while controversial because it essentially stole land from Native Americans—was popular for 125 years and included thirty states. The law was repealed in 1976, but Alaska was given an additional ten years to complete homesteading. The national monument includes exhibits highlighting life on the plains for homesteaders, as well as antique farm equipment and buildings. You can walk a trail from the visitor center, which resembles prairie grass swaying in the wind, to the education center that takes you through Freeman's homestead, including the spot where he was buried. A one-room schoolhouse is located near the homestead. nps.gov/home/index.htm

Learn about the history of Beatrice and other area communities at the **Gage County Museum**. Located in a refurbished train depot, the museum covers area history from the pioneer days, railroads, industry, agriculture, and medical advancements. gagecountymuseum.info

You must take a swing on the **world's largest porch swing** in **Hebron**. Built in 1985, the swing, which uses an irrigation component as the overhead span, can seat sixteen adults or twenty-four children. Other cities have challenged the swing's status, but it continues to remain the world's largest porch swing. It's located in Hebron's city park.

Celebrating his life and baseball career, the **Russ Snyder Museum** in **Oak** is a must for any baseball fan. Snyder spent twelve seasons—1959–70—in Major League Baseball with five teams, winning the 1966 World Series as a member of the Baltimore Orioles. He played in 117 games that season, with a .306 batting average. Besides the Orioles, Snyder played for the Kansas City Athletics, Chicago White Sox, Cleveland, and Milwaukee. Staying in Nuckolls County, the historical society manages eight unique buildings, including the first post office in Superior, a log cabin.

The childhood hometown of Pulitzer Prize–winning author Willa Cather, **Red Cloud** offers more than forty locations that were inspirations for characters or locations in her books. Cather explored life on the prairie in six novels, including *O Pioneers!* and *My Antonia*. Guided tours of the attractions, such as the Cather home in which she grew up, the Cather Second Home, and the Opera House, are offered through the **National Willa Cather Center**. The center, which opened in 2017 to serve as a living memorial to the author, is home to a public museum, archive, and research center, as well as meeting space and performing arts center. You can even reserve an overnight stay at the Cather Second Home, which serves as a bed and breakfast inn. willacather.org

A visit to Red Cloud includes more than learning about Willa Cather (though, isn't that impressive enough?). Three murals, completed during the Great Depression as part of the Works Progress Administration, are located at the local post office. A rural schoolhouse—the Yost Farm School—was used to teach children from 1887 until 1959. The building was moved to the Yost farm in 1989. Measuring 130 feet in diameter and standing three stories tall, the **Starke Round Barn** is one of the largest in the United States. The barn, more than one hundred years old, is open for visits by appointment.

A short drive south of Red Cloud, the **Willa Cather Memorial Prairie** consists of more than 600 acres of never-plowed prairie land. With grasses native to Nebraska, wild flowers, and other plants, the view is not only breathtaking, but historical. It's not often you'll come across land that has not been used by European-American settlers. The prairie is also home to several birds that will excite birding enthusiasts. visitredcloud.com

Less than an hour west of Red Cloud, the Harlan County Reservoir is a nature enthusiast's dream come true. With a large lake created by the dam along the Republican River, near the Kansas border, the area offers swimming, fishing, boating, hiking, hunting, and camping. Birdwatchers will enjoy the opportunity to catch glimpses or take photos of waterfowl, such as pelicans, osprey, gulls, ducks, and more than 300 other bird species. During the summer months, the Army Corps of Engineers hosts guided tours of the Harlan Dam each Sunday. facebook.com/harlancountylake

Outlaw Trail Scenic Byway

During the 1800s, outlaws, such as Jesse James and his brother Frank, would use the woods, gorges, and hills of northeast Nebraska as hideouts from posses fast on their tracks. It's part of tribal history that Jesse James married a member of the Isanti Dacotah (Santee Dakota) tribe during his time in the infamous Devil's Nest region of Knox County. As part of the lore of bad guys hiding out along the Missouri River region, the Outlaw Trail Scenic Byway was created to celebrate the northern edge of Nebraska—with most communities within ten miles of the South Dakota border. Covering 231 miles from South Sioux City to Valentine, the trail travels mostly along Highway 12. You'll find everything from vintage windmills at a landfill to the smallest town in America and take in Nebraska's famous Sandhills, as well as cultural celebrations, such as powwows with the Santee and Ponca tribes. nebraskaoutlawtrail.org

As you travel from the east along Highway 20, check out the classic **Jackson Windmills** in front of LG Landfill near **Jackson**. It's home to more than twenty windmills dating from the 1880s through the 1930s; the windmills have been collected over a twenty-year period. While some still work, most are available for viewing. Feel free to pull over and take a walk through agriculture history.

Ponca State Park is one of the more popular parks in the state's system. The park honors Native American history with a sculpture and waterfall display near the main entrance. Inside the park, you'll be a few feet from the scenic Missouri River, at a site which has been redesigned to reflect its earlier life reminiscent of the Lewis and Clark expedition. With ample hiking, fishing, swimming, and boating available, you can spend a few days at this state park. Primitive hiking trails take you through deep woods, with tall trees and brush. During your hike, be on the lookout for wildlife, such as deer, raccoons, and foxes. Camping is available, as well as cabins which can be rented. Enjoy wildlife viewing, with deer, pelicans, and several bird species present. The park is home to one of the oldest trees in Nebraska, with the Old Oak Tree dating back to 1644. outdoornebraska.gov/ponca

A drive along the **Outlaw Trail** will take you through several small towns with unique attractions. **Newcastle**, with a population of about 350, is home to the Ionia Volcano. Err, the volcano that wasn't a volcano. During the Lewis and Clark expedition, William Clark noted that a nearly 200-foot tall bluff seemed to be on fire. Fur traders often noticed dense smoke and fire in the area. The bluff collapsed in the late 1870s after the Missouri River had eroded its base. Scientists later determined the eruption and smoke were likely caused by heat created by the oxidation of pyrite and other shale as part of the bluff's erosion. nps.gov/places/ionia-volcano.htm

Maskell is home to the "Smallest City Hall in the US." At ten feet by ten feet, it's a tight fit for the village's five board members and village clerk.

A visit to **Crofton** combines history with nature. It's mere minutes from the Missouri River, so you can take a side trip to **Gavins Point Dam**, where you can enjoy fishing, boating, swimming, and relaxing at **Lewis and Clark Lake**. Wildlife enthusiasts will enjoy the sight of bald eagles, deer, coyotes, and several types of birds. You can camp near the spot where Lewis and Clark spent time. Back in town, tour the historic downtown, where the city celebrates its history with a mural detailing key events and attractions, including the lone tree that once sat in the middle of a street. The town is home to an antique pulley museum, which is worth at least a pop-in to view the many pulleys hanging from the ceiling and walls. No visit to Crofton is complete without spending at least one night at the **Historic Hotel Argo Bed and Breakfast**. It's considered to be the most haunted hotel in Nebraska. The owners believe the B&B may be haunted by the ghosts of children, who pose no safety risk. But, the Hotel Argo dates back to the railroad days when passengers wanted their own hotel in which to stay. Today, with nine rooms and suites, the Historic Hotel Argo celebrates the life of Hollywood actress Leslie Brooks, who lived at the hotel with her mother and grandparents before she and her mother moved to Hollywood. Later, after graduating high school, the actress, born Virginia Leslie Gettman, changed her name to Leslie Brooks and appeared in more than thirty movies. The B&B's owners enjoy sharing the history of the hotel with guests and offer tours of the building. outdoornebraska.gov/lewisandclark; facebook.com/TheHistoricHotelArgo

The **Santee Dakota** were forcibly relocated to Knox County in 1867 after the US-Dakota War in Minnesota five years earlier. Today, **Santee** is home to the **Ohiya Casino and Resort**, along Highway 12. The tribe dedicated a **veterans memorial** in 2019, which includes a special memorial for the thirty-eight tribal members executed in Mankato, Minnesota, in 1862. It was the largest mass execution in American history, following their alleged roles in the war. The memorial also honors veterans from the Civil War through the recent Middle Eastern conflicts. The tribe's headquarters building is home to the **cultural center**, which includes historical and cultural exhibits, including the rifle that once belonged to Chief Little Crow. The Santee tribe hosts an annual **wacipi** (Dakota for powwow) each June, as well as in November for Veterans Day. ohiyacasino.com; santeedakota.org

Explore Missouri River bluffs at **Niobrara State Park**, where the Niobrara and Missouri rivers meet, you can enjoy fishing, swimming, boating, and hiking several trails. RV camping, primitive camping, and cabins are available at the park. While in **Niobrara**, visit the **Niobrara Museum**, which includes a look into the area's history. You can pay your respects at the **Sage Brothers Memorial** near the museum. Three Sage brothers served aboard the same ship, which sank in the Pacific Ocean when it was struck by an Australian ship. The brothers are considered the largest single family wartime loss in Nebraska history. outdoornebraska.gov/niobrara; facebook.com/niobrarahistoricalsocietymuseum

While in Niobrara, the third-oldest town in Nebraska, you may think you've reached foodie overload with excellent choices, such as **Sportsmen's Bar and Two Rivers Hotel**, home to outstanding steaks, prime rib, and burgers. The **Country Café** prides itself on its farm-to-table menu, serving large portions at reasonable prices. The **Trading Post** will change your mind about gas station food, or at least this one. With outstanding barbecue ribs, broasted chicken, burgers, handmade pizza, and breakfast sandwiches, you might mistake the convenience store for a takeout restaurant. bit.ly/sportsmensbar; eatcountrycafe.com; facebook.com/lancetinalundberg

Once banished from its Niobrara homeland to the plains of Oklahoma, the **Ponca** tribe reclaimed parts of its lands in a major Congressional act in the 1990s. Today, the tribe has its headquarters a few miles south of Niobrara State Park, not far from the Niobrara River. A sculpture of **Chief Standing Bear** overlooks the area. Standing Bear won the first major civil rights lawsuit involving Native Americans when, in 1879, a judge in Omaha ruled that Native Americans were to be considered people under the Constitution. The Ponca host a powwow each August. poncatribe-ne.org

Monowi is considered the smallest town in America, with one resident—Elsie Eiler: town mayor, treasurer, clerk, librarian, and tavern owner. Stop in at the **Monowi Tavern** and say hi, as well as order a burger and drink. The town is about a block long. Besides the tavern, there's **Rudy's Library**, named for Elsie's late husband, which has thousands of books. The town—and Elsie—have been featured in national ads. bit.ly/monowitavern

Lewis and Clark saw a prairie dog for the first time during their expedition near modern-day **Lynch**. There's a historical marker recognizing the event on the east end of town. Take a drive downtown and check out the train mural.

Nature is the name of the game in **Valentine**, on the western edge of the Outlaw Trail. With so much to do, it may be a challenge to explore, but take the time to visit the city. A few miles east of Valentine, **Smith Falls State Park** is a gateway to the scenic Niobrara River, perfect for canoeing, kayaking, and rafting. But first, visit **Smith Falls**, Nebraska's tallest waterfall at seventy feet. The falls' water consistently stays cold due to its location among shady trees. Smith Falls State Park is perfect for hiking and camping, too. Nearby, enjoy a leisurely drive through **Fort Niobrara National Wildlife Refuge**, where you can see bison, elk, and prairie dogs. Explore the trails along the Niobrara River, such as the one leading to Fort Falls. You can also access the Niobrara River for boating from near the refuge's entrance. The **Cowboy Trail** is a bicycle/walk path from Norfolk to Valentine, with plans to expand even farther west to Chadron. outdoornebraska.gov/smithfalls fws.gov/refuge/fort_niobrara; bikecowboytrail.com

Known as the "Heart City," Valentine celebrates its name with red hearts painted on sidewalks, as well as displayed on street signs. Take a selfie in front of the giant heart downtown. With a variety of businesses, you can buy almost any western-related clothing or gear available at **Young's Western Wear**. Book and wine enthusiasts will enjoy a stop at the **Plains Trading Company Booksellers**. While in town, grab a meal at the Frosty Drive-in or grab a bigger meal at the **Bunkhouse Restaurant and Saloon** or **Peppermill Restaurant**. facebook.com/YoungsWesternWear plainstrading.com; bit.ly/frostydrivein; facebook.com/BunkhouseNE; Peppermillvsalentine.com

As you explore Nebraska's scenic highways and byways, you may want to consider these additional byways:

Bridges to Buttes Scenic Byway—From Valentine to the Wyoming border, about 200 miles of beautiful scenery awaits, with attractions such as Toadstool Geologic Park.

Gold Rush Scenic Byway—This runs almost 160 miles through Nebraska's panhandle, with attractions such as **Carhenge** and the **Museum of Fur Trade**.

Loup Rivers Scenic Byway—America's popcorn capital awaits you as it covers 150 miles along the Loup River valley. Among the stops you'll enjoy are Happy Jack Chalk Mine and the Museum of Nebraska Major League Baseball.

Sandhills Journey Scenic Byway—From Grand Island to Alliance, the Sandhills byway includes about 270 miles of interesting scenery, including attractions, such as the Nebraska National Forest and Grasslands.

Western Trails Scenic and Historic Byway—Covering almost 150 miles from Ogallala to the Wyoming border, attractions along this byway include the Petrified Wood Gallery in Ogallala, Chimney Rock National Monument, and Scotts Bluff National Monument.

Tim and Lisa Trudell are the brains behind the popular Midwest Travel Blog, thewalkingtourists.com, and a valuable member of the Midwest Travel Network. In addition to their love of all things travel, the Trudell's enjoy football, movies, and spending time with family. You might have also come across their work in: 100 Things to Do in Omaha Before You Die, Unique Eats and Eateries of Omaha, *and* 100 Things to Do in Nebraska Before You Die, *when they have been featured on Omaha news channels KMTV, WOWT, KETV, or Fox 42 News, or across mutual travels. Above all, Tim and Lisa hope that travel helps you explore the Midwest and beyond, and that this book helps you do just that. Learn more about Tim and Lisa at* thewalkingtourists.com.

NORTH DAKOTA

N orth Dakota is a road-tripper's dream. Its wide-open spaces are dotted with laid-back cities, untamed landscapes, quirky roadside attractions and stoic settings straight out of Great Plains history. Just over 760,000 people live here, so there's plenty of room to roam under the endless sky.

It entered the Union on November 2, 1889. That's the exact same date its neighbor, South Dakota, became part of the United States. And since nobody knows which order was signed first, North Dakota is either the thirty-ninth or fortieth state. This nearly simultaneous signing set both states up as good-natured rivals (that just happen to have a lot in common) from the very first moments of statehood.

Basic North Dakota Facts:
- The North Dakota state capital is Bismarck.
- The state motto is "Liberty and union, now and forever: one and inseparable."
- The state bird is the western meadowlark, a grassland bird with a bright yellow belly and a distinctive, musical song.
- The state flower is the prairie rose, which you'll find growing wild all over North Dakota.
- There are seven Highways and Byways to explore in North Dakota. You'll find four of them detailed in this chapter. The rest are listed in the index in the back of this book.

Fun North Dakota Facts:
- Remembering phone numbers in North Dakota is easy, since there's only one area code (701) for the entire state.

- The International Peace Garden near Dunseith straddles the Canadian border—and you can too. Visitors pose with one foot in North Dakota and the other in Manitoba.
- Local farmers sell their wheat to the only state-owned mill in the nation. Pick up a bag of flour from the North Dakota Mill at the grocery store for an unusual (and useful) souvenir.

Badlands buttes, backroads and the Theodore Roosevelt National Park North Unit Scenic Byway

For the most striking scenery in the state, take the highway, scenic byway and the backroads along the Badlands of North Dakota's western edge. Rust-red scoria roads and one of the most storied single-track trails in the country wind between two units of Theodore Roosevelt National Park, where graceful wild horses, chattering prairie dogs and lumbering bison seem to outnumber visitors. The route is bookended by the folksy western town of **Medora** in the south and **Watford City**, just over eighty-two miles north on Highway 85.

Medora sits just steps away from the entrance of the South Unit of **Theodore Roosevelt National Park**. This is the most-visited spot in North Dakota, so there's plenty to see and do. Spend half a day here at the absolute minimum. Shopping, strolling the wooden sidewalks, and popping into the shows, restaurants and attractions in this tiny town can easily fill a leisurely weekend. nps.gov/thro/index.htm

Most visitors encounter the region's Badlands buttes for the first time during a slow car cruise along the South Unit's thirty-six-mile **Scenic Loop Drive**. The ancient remains of coal, quartz, and volcanic ash paint these eroded rock formations in stripes of brick, grey, black, and bone. The Scenic Loop Drive isn't technically a loop at the moment (erosion has closed a stretch of road between mile markers 24 and 28 for the foreseeable future) but the out-and-back route is still one of the prettiest drives in the state. The speed limit is twenty-five miles per hour, so allow at least a couple of hours (and ideally more) to pull over to watch the prairie dogs scurry around their roadside settlements and photograph the wild horses that roam the park.

Even casual hikers can enjoy the self-guided nature trails that are located just off the driving route. They're short—the **Ridgeline Nature Trail** is 6 miles and the **Coal Vein Trail** (which explores the unique geology of a once fiery gulch) is .8 miles—and accessible for hikers of most abilities.

Bring your camera, because scenic views abound. Scamper up **Buck Hill**, the highest point in the park, or take it easy on the **Boicourt Overlook Trail**. The .2-mile trail is both paved and handicap accessible, so it's a great spot for a mini hike that the whole group can enjoy. It's especially pretty at sunset.

The rangers also recommend watching the sun set at **Wind Canyon**, an overlook that you'll soon recognize on postcards and tourism brochures. The nearly half-mile trail is appropriate for beginners, but it's briefly steep. The picturesque view of the Little Missouri River Valley is worth the effort.

Even if you can't stay long, make time to walk around Medora and soak up the Wild West ambiance. (High season runs from May through September, so research to see what's open, and when, before you go.) The craggy canyons and cowboy culture of the American West color everything in this hamlet, including the contemporary paintings and sculptures on display at **The Capital Gallery West**. facebook.com/thecapitalgallerywest

The same goes for the gifts and titles on the shelves at **Western Edge Books, Artwork, Music**. Every item is grounded in a deep sense of place. facebook.com/westernedgebooks

Pop into **Medora Boot & Western Wear** to score a pair of intricately detailed cowboy boots. Clothing for men and women is also for sale. medoraboot.com

Show off your new look as you browse the exhibits at the **North Dakota Cowboy Hall of Fame**. (Just remember, breaking in boots can take a while.) northdakotacowboy.com

Wind down with a bison burger and a local beer on the patio at **Boots Bar and Grill**. Brews from North Dakota and eastern Montana are both considered local in a place where thirty miles might stretch between ranches. bootsbarmedora.com

Those boots will also come in handy on a backcountry Badlands ride with **Medora Riding Stables and Trail Rides**. Don't worry if you're new to the saddle; the horses are gentle enough for kids seven and older to ride. bit.ly/medorastables

Theodore Roosevelt wasn't yet president when he first arrived in Dakota Territory in 1883, but this place changed his life and his way of thinking. Make the scenic drive to the remote **Elkhorn Ranch** where he lived as a young man. bit.ly/elkhornranchnd

Or stay in town and shop for souvenirs at **Joe Ferris General Store**. It was built by his guide and friend in the 1880s. Roosevelt's original cabin is located near the South Unit Visitor Center. bit.ly/joeferris

Read the largest private collection of Theodore Roosevelt books in the lobby of the gracious **Rough Riders Hotel**. It's named for Roosevelt's cavalry unit (the only one to see combat in the Spanish-American war), but it offers the swankiest digs in town. medora.com/stay/hotel/rough-riders-hotel

On the opposite end of the spectrum, the **Shepherd's Wagons** invites visitors to bed down in covered wagons for a decidedly no-frills glamping experience. (Electricity and shower facilities are provided.) custerscottage.com/options.php

If that's still not enough history for you, check out the one-man **Teddy Roosevelt Show** at the Old Town Hall Theatre. Or chat Teddy and his wife Edith as they walk through the streets. medora.com/do/entertainment/the-teddy-roosevelt-show

Similar living history presentations occur on the steps of the **Chateau de Mores State Historical Site**, the hilltop home of the hot-headed Marquis de Mores. He named Medora for his trailblazing, sharpshooting wife. history.nd.gov/historicsites/chateau

The **Medora Musical** changes every year, but the rousing review always honors Theodore Roosevelt's Badlands sojourn. A trip to the outdoor amphitheater is an annual pilgrimage for many superfans. medora.com/do/entertainment/medora-musical

Eating at the **Pitchfork Steak Fondue** before the show is another time-honored tradition. The alfresco meal includes a buffet-style dinner of cowboy classics, including steaks that are grilled on pitchforks and served atop a bluff. medora.com/eat/family/pitchfork-steak-fondue

Prefer a more elegant atmosphere? Try succulent buffalo osso bucco, an artful salad or a juicy steak at **Theodore's Dining Room**. medora.com/eat/family/theodores-dining-room

Then play a round at **Bully Pulpit Golf Course**. This is one of America's Top 100 Public Golf Courses—and a stunner. The eighteen-hole course is carved out of the rugged landscape, following the contours of the buttes and river valleys. Holes 14 to 16 take golfers through a gorge for maximum drama. medora.comdo/outdoor/bully-pulpit-golf-course

Nearby **Sully Creek State Park** offers more placid Little Missouri views. It's North Dakota's only State Scenic River, so the park is very popular with paddlers. parkrec.nd.gov/sully-creek-state-park

It's also one of many western North Dakota spots with access to the **Maah Daah Hey Trail**, which snakes through the Badlands, from here to just south of Watford City. It's one of the most brutal and beautiful single-track mountain biking trails in the nation. mdhta.com

Rent bikes from **Dakota Cyclery** if you're up for the challenge. The route is just as gorgeous—but less strenuous—for hikers and equestrians. dakotacyclery.com

Even if you step out into the backcountry for only a few minutes, bring plenty of water, snacks and a fully charged phone. Bring a map and tell someone where you're going and when you expect to return, since cell service is spotty, water stops are scarce (or nonexistent) and the arid terrain can be hot and windy.

Daredevils who favor dirt roads so rustic that they're essentially just overgrown trails will love the route to **Devils Pass**. Locals call this steep, 150-foot gorge the Grand Canyon of North Dakota. To get there, take Highway 85 north, turning onto Lower Magpie Road north of Fairfield. Drive west on Goat Pass Road (US Forest Service Road 711) until the road ends, park and hike out onto the narrow ridgeline trail that connects two bluffs. You can also hike in on the Maah Daah Hey Trail. mdhta.com/points-of-interest/devils-pass

The roads are often slippery and they're not suitable for large vehicles such as campers. If you want to experience the Badlands scenery without the extra element of danger, keep cruising north along Highway 85 to the much more accessible **Long X Trail**, the northern end of the Maah Daah Hey Trail. To find it, continue north on Highway 85, take a left just south of the Long X bridge and park at **CCC Campground**. fs.usda.gov/dpg

The **North Unit of Theodore Roosevelt National Park** is just on the other side of the bridge. The scenery here is lusher and greener than its more visited southern counterpart. And since eighty-two percent of the land is designated as a wilderness area, you'll likely have less human company as you make your way along the **Theodore Roosevelt National Park North Unit Scenic Byway**. nps.gov/thro/planyourvisit/north-unit.htm

This twenty-eight-mile out-and-back byway bursts with wildlife viewing opportunities. Give yourself at least two hours to properly take it in—and more time if you plan to explore the hiking trails along the route. It's suitable for all vehicles (including RVs) and cyclists, with just one short unpaved stretch.

Take it slow to watch longhorn cattle snoozing in the grasslands, elusive bighorn sheep navigating the craggy outcroppings, and lumbering bison (which often outnumber cars) calmly crossing the road at their leisure, creating North Dakota–style traffic jams. Give the latter plenty of space. Bison look awkward and almost cuddly, but they can run as fast as thirty-five miles per hour.

The Theodore Roosevelt National Park North Unit Scenic Byway starts at the park entrance and quickly whisks visitors past the smooth, spherical **Cannonball Concretions**, geological oddities formed as sediment tumbles down the bluffs. To see the terrain on foot, try the **Little Mo Nature Trail**. This easy, 1.1-mile hike includes a .7-mile inner loop that's both paved and ADA-accessible so everybody can join in. The 1.5-mile **Caprock Coulee Trail** is a little more challenging, but the views from the ridgeline are worth every step.

If you want epic views with minimal physical exertion, you're in luck; the **River Bend Overlook** is perhaps the prettiest panorama in the state and it's just steps from the byway. The sight of the Little Missouri River flanked by craggy cliffs and a lush ribbon of trees is a sight worth savoring. The **Oxbow Overlook** marks the turnaround point on the scenic byway and also offers striking views without much effort.

If you're hungry, continue fifteen miles north on Highway 85 to **Watford City**. Another recent oil boom flooded this no-nonsense city with a new crop of oilfield workers, support staff, and their young families. It's been a gathering place and shopping spot for farmers and ranchers for generations, so the vibe is resolutely practical. This results in some unique business models. visitwatfordcity.com

For example, you can see a sixty-million-year-old petrified tree stump that weighs in at a mind-boggling seventeen thousand pounds at the **Pioneer Museum of McKenzie County** inside the **Long X Visitor Center** and then stock up at the liquor store around back. (Grab coffee, ice cream and local gifts, music and books before you go.) facebook.com/pioneermuseummckenziecounty

A few steps away, **Burritos Bros.** sells tacos, burritos, and hearty quinoa gumbo year-round. You can also rent snowshoes for winter hiking. burritobrosnd.com

Six Shooters melds a café and movie theatre. It's a solid bet for rainy weather when you can't get on the trails. sixshootersnd.com

Drive deeper into town to **Stonehome Brewing** for dinner and local craft beer. Try Maah Daah Hey Red Rye IPA—a portion of sales help maintain the trail. stonehomebrewing.com

Or grab coffee or chai at **Door 204**. The new Linda Roesch mural on the outside wall of the coffeeshop is a great photo opportunity. facebook.com/door204/

Then retire to **Roosevelt Inn and Suites**, which boasts contemporary rooms, a collection of Teddy Roosevelt memorabilia inside and a strangely massive bust of the twenty-sixth president in front of the building. It's the perfect place to end your rugged western North Dakota adventure. rooseveltinn.com

Other great eats along the way:
Medora Fudge and Ice Cream Depot—House-made fudge and hand-scooped ice cream showcase prairie ingredients like chokecherry and rhubarb. People watching from the patio is practically a Medora rite of passage. medora.com/eat/family/medora-fudge-and-ice-cream-depot

The Farmhouse Cafe—This intimate Medora spot is open for lunch, but it really excels at breakfast items like croissant French toast with house-made chocolate sauce, stuffed hashbrowns and maple bacon donuts. facebook.com/thefarmhousecafe

Medora Uncork'd—Intimate and upscale, this wine bar is a break from Medora's cowboy vibe. Look for a solid wine list (including bottles to take home) and small plates such as Thai flatbread and charcuterie trays. medorauncorkd.wine

Outlaws Bar & Grill—This Watford City joint offers a family-friendly meal with a Western flair. Favorites include thick and juicy ribeye, bison and frybread tacos, or a half-pound (!) chocolate chip cookie for dessert. outlawsbarngrill.com/owc

Connect your trip:

Massive sculptures, more pioneer and Western history, and small-town surprises like a pottery studio and prairie abbey are just a short drive away. Hop on the **Old Red Old Ten Scenic Byway** in **Dickinson** (thirty-seven miles east of Medora) or the **Enchanted Highway**, about twelve miles east of Dickinson. Read on to learn more.

Folk art along the backroads: The Old Red Old Ten Scenic Byway and the Enchanted Highway—If you love an old-fashioned car cruise topped with a healthy helping of roadside kitsch, you'll flip for this laid-back road trip. The route starts in **Mandan** in the central part of the state, rambles west into the Mountain Time Zone and ends in proud but diminutive **Regent**. This low-key itinerary gets you off the interstate and onto the backroads by combining the charming, one-hundred-mile-long **Old Red, Old Ten Scenic Byway** with the oversized folk art along the **Enchanted Highway**—easily the state's quirkiest thoroughfare.

Breezing through without stopping would require a whole afternoon. But stopping is the entire point of this journey, so allow at least one long, lazy day to see everything along the route. Lodging in Dickinson or Regent allows you to break up the trip if you'd prefer a slower pace.

Start with massive omelets or a stack of impossibly dense pancakes at **Kroll's Diner**. It offers '50s-style diner classics as well as German-influenced comfort food like *knoephla* soup, *fleischkuechle*, (a type of meat pie) and cabbage rolls. sitdownandeat.com

If you get a later start, join the drive-through line at the **Bismarck Big Boy** for the most nostalgic lunch that money can buy. The menu features retro throwbacks like a purple cow (grape juice shakes) and local favorites like fries and gravy and pizza burgers served flying style (in a sandwich press). bismarckbigboy.com

That nostalgia deepens as you journey to **Dickinson** on the **Old Red Old Ten Scenic Byway**. The very name of this thoroughfare is pulled from two eras of transportation history. It started as one of the color-coded trails that crisscrossed the country in the days before cars, reaching from Seattle to New York in its heyday. Then it transformed into Highway 10, which ran between Washington and Michigan. oldredoldten.com

Information about the backroads, quiet towns, roadside stops and pastoral scenery is interpreted through the **Talking Trail**. Just dial (701) 566-5566 and the number on the sign in front of you to learn about the context, culture, and history of every stop along the way.

Start at the **Mandan Depot**, a handsome brick Queen Anne–style building that saw its last train in the 1970s. Cross the street to **Native Artists United** to purchase beadwork and jewelry from Indigenous artists. facebook.com/nativeartistsunited

The region's Indigenous residents are honored in *The Trail of Tears* sculpture at Sixth Avenue and Third Street. It's part of Peter Wolf Toth's Whispering Giants series that honors Native Americans in the US. North Dakota's favorite adopted son, Teddy Roosevelt, is honored in bronze in the *Rough Rider* statue on Main Street and Third Avenue.

For art that's decidedly less high-brow, head west on I-94 to meet *Salem Sue*—the world's largest Holstein Cow. This fiberglass giantess was erected in the city of **New Salem** in 1974. Drop your donation in the box to picnic and take selfies with Sue.

If you prefer a more picturesque backdrop, continue to **Gaebe Pond** outside of New Salem or head to **Lover's Cliff**, a rocky outcropping south of Almont. Couples have carved their initials into the sandstone here for generations. After **Almont**, the trail leaves Interstate 94 and continues west, escorting you down quiet country lanes.

Twin Buttes and Trails, six miles east of **Glen Ullin**, offers a peek back into history. Look north to see the route General Custer took to march his troops into Montana. The view to the southwest includes a tableau of scoria rock, which paints much of western North Dakota in subtle shades of pink, yellow, and rust-red.

Potter Robin Reynolds uses local clay to create graceful clay vessels, rustic stains and rich glazes at **Dacotah Clayworks** in the city of **Hebron**. Drop into the retired Texaco station for studio tours, demos, and unique pottery shopping. ndclay.net

Grab coffee, freshly baked cinnamon roll cake or monster bars from **Dark Side of the Brew** on your way out of town. It's hard to resist North Dakota's only coffeehouse homage to a Pink Floyd song. facebook.com/ thedarksideofthebrew

Along the road to **Richardton**, you cross over into the mountain time zone. You gain an hour, but it feels like you're going back in time as you enter the subtly majestic **Assumption Abbey**.

A small community of Benedictine monks has maintained the soaring sanctuary since it was first used for midnight mass in 1908. The Romanesque-style sanctuary contains twenty-three stained glass windows and echoes the color palette of western North Dakota— sky blue, scoria red, and the soft gold of wheat and prairie grasses. Spartan rooms and meals are available for pilgrims and travelers seeking rest and solitude. The monks also sell wine and bread. assumptionabbey.com

These souvenirs make a nice picnic at **Schnell Ranch Recreation Area** just outside of town. It also offers two thousand acres of public land for fishing and camping and trails for hiking and horseback riding. blm.gov/visit/schnell-ranch-recreation-area

Learn about the history of one room schoolhouses and the Northern Pacific Railroad in **Taylor**. Or push on to **Gladstone** to see how stagecoaches linked the region's farms and ranches in the earliest days of the Dakota Territory.

The Old Red Old Ten Scenic Byway ends in the small city of **Dickinson**. Bring a cooler to stock up on *varenyky* or *pyrohy* (cheese buttons) at the **Ukrainian Cultural Institute** after taking in the folk art and *pysanky* (intricately painted Easter eggs) on display. visitdickinson.com

The twelve-acre **Dickinson Museum Center** campus includes three history museums (**Joachim Regional History Museum**, **Pioneer Machinery Hall** and **Prairie Outpost Park**) that present exhibits and artifacts from the region's settlement era and beyond. **The Badlands Dinosaur Museum** goes much further back in time, drawing visitors in with hands-on exhibits and the largest collection of dinosaurs in the state, including complete *stegosaurus* and *triceratops* skeletons. dickinsonmuseumcenter.com

Food and fuel options are minimal along the second leg of your route, so fill up on both in Dickinson. The gracious patio at **Fluffy Fields Vineyard and Winery** cultivates a unique atmosphere. Stop for fresh daily specials, small plates, and wine made from the vineyard's grapes, North Dakota rhubarb and aronia berries. fluffyfields.com

To acknowledge the end of the Old Red Old Ten Scenic Byway in true historical style, eat at **The Brew**. This intimate coffee shop and restaurant serves up salad and sandwich lunches, a variety of teas and espresso drinks and thick slabs of Scotcharoos and gooey seven-layer bars inside a former church where Teddy Roosevelt used to worship. facebook.com/thebrewcoffee

Then drive back east to explore North Dakota's most utterly remarkable roadway—the **Enchanted Highway**. It begins on I-94 at the Gladstone exit. You'll see the highway's most famous attraction well before you turn off.

Soaring 110 feet tall, Birds in Flight was deemed the World's Largest Scrap Metal Sculpture by the Guinness Book of World Records. Enchanted Highway creator and sculptor Gary Greff had no formal art training when he taught himself to weld these massive creations from wire, pipes, and old oil drums. He just wanted to entice people to drive to his town, **Regent**, thirty-two miles down the road.

It takes a minute to truly process the sculptures' size. ***The Deer Family*** (the second sculpture off of Interstate) was so large, the seventy-five-foot buck had to be dismantled and reassembled so it could fit down Regent's streets. ***Grasshoppers in the Field*** is constructed from discarded oil wells and fuel tanks. Your sense of scale is thrown all out of whack when you realize that the tiny boat dwarfed by a seventy-foot rainbow trout in ***Fisherman's Dream*** is an actual, functioning watercraft. The birds in ***Pheasants on the Prairie*** clock in at a combined thirty-five thousand pounds. A talking trail gives some background and insight into each creation.

A final whirligig sculpture cranks into motion at the **Enchanted Highway Gift Shop** at the end of the trail in Regent. If you stop to purchase gifts or ice cream, Greff might very well be the one ringing up your purchase. Be sure to sign the guestbook. Thousands have completed the Enchanted Highway trek, including visitors from South Africa, the United Kingdom and pretty much every US state.

If you need a cold drink, a bite to eat, or a room for the night, head to (what else?) the **Enchanted Castle**. The community's former school has been repurposed into a hotel and Medieval Tavern. It's an appropriately fanciful way to end this admittedly quirky quest. enchantedcastlend.com/rooms

More good eats along the way:
Copper Dog Waffles and Coffee—Photogenic gourmet waffles at this Mandan eatery range from sweet (chocolate-drizzled s'mores and addictive apple pie) to savory flavors such as biscuits and gravy and pepperoni pizza. copperdogcafe.com

Laughing Sun Brewing Co.—This family-friendly spot in Bismarck features a deep selection of beer brewed on-site and St. Louis–style barbeque that the locals vote the best in town. laughingsunbrewing.com

The Wurst Shop—Pull over in Dickinson to pack your cooler or RV fridge with German-style sausages and homemade jams and jellies. The sign also makes an amusing photo opp. thewurstshopindickinson.com

LaVonne's Cheese Button Factory Plus—Stop by the factory to score silky sweet, fruit-studded *kuchen* (German for "cake") and comforting cheese buttons straight from the source at the Bismarck factory. (701) 223-3640

Connect your trip:
Explore Indigenous culture, art and history along the **Standing Rock National Native American Scenic Byway** and the **Sakakawea Scenic Byway**. An itinerary that links both byways (and includes the communities of Bismarck and Mandan) is covered in these pages.

Along the Missouri River: Sakakawea Scenic Byway and Standing Rock National Native American Scenic Byway

For a historically resonant road trip, follow the Missouri River through the center of the state and into the past. Quintessential American author John Steinbeck said that the Missouri is the dividing line between east and west. The idea holds water; this does feel like some great, unspoken boundary between more genteel Midwestern sensibilities and the harsh beauty of the Great Plains.

This river first attracted the attention of the young nation when President Thomas Jefferson sent Captain Meriwether Lewis and Second Lieutenant William Clark to scout the land from just north of St. Louis to the Pacific Coast. Their Corps of Discovery literally put the land that would become North Dakota on the United States map. But this wide, rambling river has been a vital part of life for Indigenous peoples for thousands of years.

This road trip keeps the Mighty Mo's waters close as it retraces Lewis and Clark's route, curving past scenic overlooks and the riverfront sites of once thriving Mandan, Hidatsa, and Arikara villages like the one where the explorers first met Sakakawea, the interpreter who would help them move west. It contains the **Sakakawea Scenic Byway** in the central part of the state and the **Standing Rock National Native American Scenic Byway**, which runs through the land of Sitting Bull in the south.

Since this road trip involves rural locations several hours apart, you can tackle the journey in a few different ways. It's possible to visit selected attractions while cruising through from north to south (or vice versa) in one abbreviated (and busy) day. But to enjoy the route in chronological order (more or less), make **Bismarck** (the state's capital) or its sister city of **Mandan** your base for a multi-day journey. noboundariesnd.com

No matter which option you choose, this road trip leaves the actual road behind as much as possible and remains firmly river-focused. Take it slow so you can ponder the intertwined nations and contrasting worldviews that now share the state's borders. But this isn't some academic exercise; you can actually get out and walk the trails, explore the recreated forts and Indigenous villages and splash in the storied waters of the Mighty Missouri for yourself.

Start with panoramic river views from **Chief Looking's Village** on the Bismarck side of the Big Muddy. (The Missouri has a host of affectionate nicknames.) The park honors a Mandan Chief and includes a memory garden and interpretive trail detailing the history of the Mandan people who inspired the city's name. This is a spot where locals take out of town guests to wow them, so pick up rich caramel rolls or hearty Maah Daah Hey Trail bread from **Bread Poets** for a pretty picnic. breadpoets.com

Or get your sugar fix at **Bearscat Bakehouse**. Find them at the Bismarck and Mandan shops or at CashWise Foods. bearscatbakehouse.com

Then cross the river and spend the morning at Mandan's **Fort Abraham Lincoln State Park**. Indigenous oral history places the Mandan along the banks of the Missouri as early as 1000 AD. The Hidatsa arrived about six hundred years later, followed by the Arikara, who call themselves the Sahnish. Indigenous women and girls were the region's first farmers. They grew corn, beans, and squash along the fertile riverbanks. **On-a-Slant Village** allows visitors to tour reconstructed earth lodges like the ones they lived in. parkrec.nd.gov/fort-abraham-lincoln-state-park

The greatest oppositional force to Indigenous life—the military might of the new United States government—is also on display here. Tour a replica of the house where General George Armstrong Custer lived before he led his troops into defeat at Little Bighorn, see the reconstructed barracks and cavalry post, and stock up on historical reading material at the **Commissary Bookstore**. At the top of the hill, historical placards explain the crumbling foundations that are all that remain of this frontier **infantry post**. Climb the reconstructed blockhouses to see for miles in every direction.

For postcard pretty views of the confluence of the Heart and Missouri Rivers, set out on foot. Take **Bob-Tailed Trail** past the **Post Cemetery** to

Little Soldier Loop. This hard-packed single-track trail is lined with waving grasses, a sprinkling of pale pink prairie roses (the state flower) and the occasional cactus. You can go out and back or hike a roughly six-mile loop that descends along the buttes, down through the riverside campground (where you can book a stay in a cabin or tipi), and back up to the hilltop.

Lewis and Clark first met Sakakawea in a Hidatsa village much like the one you just toured. She was the daughter of a Lemhi Shoshone Chief in what's now Idaho, but she came of age in what would become North Dakota. The presence of a woman and her baby son signaled that the group was peaceful.

Her second home is now part of the **Knife River Indian Villages National Historic Site** just outside of **Stanton**, an hour northwest of Bismarck. The twenty-three-mile **Sakakawea Scenic Byway** links Stanton and nearby **Washburn**. These Hidatsa settlements were part of a vast trading empire that reached from the Gulf Coast to the Pacific Northwest before a series of disease outbreaks devastated the nation. Just a museum, a reconstructed earth lodge and gardens, and quiet hiking trails remain. nps.gov/knri/index.htm

The **Fort Clark State Historic Site** west of Washburn is a vast, solemn plain that silently memorializes the Mandan and Arikara residents killed by smallpox and cholera that spread through the nearby trading post. The survivors of all three nations moved to Like-a-Fishhook Village near what's now **Fort Berthold**. They're still linked today as the MHA Nation (Mandan, Hidatsa, Arikara) or the Three Affiliated Tribes. history.nd.gov/historicsites/clark

The sixty-four-mile **Killdeer Mountain Four Bears Scenic Byway** between Manning and New Town offers a scenic drive, important landmarks and additional insight into this new era of the tribes' history. It's beyond the scope of this itinerary, but a worthwhile addition for travelers interested in authentic Indigenous history. bit.ly/killdeermountainbyway

The Corps of Discovery wintered near present-day **Washburn**. Tour a full-size reconstruction of the camp at **Fort Mandan**. Seeing their bunks, the stores of food and the games they played to pass the time let you step into their boots and imagine what this remote setting felt like years ago.

That sense of historical immersion deepens at the **Lewis and Clark Interpretive Center**, where interactive exhibits display artifacts the exhibition would have used and detail the bustling world of Mandan and Hidatsa commerce. The collection also includes eighty-one original aquatints by Karl Bodmer and Prince Maximilian, artists and explorers who followed Lewis and Clark west. parkrec.nd.gov/lewis-clark-interpretive-center

The purpose of the expedition was to usher in a new age of settlement, primarily by white immigrants of European descent. North Dakota's capital was named after German Chancellor Otto von Bismarck, so it's no surprise that many residents have German ancestors. Tuck into *sauerbraten* or a chicken *schnitzel* sandwich on the **Ale Works** terrace to taste that culinary heritage yourself. bismarckaleworks.com

If you'd rather keep the river in your sights, try the **Paddle Trap** patio in Mandan for clam chowder, hearty sandwiches and brunch with a Missouri view. This family-owned joint offers boat-in service if you want to join the crowd and eat out on the water. thepaddletrap.com

Many marine dealers offer short-term boat rentals. Travelers with a sense of adventure can rent kayaks, canoes, and paddle boards from **Paddle on North Dakota** in **General Sibley Park**. paddleonnd.com

Start your next day of sightseeing with cheddar scones or almond milk smoothie bowls topped with house-made granola from **Terra Nomad**. The lattes with house-made vanilla or lavender syrup are especially tempting. terranomadcompany.com

Or try a perfectly flaky croissant or cheese Danish at **Brick Oven Bakery**. You can order quiche, pastries, and plump loaves of fresh baked bread online. Brickovenbakerynd.com

Then explore the **North Dakota State Capitol** grounds. The **Arboretum Trail** identifies seventy-five types of trees and shrubs and several sculptures and monuments, including a bison rendered in steel and tributes to Sakakawea and local veterans. bit.ly/arboretumtrail

Dig into six hundred million years of history at the **North Dakota Heritage Center and State Museum**. Guests can see T-rex and mastodon skeletons, hear Indigenous words spoken, climb inside a tractor simulator and peek into a '50s malt shop. Admission is free. The **Museum Shop** is an excellent spot to score local books, food, art, and music. statemuseum.nd.gov

To experience Dakota and Lakota culture, head south to the **Standing Rock Sioux** reservation, which stretches across the South Dakota border. Before white settlement, the Dakota hunted buffalo and farmed, while the Lakota were horsemen as well as buffalo hunters. standingrock.org/content/visit-us

One of the strongest voices against forced resettlement, the foreign notion of a permanent residence and cultural assimilation in general was Tatanka Iyotake—also known as Sitting Bull. The Standing Rock National Native American Scenic Byway runs the land where the great Hunkpapa Lakota leader lived and died.

The thirty-five-mile byway isn't a difficult drive. But since most sites are more than an hour south of Bismarck and the route runs almost to the state line, allow sufficient travel time.

Pack a picnic to enjoy at **Prairie Knights Marina** in **Cannon Ball**, bring your boat to **Lake Oahe**, or hike the **Lewis and Clark Legacy Trail**. Three nature trails detail different prairie plants and their purposes in traditional Indigenous medicine.

Continue south to **Fort Yates**. The reservation's largest town and tribal headquarters is named for the **Standing Rock Monument** on the banks of the Missouri River. **Standing Rock** has a history of environmental advocacy and is one of just a handful of Kennedy Center's Turnaround Arts communities in the country. This artistic legacy surfaces in **murals** at Hagel's and White Buffalo Foods.

You can try buffalo yourself at R&B's Grill. It offers café classics like burgers as well as specials like traditional bapa soup and fry bread. facebook.com/rbsgrill

Sitting Bull was killed just outside of Fort Yates. Pay your respects at the **Sitting Bull Burial Site**. There's quite a debate about where his remains rest today—another Standing Rock Sioux community just across the border in **Mobridge**, South Dakota also has a memorial site.

Book a room (or a luxury suite with a whirlpool) at **Prairie Knights Casino** for an evening of gaming. Its **Hunters Club** restaurant is your best bet for fine dining. prairieknights.com

Or head north to Bismarck's **Peacock Alley** to dine on aged Angus beef and decadent desserts inside a former hotel that doubled as a speakeasy and gambling den during prohibition. Speaking of speakeasies, the **510.2 Speakeasy** hides in plain sight just across the street—if you can find it. peacock-alley.com

Start your trip the same way it began—with views of the Missouri River. **Keelboat Park** is just a few blocks down the hill from where your journey started. See the colorful and stylized Lewis, Clark and Sacagawea statues, climb into a fifty-two-foot replica of their boat or walk or bike the riverfront **Missouri Valley Millennium Legacy Trail**. bisparks.org

Boarding the **Lewis and Clark Riverboat** is like stepping back in time. Seeing the city lights flicker and glow as the paddleboat glides along the Mighty Missouri is a fun and historically accurate way to end your journey along one America's most famous rivers. lewisandclarkriverboat.com

More good eats along the way:
Noodlezip—Seasonal menus feature made-from-scratch pan noodles, stir fry, soups, and sides from Korea, Thailand, China, Vietnam, and Japan right in downtown Bismarck. noodlezip.com

The Walrus Restaurant—This eclectic neighborhood spot in Bismarck serves up pasta, sandwiches, veggie-packed salads, and an eye-popping array of beer for anyone willing to get off the beaten path and settle in. thewalrusrestaurant.com

Fireflour Pizzeria & Coffee Bar—Wood-fired Neapolitan pizzas prioritize ingredients like organic tomatoes and hand-stretched mozzarella. Small plates, gelato, and espresso round out a menu that Bismarck foodies love. fireflourpizza.com

Dakota Farms Washburn—This friendly, no-frills café has been serving up homemade soups, all-day breakfast, fresh-baked pies, and German specials along Highway 1804 in Washburn for more than forty years. facebook.com/DakotaFarmsWashburn

Connect your trip:
The **Standing Rock National Native American Scenic Byway** links directly to the **Native American National and State Scenic Byway** at the South Dakota border. It traverses the Crow Creek, Yankton, Lower Brule, Cheyenne River, and Standing Rock Sioux land that shares its geography with South Dakota.

Mandan is also the starting point for the **Old Red Old Ten Scenic Byway**, which connects with the **Enchanted Highway**. This art- and history-filled road trip is detailed earlier in this section.

Head east for public art and urban eats

For a completely different atmosphere, landscape, and cultural experience, try an art-packed culinary trip between Fargo and Grand Forks. Located about an hour apart along the state's eastern border with Minnesota, these cities buzz with creative and entrepreneurial energy that's fueled by numerous startups, fresh waves of college students that pour in every year and thriving art and food scenes.

You won't find dramatic plateaus and rugged scenery or here; the Red River Valley is pancake-flat. This was once the bottom of a massive Ice Age lake. The nutrients deposited then—and during subsequent floods—make this some of the richest farmland in the world.

Start your road trip in **Fargo**, the largest city in the state. Fargo was made famous (or infamous) by the 1996 Coen brothers' film of the same name. Locals love to hate this connection, pointing out that not a single scene was filmed in the city.

The **Fargo-Moorhead Convention and Visitors Bureau** embraces the movie, inviting travelers to pose with not one but two **woodchippers**, a macabre and pivotal set piece in the film. The woodchipper in the lobby was actually in the movie. The outdoor model, surrounded by the **Celebrity Walk of Fame** hand and footprints, is a replica. fargomoorhead.org

Superfans should snag Woodchipper IPA from **Fargo Brewing Company** as a memento. If it's not on tap at the brewery, try the mammoth **Happy Harry's Bottle Shop** on Forty-fifth Street. fargobrewing.com/therealfbc

If North Dakota is the fiftieth state you've visited, don't leave without joining the Convention and Visitors Bureau's **Best For Last Club**. You'll score a T-shirt and certificate. (North Dakota elevates wry self-deprecation to an art form.)

The public art tour continues in **downtown Fargo**, the creative epicenter of the city. Located along the western banks of the Red River, this walkable district is packed with public art, sidewalk cafes, and window-shopping experiences. It was the first neighborhood established in the city, so it's been a prime place to people watch since the 1870s. downtownfargo.com

Start on the **Veterans Memorial Bridge** that separates Fargo from **Moorhead**, Minnesota. Interpretive panels detail the history of the Red River and sidewalk mosaics show a map of the sister cities' historic buildings and the river's path north into Canada.

Pose with the **Statue of Liberty** on Main Avenue on your way to **Sandy's Donuts**. Lemon blueberry donuts, maple bacon long johns, and angel icing bismarcks have inspired a passionate following since 1983. sandysdonuts.com

Or order **Boiler Room** all-day brunch favorites. The subterranean restaurant's rumchata French toast, deep-fried Scotch Eggs, and three cheese tater tots are local obsessions. boilerroomfargo.com

Bring your picnic to **Island Park**, looking down to spot the poems pressed into the sidewalk that runs parallel to Fifth Avenue. The city's oldest park is full of shady spots, a playground, and **sculptures**, including a tribute to Norwegian writer Henrik Wergeland. The first Red River Valley immigrants were from Scandinavia and the British Isles. Now you'll hear Arabic, Somali, Nepali, Tagalog, Swahili, Spanish, Kurdish, and a host of other languages in the city. fargoparks.com/facilities-recreation/island-park.html

Walk or drive north to **Front Street Taproom** to try regional craft beers and ciders. A large **Greta Thurnberg portrait** by North Dakota photographer Shane Balkowitsch graces the alley behind the building. frontstreettaproom.com

Continue west to where the alley meets Eighth Street to photograph the quirky **Penguin Mural**. Cross Eighth to snap up almost impossibly pretty tarts, eclairs other decadent treats at **Nichole's Fine Pastry**, then pose in front of the **Wildflowers Mural** at the south end of the block. nicholesfinepastry.com

Take a few photos of the colorful **bison sculpture** and **painted boxcars** at Main and Broadway. Continue north on Broadway, noticing the art on the **electric boxes**, the **historical markers** on each street corner, and **sidewalk mosaics** under your feet at the intersections as you head to the **Art Alley** along First Avenue North between Fourth and Fifth Streets. The colorful illustrations change constantly, and anyone can contribute, so bring paint or markers to make your mark.

Fargo's most iconic sculpture, *The Sodbuster* by Luis Jimenez, is on display in front of the Fargo Public Library. It's surrounded by a Native American medicine garden. The **City Hall Art Panel Project** is visible from the patio.

Pose in front of the angel wings at the **Silver Lining Creamery** while ordering small batch salted caramel or rosewater ice cream from the walk-up window. Look for the **ASL Bike Rack** outside and the **skyway mural**. silverliningcreamery.com

There's a set of red, white, and blue wings across the street at the **Fargo VFW**. Turn down **Roberts Street Alley** to spot a few more several more paintings, including the **Postcard Mural**. Notice the undulating sculptures atop **Roberts Street Chapel**, then continue north on Roberts Street to photograph the **Peacock Mural** at Roberts Street Studio and the **Meadowlark Mural** across the street.

Turn back toward Broadway and continue south. Stop to shop for quirky and cool creations from Midwestern artisans at **Unglued**. ungluedmarket.com

Take a photo of the **Fargo Theatre** marquee, the most photographed spot in town. Then pop into the alley behind **Pickled Parrot** to jump into a video game scene in front of the **Mario Wall**. fargotheatre.org

To track down even more public art, visit **Fargo Walking Tours**. The website profiles three public art walks, a geocaching adventure, and a historic architecture tour. fargowalkingtours.com

Or purchase local art and gifts to take home at **Gallery 4**. It's the oldest co-op gallery in the state. gallery4fargo.net

Order lunch from the **Hotel Donaldson**. The eclectic boutique hotel, restaurant, and lounge are decorated entirely by regional artists. hoteldonaldson.com

If you'd rather support a small-town eatery, stop at the **Hillsboro Café and Bakery**. It's right between Fargo and Grand Forks as you drive north along Interstate 29. Buy a cupcake for the road—proceeds go to kids who can't afford school lunches. hillsborocafe.com

Or enjoy upgraded pub grub like bangers and mash and squeaky cheese curds from **Rhombus Guys Brewing** in downtown **Grand Forks**. This former opera house is the grandest brewery in North Dakota and one of the few historical structures to survive the flood and fire that devastated downtown in 1997. rhombusguysbrewing.com

Save room for goodies from **Widman's Candy Shop** down the street. Displays are stocked with chocolate-covered everything—from blueberries and marshmallows to pickles and coffee beans. Salty sweet Chippers (chocolate dipped Red River Valley potato chips) are a fan favorite.

Fargo is known for its murals, but **Grand Forks** is a sculpture city. Savor your treats in downtown Grand Forks' pocket parks, where public sculptures, winding paths and ivy colored walls create an art-filled respite in the middle of the city. Find **Loon Park** along South Third Street. visitgrandforks.com

The **BIG Heads** (oversized blue noggins that sport flowers for hair in the summer) are the city's biggest conversation pieces. Find the first at Fourth Street and Kittson Avenue, in front of the Grand Forks MTC. It's just across the street from **Browning Arts** and **You Are Here**. Paintings, collages and sculptures frequently spill out of these galleries and onto the sidewalk. browningarts.com/gallery

The University of North Dakota art collection includes works by Dalí, Warhol, and other giants of contemporary art. It's displayed at **Empire Arts Center Gallery**, part of the **Empire Arts Center**, which also hosts a resident theatre company and traveling productions. empireartscenter.com

The second blue head is by **Town Square**, where a paddle wheel fountain serves as a meeting place and local landmark. This bustling public square hosts outdoor concerts during steamy summer Saturdays and ice skating in the winter.

Take a short walk to the **Flood Memorial Monument** near DeMers and Third Street. This obelisk illustrates just how high the 1997 flood waters rose. This riverfront landmark is located on the **Greenway**, a 2,200-acre network of green space along the banks of the Red and the Red Lake Rivers. Twice the size of Manhattan's Central Park, the Greenway's paved multi-use paths link parks, disc golf courses, swimming pools, and picnic spots on both sides of the river. greenwayggf.com

Take a photo straddling the North Dakota–Minnesota border on the **Sorlie Memorial Bridge**, then grab a drink on one of the river-front patios in East Grand Forks. It's an easy way to add another state to your itinerary.

Or head to the **Boathouse on the Red** to rent canoes, kayaks, and stand up paddle boards to experience both cities from the water. (Daily, weekend, and ninety-minute rentals are available.) groundupadventures.com/bhotr

Boaters and anglers can get on the river in both cities. East Grand Forks's **LaFave Park** features a boat dock and handicap accessible fishing spots. **Lincoln Drive Park** in Grand Forks includes a playground, horseshoe pits, and frisbee golf. gfparks.org/parks-facilities/parks/lincoln-drive

The **Red River State Recreation Area** in East Grand Forks attracts campers and outdoor enthusiasts. This unusual urban camping experience combines the energy of the city with the stillness of the river landscape.

Water babies, families with kids, and anyone visiting during the cold winter months will love Splashers of the South Seas. The sprawling enter-tainment complex holds the largest indoor waterpark in the state, an arcade, bars, restaurants, and family suites with kid-friendly amenities like bunk beds and gaming systems. Zoran Mojislov's *Northern Rose*, a sculpture of towering granite, stands outside. canadinns.com/play/splashers-of-the-south-seas

Golf enthusiasts tee off at **King's Walk Golf Course**. Designed by the legendary Arnold Palmer, it's inspired by links courses in Ireland and

Scotland and weaves the landscape's natural prairie and hardwood forests into its layout. kingswalk.org

No matter how you choose to play, unwind at one of the city's most welcoming restaurants. **Sky's Fine Dining and Spirits and Cloud 9 Lounge** is known for creative cocktails, a romantic atmosphere, and downtown views. (The champagne brunch is also worth prioritizing.) skyscloud9.com

The **Toasted Frog** features beautifully plated steak, fish, and pasta dishes in an art-filled dining room. The restaurant's signature (and utterly addictive) fried cheesy pickles inspired a tribute from Emmy-nominated local foodie celeb, Molly Yeh. Toast this region's art and food fusion with an orchid-bedecked martini. toastedfrog.com

Other great eats:

BernBaum's—The owners' Icelandic and Jewish heritages spark inspired riffs on Jewish deli classics like blintzes topped with lingonberry sauce in this popular downtown Fargo eatery. bernbaums.com

Mezzaluna—The glam clamshell booths are the perfect place to savor steak or scallops in downtown Fargo. There's perfectly chilled vodka on tap, so the cocktails are always on point. dinemezzaluna.com

Rhombus Guys—Go for cult-classic pizzas, local beer from the sister brewery, and a broad range of imaginative meat-free pies like gorgonzola pear. There are locations in Fargo and Grand Forks. rhombusguyspizza.com

HELIX Wine and Bites—Warm and intimate, this inviting Grand Forks bistro and wine bar showcases creative dishes designed to pair perfectly with the carefully curated wine selection. helixgf.com/menu

Scenic Byways in North Dakota
- **Killdeer Mountain Four Bears Scenic Byway**—64 miles
- **Old Red Old Ten Scenic Byway**—108 miles
- **Sakakawea Scenic Byway**—23 miles
- **Sheyenne River Valley National Scenic Byway**—63 miles
- **Standing Rock National Native American Scenic Byway**—35 miles

- **Theodore Roosevelt National Park North Unit Scenic Byway**—13.7 miles
- **Turtle Mountain Scenic Byway**—53 miles

Alicia Underlee Nelson is the creator and curator of prairiestylefile.com, the co-host of the Travel Tomorrow Podcast (traveltomorrowpod.com), *a member of the Midwest Travel Network and the author of* North Dakota Beer: A Heady History. *She's contributed stories and photos to Thomson Reuters, Food Network, AAA Living, Midwest Living, Matador Network, craftbeer.com, USA Today, and numerous other publications. When she's not traveling with her husband and son, you'll find her hiking, cooking, drinking endless cups of black coffee, and reading incessantly. Alicia hopes that this book inspires you to see familiar places in a new way.*

OHIO

Ohio is an amazing state, founded in 1803. Dubbed the "Buckeye State," it's home to roughly eleven million people.

Basic Ohio Facts:
- The state capital is Columbus.
- The state motto is "With God, all things are possible."
- The state bird is the cardinal.
- The state flower is the carnation.
- There are twenty-seven highways and byways to explore.

Fun Ohio facts:
- All of Ohio's eighty-three state parks are free for everyone to enjoy, and many are located on the byways.
- Ohio gets its name from the Iroquois word ohi-yo, meaning "great river."
- Agriculture is Ohio's largest industry, and the state ranks number one in Swiss cheese production (which you can see on the Amish Country Byway).

Amish Country Byway

Come tour the scenic Amish Country Byway and visit one of the most intriguing places in Ohio. You will find the largest population of Amish in the United States located right here in Holmes County. As you drive these routes, you will fall in love with the picturesque countryside, quaint Amish roadside stops, and the delicious home-cooking at any restaurant along the way. Every mile of state and federal highway in Holmes County is designated as an Ohio Scenic Byway, and you will have 160 miles of road to explore with incredible views no matter where you go.

*Pro tip: Before you get too far along on your road trip through Amish country, take some time to see the **Amish and Mennonite Heritage Center**, where you will learn more about this plain community. A stop here will open your eyes to this unique culture's history, from its Anabaptist roots up through today. Behalt houses one of four cycloramas—panoramic images on the inside of a cylindrical platform—in North America. It is the sole work of the artist, Heinz Gaugel. If you have time after your tour, explore the **Pioneer Barn, Conestoga Wagon, Amish School**, and **Gift Shop**, which are all located on the Behalt property. behalt.com*

The main route running east to west through the middle of Amish Country is State Route 39. I call this the "heart" of Holmes County. Finding an excellent central location to stay when enjoying this area is a bonus, and the **Carlisle Inn** located in Walnut Creek is the perfect spot. The views from the balcony of this hotel are incomparable. In the evening before going to bed, head to the **Ohio Star Theater** for a fun-filled and family-friendly show.

I love sitting on the balcony and listening to the clip-clop of horses' hooves and watching the Amish bicycle by in the mornings while I sip my coffee and devour fresh donuts. Before heading out for the day, take your breakfast at the **Der Dutchman** and visit **Carlisle Gifts at Walnut Creek**, both within an easy walking distance from the inn. dhgroup.com; dhgroup.com/inns/carlisle-inn-walnut-creek; dhgroup.com/theater

You will want to start your drive on the main drag through Holmes County, State Route 39. Begin your excursion at **Walnut Creek Cheese**, one of the largest Amish grocery stores and delis in the county. You won't only get to fill your basket with delectable treats. You can also find kitchen items, candles, and every kind of gadget you would ever need for baking! walnutcreekcheese.com

After your shopping spree head to the **Farm at Walnut Creek**, for a thrilling yet educational trip through a safari right in the middle of Amish country. You will have the opportunity to view and feed more than five hundred animals from six different continents, such as buffalo, llamas, giraffes, deer, elk that live at the farm. You will have two options for feeding these majestic beasts; you can enjoy hand feeding them from the comfort of your car or on a laid-back horse-drawn wagon ride. There is something exhilarating when you hold that bucket up to these wonderful creatures. thefarmatwalnutcreek.com

Once you are back on the road, it won't be long before you come upon the **Schrock Heritage Village**. Here you will find some of my favorite shops in the community, **Berlin Antique and Craft Mall**, **Tis the Season Christmas Shop**, **Berlin Leather and Shoe**, and **Strebs's General Store**. Make sure to block enough time out of your schedule to wander through Ohio's largest year-round Christmas store, Tis the Season. I can get lost while looking at all the delightful Christmas fun and singing along to Christmas music, even if it is July. amishfarmvillage.com

Maybe you have fallen in love with this spot, and you are looking for a place to stay and kick back to take in the quiet ambiance. **Shrock's Guest House** is right here at this sprawling Amish complex. If you have your RV, **Scenic Hills RV** is right across St Rt 39, it's just the spot for some R and R by the campfire. (330) 893-3051; scenichillsrvpark.com

As you ramble along St Rt 39, you will note all the small towns, but as you come into **Berlin**, be prepared to stop and linger awhile. Have you ever ridden in an Amish buggy? If not, you can ride in an authentic Amish buggy on **Mel's Amish Buggy Ride**. As you sit back into the buggy, you can imagine what it might be like to live a little more simply. (330) 275-7896

It's time to eat, and this little town cooks up deliciousness. **Boyd and Wurthman's** is a local favorite that has been cooking phenomenal home-cooked fare for more than seventy years. As a matter of fact, you can still eat at the original, green counter built in the '40s and order a cup of coffee for just seventy-five cents. Two of my favorite bakeries are located in Berlin, and they are always cranking out the best-baked goods around. **Der Bake Oven** and **Kauffman's Country Bakery**. boydandwurthmann.com; derbakeoven.com; kauffmanscountrybakery.com

Berlin has another incredible place to stay and relax. **Berlin Grand Boutique Hotel** gives you a splendid spot to call home for the night. This hotel has all the amenities you could want in this Amish paradise. Staying here will provide you with more time to explore this little town. Conveniently located near everything, this hotel is ideally situated off the beaten path, but close enough to walk to everything on Main Street.

Millersburg is the next little town on the Amish Scenic byway, and it is the center point of the route. Enjoy a stroll through the historic downtown and walk along the cheery store-lined streets finding hidden treasures at the small shops. historicdowntownmillersburg.com

As you take in the scenery on this last leg of the route on 39, you roll into **Loudonville**. It is the perfect stop for adventurous outdoor lovers. The **Mohican State Park and Lodge** area offers kayaking and tubing, and adrenaline-pumping activities. You can ride down a zipline through the forest and enjoy the spectacular views on your hike through the luscious trails. There are thirteen miles of hiking trails within the park and thirty-two more in the adjacent Mohican State Memorial Forest. You can stay busy here, exploring the alluring forests and gently flowing Mohican River for at least a day.

So, you've driven State Route 39, and you may think you are done; however, there are plenty of other byways crisscrossing through Holmes County. These Amish Country byways all branch off ST RT 39, and you could continue touring the Amish backcountry for days on end.

ST RT 62

Are you ready for more adventure? Scenic St. Rt. 62 will take you by **Country Furniture**, 4329 County Road 168 Millersburg, OH, 44654. It is Amish-owned and has been in business for forty-one years. They carry hand-crafted hardwood furniture that is heirloom quality. Across the way, you find **Heini's Cheese Chalet** that was established in 1935 and is a third-generation, family-owned company. Heini's works with local dairy farmers to produce their cheese, and that commitment remains strong. (I think this is why the cheese is so good here!) They can make up to twelve tons of cheese in a day. I love to take the free tour and sample the delicious twenty-five different hand-crafted cheese in their showroom. 330-893-4455; heinis.com

Lastly, before you leave town, visit **Winesburg Meats**. They have been a family-owned and -operated business since 1959. All the meats and house-made products have none of the artificial preservatives, soy, gluten, or fillers found in most other products. You'll want to stop in and take a trip back in time to when food was simply better for you. winesburg-meats.com

ST RT 557

Take the beautiful and winding St Rt 557 into the quite charming town of **Charm**. On this route, you'll be tempted by the best swiss cheese in the US at **Guggisberg Cheese**. Their award-winning cheese will have you drooling for more. In the 1950s, the Amish were looking for a cheesemaker to provide a market for their milk, and Alfred Guggisberg came to the Doughty Valley to create his world-class cheese. After imbibing in all the cheese, you can be taken to the Swiss Alps for a delightful dining experience at **Chalet in the Valley**, located just across the street. Interested in staying in Doughty Valley? You can stopover for the night in this hidden Swiss oasis at the **Guggisberg Swiss Inn**. guggisbergswissinn.com; babyswiss.com; chaletinthevalley.com

The Amish-owned **Hershberger's Truck Patch** is a one of a kind all-inclusive Amish experience. If you are short on time, Hershberger's needs to make your bucket list! This Amish stop will have you taking a buggy ride through the farm, petting and feeding the animals, and wandering through their aisles and aisles of home-baked goods. While you are here, you have to try one of their locally famous fry-pies. They are the best in Amish country. (330) 674-6096

Before you leave Charm, drop in at **Keim**, a lumber, home, and hardware store, where a tradition of uncompromising quality meets modern design. Here, homeowners, and woodworkers alike can find "everything they need to build a house and make it a home." Their 125,000-square-foot showroom features kitchen and bathroom displays, an incredible woodshed stocked with 130 different kinds of wood from around the world, and aisles of just about anything you can think of for your home. You can spend a morning or afternoon at Keim. Don't miss grabbing a snack or light lunch at their

Carpenter's Café, where they offer homemade sandwiches and soups. This is the perfect Holmes County destination with something for everyone! KeimHome.com

ST RT 515

Traverse the short, but sweet St Rt 515, which will take you through more of the gently rolling hills of Holmes County. If you've made your base camp the **Carlisle Inn**, this route is just outside your room's door. **Hillcrest Orchard** is right off the road and has some of the best cider and apples you will ever purchase. Owned and operated by an Amish family, this stop is friendly, locally sourced, and has the best view from the lookout terrace at the back of the orchard. (330) 893-9906

If you are curious about how the Amish live, you can take a tour of **Yoder's Amish Home**. You will learn everything you wanted to know about the Amish here at the farm. Their local, knowledgeable guide takes you on a thirty-minute tour through both homes on the property and the barn built in 1885. The guide will explain a great deal about the history and lifestyle of the Amish people and give you ample opportunities to ask questions. yoder-samishhome.com

Have you ever heard of Trail Bologna? **Troyer's Trail Bologna** is a staple food created right here in this tiny, nondescript stop on 515. In 1912, Michael Troyer created a unique special formula that consisted of a blend of seasonings to make delicious all-beef bologna, which is made with all-natural ingredients, without any fillers. The Troyer family, now in its fourth generation, continues to produce large quantities of genuine Trail Bologna here on their property daily. troyerstrail.com

ST RT 241 Mount Hope

As you continue to explore Holmes County, you'll continue to pass through the beautiful countryside. St Rt 241 is dotted with many small Amish roadside stops, and even though the route is short, you'll find yourself on it for a while, as you pick and choose your detours. A few places to make sure to stop include the **Ashery Country Store**. Then have a delicious meal at **Mrs. Yoder's Kitchen**, which is one of my family's personal favorites. Next, take a look-see at the heirloom furniture at **Homestead Furniture** before you end your day of driving. asherycountrystore.com; mrsyoderskitchen. com; homesteadfurnitureonline.com

You might think so many of these country markets, Amish stores, and the crazy number of restaurant stops might be repetitive and the same. They are not; each one is unique and has a convivial flair! Grab an old-fashioned map of the roads and drive them all. Each one has a distinctive flavor, and you will enjoy every Amish home and perfectly manicured flower bed and yard you pass. Holmes County and her scenic byways will have you coming back for more, because one trip here does not even scratch the surface of the hidden treasures that this beautiful area of Ohio holds.

Pro tip: Please make sure to note that most places are closed Sunday on these Amish Scenic byways. You will see "No Sunday sales" and "No Sunday check-in" signs along these routes.

Perhaps you want to have someone personally take you through Amish country and share all their favorites. You can have a meal served in a real Amish home cooked by a local family on one of these tours, so will want to bring your appetite and be ready to see Amish Country in this truly special way! Book your outing through the byway with **Troyer's Amish Tours**— owned and operated by Rich Troyer, who was born and raised Amish in Holmes County—or **All About Amish Backroad Tours** by DAT Travel. TroyersAmishTours.com; Dattravel.com

Lake Erie Coastal Ohio Trail Scenic Byway
Ohio's Lake Erie Coastal Trail is more than a byway; it's an experience! Every moment of this drive along the vast coast of one of North America's Great Lakes is exhilarating and inspiring. You will drive through idyllic harbors, historic residential areas, beautiful state parks, sprawling vineyards, and miles of breathtaking views of Lake Erie.

*Pro tip: Do not start this byway without this map, and keep
an eye out to follow the green signs marking the byway; or
you can download the app. bit.ly/lakeeriebywaymap*

Northeast Region

Traveling from east to west, you will start your driving adventure in the small
town of **Conneaut**. Before you begin westward, you may want to meander
through this inviting town. Located here, you have a beach that is one of the
best for finding beach glass. What is beach glass? **Beach glass** is created in
freshwater as it is tumbled and smoothed by the rolling waves, particularly in
the waters of the Great Lakes.

While you're in **Ashtabula**, you won't want to miss the historic harbor
right on the byway. If you're lucky, you will see the bascule drawbridge in
action while enjoying coffee from **Harbor Perk** or while eating at **Bascule
Bridge Grille**, which has a playful yet elegant atmosphere to go along with
their creative fare. You will be in a foodie's dream! It's so good you will
want to lick your plate. Before you head out of town, take a sunset paddle-
board or kayak float out to the lighthouse with **Harbor Yak**. This will be a
once-in-a-lifetime experience here on Lake Erie's shores with the charming
harbor town in the background. Harborperk.com; basculebridgegrille.com;
harboryak.com

As you head into **Geneva-on-the-Lake**, you might be taken off guard as
you come into a five-block "strip" loaded with things to do and see. You'll be
drawn away from the lake views to capture moments of food and fun. You
will want to stay here a day or two, so you can enjoy everything this Ohio
gem offers. You can choose from three flavors when picking out lodging here,
because you can stay in cozy cottages, an upscale lakeside inn, or the State
Park lodge and marina.

Quaint, clean, and right on the lake, you will find **Abigail's Lakeside
Cottages** with a lovely sundeck and firepit right on the lake's shores. If you
like more of the boutique resort, you will enjoy the **Lakehouse Inn**, with its
farm-to-table restaurant and winery right on the property and a sprawling
patio where you can sip a glass of wine as you watch the sunset. This perfect

spot on Lake Erie houses a spa where you can unwind after your day of sight-seeing and driving. The **Lodge at Geneva-on-the-Lake Marina** is one of Ohio State Parks' premiere lakeside destinations and books up months in advance. You can enjoy boating, fishing, hiking, and waterside sunset views within walking distance from your room. No matter what kind of lodging you are looking for, Geneva-on-the-Lake has it all! abigailslakesidecottages.com; thelakehouseinn.com; thelodgeatgeneva.com

Once you settle on lodging, pick a few things to do here in Geneva based on the amount of time you have. If you love fishing, **DB's Fishing Charter** is one of the best on the lake. If fishing is not your thing, they offer relaxing sunset cruises that can be enjoyed by the whole family. dbsportfishing.com

Fairport Harbor boasts one of the many lighthouses you will find along this trail. Grab some ice cream from **Fairport Creamery** and then head to the **Fairport Harbor Marine Museum and Lighthouse** for a tour. If you have time, wander the unique shops along the historic harbor before heading toward the bustle of Cleveland. fairportharbortourism.com; fairportharbor-creamery.com

North Central Region

One of the best beaches on the byway is **Headlands Beach**; you will find many Ohio State Parks along this coast. Here you can sunbathe, hike the dunes, or look for the beautiful beach glass along the shore. This is the perfect stop to stretch your legs and walk the pebbled beach before heading farther.

Cleveland and surrounding areas—Cleveland rocks! This thriving coastal city is alive with everything urban. You can sleep in luxury along the lake with upscale places to stay like the **Kimpton Schofield Hotel** and the **Metropolitan at The 9**. theschofieldhotel.com; metropolitan-cleveland.com

Dining in this lakeside metropolis is incomparable; you can choose from casual dining to dressed-to-the-nines–style restaurants. **Alley Cat Oyster Bar** has a So-Cal feel that meets New England comfort food, or try the **Collision Bend Brewery**. It is named after the notoriously hard to navigate section of river it overlooks, Collision Bend was built in 1863 and offers you waterfront dining on an outdoor patio. You won't be disappointed with the craft beers and wood-fired pizza! Alleycatoysterbar.com; collisionbendbrewery.com

With food and lodging figured out, you can set your sights on the fantastic culture and museums in Cleveland. You'll find the **Cleveland Museum of Art** in the North Coast Harbor. This museum brings the classics to life with their cutting-edge interactive technology that helps you engage with the intriguing exhibits. You can walk among dinosaurs at the **Cleveland Museum of Natural History** or the **Cleveland History Center**. You'll learn about the city's roots with stories from the 1790s leading up to today, engaging you in hours of exciting historic moments caught in time. clevelandart.org; cmnh. org; wrhs.org

Are you looking to camp along the shoreline of Lake Erie? **Neff Brothers RV Rental** located in **Lorain** can have an RV set up and ready for your arrival at one of the many campgrounds along the trail. Choosing this way to stay on the byway gives you the opportunity to kick back by the shore and sink your toes in the sand. Lake-view campsites can be found at East Harbor State Park or on South Bass Island. neffbrosrv.com

I would be remiss if I did not take you off-trail for a moment to the **1830 Hallauer Bed and Breakfast** located in **Oberlin**. Here you can see how the Ohio River Scenic Byway and the Lake Erie Coastal Trail intersect with underground railroad history. The B and B owners are retired teachers and are eager to share the home's history and Oberlin's vibrant past with you! hallauerhousebnb.com

Northwest Region

As you make your way into the region, you will be in an area that touts itself as the "Walleye Capital of the World." You will find fishing charters, plenty of parks, beaches, and historic lighthouses dotting the shores.

If the byway hasn't captured your heart by now, as you head into **Vermilion**, that's all about to change. Here in this coastal town, you can let your adventurous side come out by renting a Waverunner for a day on the lake with **Erie Shore Wave Runners**, or catch the paddle boat for an evening cruise on the **Mystic Belle**. erieshorewaverunners.com; donparsonsmarina.com

Stroll along **Main Street Beach** and take a photo of the **Vermilion Lighthouse** before you shop downtown at the delightful stores lining the way. One of my favorites is **Brummer's Chocolates**. No stop in Vermilion is complete without eating at the local soda fountain, **Big Ed's Mainstreet Grill**, or having a high-end dining experience inside an old bank vault at the **Wine Vault**. brummers.com; (440) 967-4002; (440) 963-7443

If that isn't enough about this quaint town, let me tempt you to stay the night in the **Old Vermilion Jailhouse Bed and Breakfast** in the heart of the harbor district. Built-in 1910, this jailhouse has been renovated into a perfect place to relax before continuing on your journey. jailbed.com

Huron chalks up the delightful **Nickel Plate Beach**, where you can take pictures at the Lake Erie Love sign and sit for a moment in the sun. Don't miss the **Huron Pier and Lighthouse**, just a short drive down the road where you can check another lighthouse off your list.

Known as the "Roller Coaster Capital of the World," **Sandusky**, Ohio, is home to **Cedar Point**. Take a ride on the heart-stopping Millennium Force, where you can see most of Lake Erie before you plunge down at the top of the peak. It would be almost a sin not to take in the beach vibes of 150-plus years of entertaining fun at **Hotel Breakers**. cedarpoint.com

While this town might have roller coasters to brag about, you'll find it has a lot more to offer. You'll want to visit the **Maritime Museum** of Sandusky, take a Segway tour of the Sandusky Bay Pathway through downtown, and visit Jackson Pier for a cruise with **Goodtime**. sanduskymaritime.org

As you continue to snake your way along the coast, you will come to the most quintessential lighthouse on the trail at the stunning **Marblehead Lighthouse State Park**. You will see the completely renovated lighthouse, the lightkeepers' home, and the museum where you can learn the history of this classic stop. Pack a picnic, then climb to the top of the lighthouse for stunning views of the lake.

East Harbor State Park is a short seven miles from here, and it is home to some of the best shoreline fishing on the trail. Here among the wooded marshlands you can find places to drop in your boat, find a dreamy spot to set up for camping, take a dip swimming at the beach, play a round of disc golf, go for a nature hike, or look for the abundant wildlife within the park.

> *Bonus Region: Take a break from driving in your car to tooling around an island in a golf cart and visit **Put-in-Bay** on South Bass Island. Grab a ride on **Miller Ferry** for a short eighteen-minute trip over to an island oasis. Rent a golf cart as soon as you disembark at **E's Golf Cart Rental** to make your day trip accessible to all the island attractions. Visit the delightful wineries, check off another lighthouse, and see **Perry's Victory & International Peace Memorial**, where Oliver Perry's cry of "We have seen the enemy, and they are ours" reverberates in history. Walk the shop-lined downtown, and before you leave, eat some of the best lobster bisque at the **Boardwalk**. millerferry.com; esputinbaygolfcarts.com; the-boardwalk.com*

Port Clinton is a hub for fishing charters, and anglers flock here to drop a line in Lake Erie's bountiful waters. Among the Great Lakes, Lake Erie locals proclaim itself as the premier spot for sport fishing. Here in the lake's western basin, the popularity is evident by the plethora of marinas and fishing charters that have sprung up over the years along the shoreline. One such marina is **Tibbles**. They have been in business since 1921, and continue to serve anglers and sight-seekers every year. tibbelsfishing.com

Before leaving town, take a quick stop at **Port Clinton Lighthouse** to check another lighthouse off your list and grab a photo before continuing on.

Up till now, you might have passed by the many water sports locations in your effort to drive the trail. However, it is high time to get out on the water, and the **Portage River Paddle Co.** located on the Portage River is one of the best places to get out there. A short paddle away from where you get in, you will see eagles, blue herons, turtles, and maybe a Lake Erie water snake. portageriverpaddlingco.com

Did you know that Ottawa County was named one of the hottest bird-watching areas in the Midwest? You have now entered the warbler birding capital of the world. Thousands of people descend here in the spring at **Maumee Bay State Park and Lodge** to view the migrating birds. Get back to nature with a walk-through **Magee Marsh** and **Ottawa National Wildlife Refuge** and experience this natural phenomenon for yourself. maumeebaylodge.com

You will have not even touched the surface of all the wondrous and unusual things to do on the Lake Erie Coastal Byway Trail. Hidden harbors, coastal beaches, and quiet marshes will be waiting here for you to experience on your next trip to this nautical wonderland.

Ohio River Scenic Byway

This history-rich 452-mile scenic byway meanders along the banks of the Ohio River. As the road winds its way along the river's banks, it offers stunning views as you cruise along. You will find the bountiful history of the region in the rural landscapes and quiet, friendly communities. Venture west along the river in the spirit of trailblazers and freedom seekers, the beauty of this drive will inspire you to blaze your own trail.

The **Ohio River Scenic Byway** is a fourteen-county jaunt along the mighty Ohio River that lies on the southern border. You will start your journey westward in **East Liverpool** on ST RT 7. This historic town is known as "America's Hometown" and has the distinction of being the "Pottery Capital of the World." Clay was discovered in the area in the mid-1800s, and more than two hundred pottery factories popped up throughout the city over the years.

Before you get too far down the road, make sure to visit some of the spots in this charming town. The **Museum of Ceramics** is one of the best places to learn about the pottery they have been churning out of this town for 150-plus years. This museum boasts the largest display of Lotus Ware in the world and has a 170-year old "Great Wheel" (potter's wheel), which is one of the last six remaining in the US. Then mosey through the clay shop and take home a piece of East Liverpool clay history. themuseumofceramics.com

As you wind your way down ST RT 7, you will begin to appreciate the beauty displayed along the banks of the Ohio River. You might be taken by surprise as you come into **Steubenville**. It's here you will find **Fort**

Steubenville. This fort was built in 1786 by the First American Regiment to protect surveyors who had been sent by the Continental Congress to map the Northwest Territory. On this property, you will also find the **First Federal Land Office** west of the Allegheny Mountains. The building is made from the original logs dating around 1801 and houses furnishings and items inside are what would have been found in a frontier settlement at the turn of the nineteenth century. oldfortsteuben.com

The stretch of road between Steubenville and Marietta, Ohio extends some of the best views of the byway, on one side you have the Ohio River and on the other are the forested hills of Wayne National Forest. You might find yourself engaged in the beauty and miss a sweet little stop on your way towards Marietta, so be on the lookout for Sardis's tiny village. I pumped the brakes and turned off the byway and pulled my car to a stop in the town center. Here you will find a historical marker about the **Sardis Town Pump**, located in a charming white gazebo in the middle of the street. Read the historical marker about this pump and then fill your water bottle, like many locals still do today.

Once you have capped the lid, stroll over to **Marv's Place Café** where you can dine in a fully restored restaurant that is full of history. This historic building was built in 1894 and has housed a department store, shirt factory, was an assembly point for Ford Model As, casket factory, apartment building, and poolroom! While you enjoy your break in this historic building, talk to the owner and have her share her story about the renovations and how Marv's came to life. To give you a small taste of her wit, she told me that "Marv's Place is an acronym for Marvin's Aging Relatives Venture." marvsplace.com

If you have been captured by the picturesque small town here, take a room at the **Orchard Bed and Breakfast** on the edge of town where you can sink into an antique clawfoot tub before your head to bed. theorchardbedandbreakfast.com

I was told that the Ohio River's best view is in the Sardis Cemetery off of 255, and they were not lying! This view is known as the **Long Reach of the Ohio River**, where you can see for miles and miles. Stop and linger for a moment here, you won't be disappointed.

Camping on this journey? There is a hidden gem to share. **Leith Run Recreation Area Campground** is located right on the river with hiking, fishing, and boating right at your fingertips! The best part of this campground is that it is only twenty dollars a night.

Next up is Ohio's first adventure, **Marietta**. It was established in 1788 and is the oldest city in the state of Ohio. Celebrated as the "Riverboat Town," it is located at the confluence of the Ohio and Muskingum rivers. Before your trip along this byway, read *The Pioneers* by David McCullogh, and it will give you a deep appreciation for this fantastic town along the Ohio River.

Spend a day and night in Marietta. I recommend staying in one of the two historic buildings: **Lafayette Hotel**, located on the Ohio river with rooftop views of the sunset or **Hackett Hotel** situated in the heart of downtown. Both are teeming with character. lafayettehotel.com; thehacketthotel.com

You will want to take a ride on the **Valley Gem Sternwheeler**, see the city on the **Trolley Car**, soak in the history at the **Campus Meritus** or **Ohio River Museum**. Take time to relax at **Muskingum Park**, where you can see the **Westward Monument** sculpted by **Gutzon Borglum**, the same artist who created Mount Rushmore. No visit is complete unless you stop at the oldest family-owned business located in Ohio, **Schaffer Leather**. They have been in business for more than 150 years, and its fifth generation curates it! valleygemsternwheeler.com; mariettamuseums.org/campus-martius; schaferleather.com

Marrietta has the market on delicious food. Stop in to enjoy a unique dining experience at **Busy Bee**, a farm-to-table establishment where everything is house-made and locally sourced, or **Austyn's** for an elegant dining experience. If you're looking to wet your whistle, imbibe at **Marietta Brewing Company**, where they craft their fresh brews on the property. busybeerestaurant.com; austyns.com

As ST RT 7 continues to take you along the river, you will find yourself in **Gallipolis**. While this is just a short stop on the byway, don't miss it. Gallipolis means "City of the Gauls," and began as a speculation project of the Scioto Company, which encouraged investors in France to purchase lands in Ohio. Hundreds invested money, hoping to find prosperity in America;

however, upon arriving, the French found the deeds worthless. The **French Colony Arts** and **Our House Tavern** shine a light on this piece of history located in the center of town. bit.ly/ourhousetavern

Grab a coffee from **Poppy's** or a sweet confection from **Sprinkle and Pop** and sit by the river in Gallipolis City Park. You can also see the *Spirit of the American Doughboy* memorial and a high-water marker from the flood of 1913. If you've brought along your boat or kayak, you can drop in at the **KH Butler River Access** just outside of Gallipolis. 46 Court Street; 334 Second Ave

In my opinion, as you come into Lawrence County, you will have finished the most scenic part of the drive. However, going forward, make sure to see each of the five magnificent bridges spanning the river in the tri-state area, into West Virginia and Kentucky, most notable being the Oakley C. Collins Bridge in Ironton.

For a moment, you might be put off by the industrial section of the river route you are entering, but before you write off Ironton, take a slight detour off 52. Check out the **Armory Smoke House** for some of the best BBQ along the byway and drive up to **Lake Vesuvius** in Wayne National Forest. Here, you will see remnants of old iron furnaces and find some excellent hiking trails. thearmorysmokehouse.com

Of course, if you are in southern Ohio, you will want to spend some time in **Shawnee State Park**, where you can stay in the stunning lodge, play a round of golf on the course, and hike some of the most rigorous trails in this part of the state. Here at the lodge, you will have a plethora of things to do and plenty of time to relax before your next destination along the byway. shawneeparklodge.com

A unique bed and breakfast along the route is the breathtaking **Selby 100 Mile House and Mirage Champagne Bar**, located right on the banks of the Ohio. Steeped in history and clothed in luxury, this delightful location is perfect for an evening respite. Sip a glass of champagne and read about the history of one of the previous owners, Roger Selby, who was the leading importer of Arabian horses, most notably his stallion, Mirage. selby100milehouse.com

As you continue to wind your way toward Cincinnati, you quietly roll into **Ripley**. I was taken back by the charming quaintness of Front Street and the lined walks with benches adorned with blooming flowers. Ripley will share her strength with you as you take time to learn of her history. This tiny town played a role in saving and helping more than six hundred slaves through the Underground Railroad.

Start your stop here at the **John Parker Home**. John Parker was a former slave who was able to buy back his freedom and help many up to the **John Rankin House**, where together they would help these freedom seekers along their way on the Underground Railroad. johnparkerhouse.net; ohiohistory.org

Stop and browse at **Olde Piano Factory Antiques**. This historic building houses two pianos that were built here at the turn of the century, and is jam-packed full of aged treasures of days gone by.

Turning your car toward Cincinnati, you are met with continued beauty along the river. Just before you head into the downtown, you will come upon **Grant's Birthplace**. This quick stop is picture-worthy and full of presidential history. ohiohistory.org

Cincinnati is known for many things, but it should be noted above all that they love their chili, and that they played an essential role in the underground railroad.

As you begin to explore this last section of the Ohio byway, before heading into the Indiana and Illinois sections, pick your base camp for the night. Two unique and new hotels in The Banks area are the **Lytle Park Hotel** and **AC Hotel**. Both hotels offer stylish and modern rooms and have rooftop lounges, which are perfect for enjoying the skyline of Cincy and the Ohio River. thelytleparkhotel.com

Teeming with plenty of museums and history, you can check out **William H. Taft Historic Site** where you can visit the birthplace and boyhood home of William Howard Taft, the nation's twenty-seventh president and tenth chief justice of the US Supreme Court. The site was established in 1969 and stands today, sharing the past. **American Sign Museum** has one of the happiest rooms to walk into in Cincinnati. They have dedicated themselves to the art and history of commercial signs and sign-making. One of my favorite signs is the Holiday Inn arrow sign; it is like a blast from the past. americansignmuseum.org

Don't miss the **National Underground Railroad Freedom Center**. Here they celebrate the heroes who created the secret network through which the enslaved could escape to freedom in the north. freedomcenter.org

Take in the urban and local parks at **Shawnee Lookout**, **Withrow Nature Reserve**, and **Smale Riverfront Park**. No visit to Cincy will be complete without a stop at the **Camp Washington Chili** for a delightful taste of the delicious secret recipe they have been serving customers since1940. **Findlay Market** is Ohio's oldest continuously operated market and has been in the same iron-framed building since 1855. You will find farm-fresh and locally sourced foods. Many of the vendors are multi-generational and have helped keep the farmer market's historic traditions alive. campwashingtonchili.com; findlaymarket.org

This is just a sampling of the fantastic stops and finds on this byway through the southern part of Ohio. I am sure after this exhilarating journey along the Ohio portion of the river, you will be looking for more adventure along her shores. You can continue your journey along the Ohio River by reading the sections in the book's Indiana and Illinois portions.

Appalachian and Hocking Hills Byways

Southern Ohio is home to captivating scenic rolling hills, premiere hiking, delightful places to eat and stay, and my fellow history buffs will be pleased to know it's home to many of Ohio's historic destinations. Filled with happy surprises and stunning views, combining these two byways will not disappoint. You'll love every twist and turn as you make your way along the 131 miles of the Appalachian and Hocking Hill Byways.

Pro tip: The entire route is marked by the Ohio Byway signs that feature a white flower and yellow sun, making it easy to stay the course during your journey.

Getting started on one of the newest byways in Ohio is simple. A great starting point is a stay at the eco-friendly, off-the-grid but modern, **Beaver Lodge at Dragonfly Lake**. While it is not directly on the byway, it's just a short drive to Route 78. This fantastic lodge is located on a secluded and private thirty-three acres in the Appalachian Mountain foothills, where you can enjoy kayaking and hiking before your road trip toward Nelsonville. thenestlodging.com/dragonflylake

If you enjoy the outdoors, **Piatt Park Gorge**, (travel west on State Route 78 to CR30 to TR2308) is a secluded gem full of old-growth Appalachian hardwoods and majestic hemlocks. Tucked inside the park, you will find an enchanting gorge and cave area that you can trek through, and there are a handful of striking waterfalls. Hiking the trails will give you a spectacular view of the natural beauty located in Monroe County. You might even get a glimpse of wild turkey, deer, or black bear that live in the habitat of this extraordinary place.

As you continue your drive on State Route 78, you quietly enter Noble County. You will continue to see stunning beauty as you wind your way to **Caldwell**. This small town is home to the first oil well in North America: the Thorla-McKee Well, and it is commemorated in the local **Caldwell Park**. In 1814, settlers Silas Thorla and Robert McKee noticed that deer were licking a spot on the ground, and they were hopeful it would lead to an underground deposit of salt.

They were not looking for oil because it wasn't useful to settlers in 1814, however, the livestock needed salt and Thorla and McKee needed it to preserve meat for the long winter months. They drilled their well and found salt and oil. Using wool blankets to soak the oil off the salt brine's surface, they would wring out the oil because it was useless to them.

Fun Fact: They later bottled the oil and called it Seneca Oil, a digestive elixir.

The Thorla-McKee Well is located at the intersection
of State Routes 78 and 564 near Caldwell.

Continuing through town, you will want to stop at the **Historic Jail Museum & Information Center** and the **Baker Glass Museum and**

Antique Gallery. You can see the immense private collection of over 300,000 pieces from many local glass companies at the gallery, including Cambridge Glass, Heisey, Fenton, Westmorland, and Degenhart. Before you head out of Caldwell, stop at **Lori's** for a piece of homemade pie! They've been a local favorite for over thirty years. (740) 732.5288; bakermuseum.org; (740) 732-4711

Just down the road is **crash site #3 for the *USS Shenandoah***, this is a small pull-off with a sign, monument, and information about the crash. It is easy to miss, so be on the lookout for it. The *USS Shenandoah* was a massive, 680-foot-long cigar-shaped Navy dirigible with forty-three crew members aboard. It was ripped apart and pulled to the ground early in the morning of Sept. 3, 1925. You can pay tribute to the fourteen Navy men who lost their lives in this fiery crash.

Bonus Spur Route: If you have time, the Appalachian Byway has a spur off of it onto State Route 28 to the **Wilds**. You can board an open-air jeep for a safari tour where you'll see rhinos, giraffes, and many other rare and endangered animals roaming in large, natural-like habitats. While you're in Cambridge, you can check out **The Living Word Outdoor Drama** or visit the other various museums in the area. thewilds.org; facebook.com/The-Living-Word-Outdoor-Drama-150945389146

As you enter Morgan County, you will be taken to what is known as the front porch to the great outdoors. You will find a community where you can enjoy a tasty meal and stop at some of southern Ohio's most historic buildings in **McConnellsville**. This section is my favorite stretch of the Appalachian Byway because the people here are welcoming, the towns are beautiful, and it encapsulates some of my favorite activities to do in the state.

The first stop on this section of the byway is the Big Muskie Bucket at **Jesse Owens State Park**. "Big Muskie" was once the **World's Largest Earth-Moving Machine**, and what remains today is a gigantic metal bucket that rests on a rise, overlooking the beautiful valley that was previously mined by American Electric Power. This once barren mined land is now called "Re-Creation Land" because this green space is now a 5,735-acre park and wildlife area. If you have time, you can take advantage of the fishing, camping, boating, hiking, biking, and horseback trails through this expansive natural wonderland. 4470 E. State Route 78, McConnelsville, OH 43756

After all that recreating, stop in at any of the great restaurants in McConnelsville. Or if you're thirsty, swing by the **Old Bridge Brewing Company** for some locally made craft beer. Or, if you are ready for a pick-me-up after all the driving, grab some coffee from **Seraphinea's Crumb and Coffee**. It's an authentic bakery, specializing in bread and pastries. They make everything from raw ingredients on-site and they have the best muffins in town! oldbridgebrewing.com; crumbandcoffee.com

However, the locals' go-to eatery is the **Boondocks BBQ and Grill** to get some of the best BBQ you have ever had. Owners Bobby and Maria Burdette are natives to the area and came home to open this local eatery. It was their dream to offer their friends and family the same quality eats they would get in the bigger cities, at an affordable price. Boondock's motto is "Keep it simple, keep it good, keep it affordable." Favorite items on the menu that the locals love are the Pulled Pork Street Tacos and the Boondocker. theboondocksbbqandgrill.webs.com

Once you're recovered from eating, you will want to take a tour of the **Twin City Opera House** and **Morgan County Historical Society**, **Evelyn True Button House**, and **Doll House**. Do not miss seeing the old barn piece with a cannonball hole from the Civil War, which happened during Morgan's Raid. Hostile troops came through this area on July 8, 1863, led by Brigadier General John Hunt Morgan. While you are at the **Doll House**, make sure you pause a moment to see the doll that was found after the catastrophic flood of 1913. historicalmorgancounty.com

Take a break from history for a walk in the woods or a day on the lake by renting a pontoon boat at the marina at **Burr Oak State Park Lodge**. This natural playground is tucked away off the byway. The road leading up to the lodge is known as the **Rim of the World**, it's one of the most awe-inspiring passages along the way. Pull off for a moment to take in the expansive views of the gorgeous rolling hills and valleys. stayburroak.com

When you get to **Nelsonville**, you are ready to stretch your legs and walk the **Historic Public Square**. The town center is lined with unique shops and small places to grab a snack, try **Rhapsody Music and Dining**, and snap a picture of the historic **Stuart's Opera House** while in town. cityofnelsonville.com/index.php/attractions

If you're looking for an adventure on the rails, you can also book a ride on the **Hocking Valley Scenic Railway** This trip is a history-filled journey through the beautiful hills of southern Ohio. You'll enjoy the shared history from one of the many volunteers that keep this train rolling on the rails. Right next door to the train depot is the **Rocky Mountain Outlet**, which is one of my favorite places to shop for great outdoor gear and boot deals. hvsry.org; rockyoutlet.com

If you're still up for some road-tripping, a few short miles up the road is the **Hocking Hills Scenic Byway**. Running through Hocking Hills State Park is State Route 374, where you will start your drive at the **Paul A. Johnson Pencil Sharpener Museum** located at the visitor center. As you wind your way into the lush flora and fauna of the Hocking Hills region, you will begin to see the tall grand Hemlock trees and the luscious ferns along the road. 13178 OH-664, Logan, OH 43138

I have to mention my favorite stop as you head into the woods, **Hocking Hills Coffee Emporium**. We always stop and recharge when we come by. This sweet coffee shop is owned and operated by four friends, called the Jugs, (Just Us Gals) They have brought to life the best coffee in the area. I highly recommend you enjoy a cup of coffee as you drive that supports economic development and women's progress in Ohio's Appalachia. hockinghillscoffeeemporium.com

Once you're in the forest's heart, you will roll up on the **Hocking Hills State Park Visitor Center**, where you can learn more about this crown jewel of the Ohio State Parks system. If you're up for hiking, this is the start of the **Old Man's Cave** trail. The trails in the park are some of Ohio's most challenging but also some of the most stunning. I recommend you pause here to listen to nature's sounds, gaze at some of the plentiful waterfalls, catch a glimpse over the edge of the sharp cliffs, and enjoy ample wildlife. 21725 OH-374 Scenic, Logan, OH

Heading back out onto State Route 374, you will head towards **Conkles Hollow State Nature Preserve** (no dogs allowed here). This is my favorite hike in the Hocking Hills region. Why? Because it has everything I love about this area in one place. It is ADA accessible on the paved gorge portion, and if you hike upwards, it has steep trails and glorious views on the rim trail. There is a beautiful waterfall right in the heart of the rocky crevasse at the center.

You'll want to stay in this region for a few days, and my go-to places are **Hocking Hills Treehouse Cabins** and the family-friendly **River Rock Lodge**. Each one is unique and has all the amenities you will want after your winding drive through the Appalachian Byway. hockinghillstreehousecabins. com; libertyloglodging.com

Combining these two byways gives you the beauty and adventure that southern Ohio provides to visitors all in one. You will have seen the best that Appalachia offers as you have driven along her ancient paths, and you will have sampled some of the best trails in Hocking Hills. These byways will leave you mesmerized by their magnificence and looking forward to a return visit to delve deeper into their treasure troves.

Brandy Gleason is the creator of the popular Midwest Travel Blog gleasonfamilyadventure.com, and a valuable member of the Midwest Travel Network. In addition to her love of all things travel, Brandy enjoys hiking, reading in her Eno hammock, and spending time with her family. You may have also come across their work in: Ohio and Indiana tourism travel guides, online articles on Roadtrippers.com, when they have been featured on 10tv in Columbus Ohio, or across mutual travels. Above all, Brandy hopes that travel gives you the opportunity to adventure, learn about yourself, and explore more and that this book helps you do just that.

Learn more about Brandy Gleason at gleasonfamilyadventure.com

N.ZANATI

SOUTH DAKOTA

The state of South Dakota is an intriguing and sparsely populated package of breathtaking scenery, outdoor adventures, bustling cities, and acres of farmland and ranches. There are natural wonders like glacial lakes, the Badlands, the Black Hills, and Jewel and Wind Caves, and the man-made wonders of Mount Rushmore, **Crazy Horse Memorial**, and the World's Only Corn Palace. It's a place of geological, archaeological, and living history. The state is home to nine Native American tribes and has several important cultural sites. Lewis and Clark journeyed along the Missouri River, followed by settlers and homesteaders who forged their way west, many of whom chose to stake their claims.

We've chosen four scenic drives through this complex state, and they're designed to give you a taste of everything it has to offer. Whether you want to experience natural beauty, cultural history, or modern day adventures, you're sure to find it in South Dakota.

South Dakota entered the Union in 1889, and is home to nearly 890,000 people. Its official nickname is the "Mt. Rushmore State." Before that nickname became official in 1992, the state was nicknamed the "Sunshine State."

Basic South Dakota Facts:
- The state capital is Pierre.
- The state motto is "Under God, the People Rule," while the state slogan is "Great Faces. Great Places."
- The state bird is the Chinese ring-necked pheasant.
- The state flower is the pasque.
- Explore five South Dakota highways and byways. They are listed in the index in the back of this book.

Fun South Dakota Facts:

- South Dakota has more shoreline miles than Florida.
- Black Elk Peak, South Dakota's high point, is the highest-altitude spot in the United States east of the Rocky Mountains.
- South Dakota gets its name from the Dakota Native American tribe. "Dakota" means "friend" or "ally" in the Yanktonai language.

A Black Hills Road Trip

With massive mountain carvings, caves, waterfalls, the world's biggest motorcycle rally, and more, South Dakota's mountains shine. Rising from the plains of western South Dakota, the Black Hills are an isolated mountain range east of the Rockies. They aren't black; they appear black from a distance.

When you visit the Black Hills, say hello to spiraling roads that beg you to drive them. Say hello to fun!

On the Black Hills' eastern edge, Rapid City is the region's largest city. It's an excellent place for your headquarters. bit.ly/rapidcityplacestovisit

For a kid-friendly stay, the **Best Western Ramkota Hotel** is the perfect stop. bit.ly/bwramkota

Lake Park Campground and Cottages has earned twenty-five years of Great Service Awards from South Dakota Tourism. bit.ly/lakeparkcampground

Join s'mores parties, watermelon feeds, and pancake breakfasts when you camp at **Rapid City Black Hills KOA**. bit.ly/blackhillskoa

In the northern Black Hills, make the **Best Western Black Hills Lodge** your headquarters. bit.ly/bestwesternblackhillslodge

RVers will enjoy stunning Black Hills views at **Elkhorn Ridge Resort**. bit.ly/elkhornridge

Hang out with the Presidents in Downtown Rapid City, "**The City of Presidents**." Every former President has a life-sized statue on a street corner. Take a selfie with your favorite President. presidentsrc.com

Try a Cuban sandwich and the ice cream flavor of the day at **Armadillo's Ice Cream Shoppe**. armadillosicecreamshoppe.com

Drink to firefighters at **Firehouse Brewing Co.** and enjoy a tasting at **Firehouse Wine Cellar**. Eat the locally sourced buffalo burgers. firehousebrewing.com

Enjoy a superb collection of military aircraft and missiles at the **South Dakota Air & Space Museum**. Since the museum's bus tours go to **Ellsworth Air Force Base**, tour riders must show government-issued photo identification. sdairandspacemuseum.com

While the Presidents in Rapid City are life-size, the Four Presidential Faces at **Mt. Rushmore National Memorial** dominate the landscape. For the best pictures, arrive before sunrise. The morning sun shines directly on the faces. In the evening, enjoy the illuminated faces until eleven p.m. Come for the evening lighting ceremony. Walk the **Presidential Trail**, visit the **Sculptor's Studio** and learn about Native American life at the **Lakota, Nakota, and Dakota Heritage Village**. Be prepared to climb 422 steps. nps.gov/moru

The sculptural scale is big at Mt. Rushmore, but Crazy Horse Memorial's scale dwarfs the other mountain carving. Brule Lakota leader Henry Standing Bear asked sculptor Korczak Ziolkowski to create a monument to Native Americans. Ziolkowski began blasting in 1948. The work continues, funded entirely by admissions and contributions. crazyhorsememorial.org

Explore the museums and gift shops, eat at the restaurant, and watch the mountain carving.

If you hear a siren, head to the restaurant's patio. Order some *tatanka* (bison) stew while you wait for the blast that's about to occur. After a series of countdowns, you'll hear "Fire in the hole!" and will see rock flying off the mountain. Twice a year, the memorial holds night blasts and laser light shows on summer weekend evenings. For a closer view, join the **Rustic Bus Ride** to the bottom of the mountain.

Drive half an hour to **Hill City** and take a two-hour trip into the past on the **1880 Train**, the oldest continually operating tourist train. You'll pass mining operations, forests, meadows, and canyons. Passengers may see deer, wild turkeys, woodchucks, and waterfowl. In the fall, enjoy the foliage, local wines, and delicious food on the **Wine Express**. 1880train.com

From Hill City, join the **Highway 386 Wine Trail**. The route connects **Prairie Berry Winery**, **Naked Winery**, and **Stone Faces Winery** to **Belle Joli Winery** and **Schade Vineyard** in **Deadwood**. blackhillsbadlands.com/wineries

On the way, explore **Pactola Reservoir**. Underwater, visit the drowned town of Pactola. Spear fishers can track bigmouth buffalo fish, which can weigh eighty pounds. Above the water, fish for rainbow trout and pike. bit.ly/pactola

In **Keystone**, discover **Grapes & Grinds**, the Black Hills' best coffee shop. grapesgrinds.com

Ride impossible highways through **Custer State Park**. Plan at least three and a half hours for the drive, but wildlife jams may cause delays. The drive comes in three sections, **Needles Highway**, **Iron Mountain Road**, and **Wildlife Loop Road**. Please note: The roads are not RV-friendly. The winding roads might cause difficulty for those who suffer from motion sickness. gfp.sd.gov/csp-scenic-drives

Needles Highway takes drivers through pine and spruce forests, stands of birch and aspen, and meadows full of wildflowers. The jagged granite Needles seem to chew at the sky. Dive into the most beautiful swimming hole available, **Sylvan Lake**. Enjoy fine dining with fresh, locally-sourced ingredients at the **Sylvan Lake Lodge**. bit.ly/sylvanlakelodge

Don't pass by the **Needle's Eye**. Park in the lot and walk around. The short hike at **Moonlight Ridge** is challenging at first, but quickly rewards hikers with beautiful views. Rock climbers also will find rewarding routes. bit.ly/moonlightridgerockclimbing

The engineering on **Iron Mountain Road** is a work of art, and it crosses some of the Black Hills' best scenery. Three of its tunnels frame Mt. Rushmore. Those who love a bit of a driving challenge will enjoy the pigtail bridges. They twist 360 degrees for a quick altitude change. Drive slowly.

On **Wildlife Loop Road**, see Custer State Park's stars, more than 1,300 free-roaming bison. Deer and elk are out early in the morning and the late afternoon. If you're lucky, bighorn sheep or a mountain lion will come out. The park also hosts a prairie dog town and a pack of feral burros.

For uninterrupted views, and to bag the South Dakota high point, climb **Black Elk Peak**. One of the routes includes **Little Devils Tower**. At the summit, climb the stone **Black Elk Peak Lookout**. From there, hikers can see four states, Nebraska, South Dakota, Wyoming, and Montana. The Civilian Conservation Corps built the tower in the mid-1930s. They hauled the stone to the summit manually. bit.ly/sdhighpointtrail

The peak is named for Nicholas Black Elk, who experienced a famous vision on the mountain. In 2017, the Catholic Church began investigating his case for sainthood. bit.ly/blackelkbiography

While visitors must hike to Black Elk Peak's summit, **Mt. Coolidge Lookout Tower** is reachable by car. At the top, view the Needles, Crazy Horse, and even the Badlands, sixty miles east. Mt. Rushmore is also in view—very appropriately. The 1.2-mile gravel road is narrow and unsuitable for RVs and other oversized vehicles. gfp.sd.gov/csp-sights

The mountain's name was changed in 1927 in honor of President Coolidge's visit to the Black Hills. Mt. Rushmore was only a concept when Coolidge came. Some South Dakota salesmanship persuaded him to pledge the equivalent of $3.6 billion in federal funds. Ironically, Coolidge liked to cut federal spending. bit.ly/coolidgeblackhills

The Black Hills aren't only spectacular above ground. Visit **Jewel Cave National Monument** and **Wind Cave National Park** for underground marvels.

Jewel Cave is the world's third-longest cave with at least two hundred miles of passages. It's known for "cave bacon," a type of flowstone. See a ten-foot-long piece on the **Scenic Tour**. The cave's jewels are nailhead spar and calcite spar. The park also offers the accessible **Discovery Talk Tour**. The **Historic Lantern Tour** and the **Wild Caving Tour** are more strenuous. nps.gov/jeca

Underground, **Wind Cave** is best known for its intricate boxwork, frostwork, and cave popcorn. Above ground, explore the plains on thirty miles of trails. The park attracts many bird species. Larger animals include bison, pronghorns, elk, coyotes, and bobcats. nps.gov/wica

According to Lakota legend, a bear and a sea monster fought to the death. The bear's body became Bear Butte. The mountain is sacred to Native

Americans. When you climb the butte, pause to appreciate its sacredness. The 1.85-mile **Summit Trail** at **Bear Butte State Park** will take you to the top. If you see pieces of cloth, bundles, or pouches hanging from the trees, please do not disturb them. They represent prayers. bit.ly/bearbuttesp

Nearby **Sturgis** is the home of the famous **Sturgis Motorcycle Rally**. Thousands of bikers flock to the Black Hills each August for the rally. At the **Sturgis Motorcycle Museum and Hall of Fame**, watch biker movies and explore their motorcycle collection. sturgismuseum.com

Eat a Popper Burger at the **Knuckle Saloon** in Sturgis. theknuckle.com

In 1892, Col. Caleb Carlton gave "The Star-Spangled Banner" its first push toward national anthem status. He ordered that the song become the official music for Fort Meade's evening retreat ceremony. Fort Meade's soldiers weren't fond of the Ku Klux Klan, and they broke up a cross-burning with machine guns. Learn about these stories and more at the **Old Fort Meade Museum**. fortmeademuseum.org

Get your first hole-in-one at the **Sanford Lab Homestake Visitor Center** in Lead. Trust us: You can't miss a hole that's a mile wide and a mile long. The "hole" is the **Homestake Mine**, the Western Hemisphere's most extensive. In 2001, it ran out of ore. Sanford Lab now runs cutting-edge physics experiments in the mine's depths. The center also offers Lead trolley tours and bike rentals. sanfordlabhomestake.com

Ride the bikes on the nearby **George S. Mickelson Trail**, which provides eighty miles of outdoor recreation. bit.ly/mickelsontrail

The **Homestake Trail** offers good views of the mine. northernhillsrec.org/trails

In 1876, prospectors entered a ravine full of dead trees—with a creek full of gold. And **Deadwood** was born. Deadwood is very proud of its history. After all, the entire town is a National Historic District. deadwood.com

Wild Bill Hickok came to Deadwood seeking his fortune. Instead, Jack McCall shot him. Hickok was left holding the Dead Man's Hand, aces and eights. The town daily reenacts the assassination and McCall's subsequent trial. bit.ly/deadwoodreenactments

To fully enjoy Deadwood, take the tours, including a private gold-mining lesson. bit.ly/deadwoodtours

Deadwood shopping is prime. Your jewelry box needs some Black Hills Gold. Find it at **Berg Jewelers**. bergjewelers.com

Eat homemade pasties at **Lou Lou's Bombdiggity's**. The pasties are large meat pies with hilarious names like Meathead and Miss Priss. bit.ly/loulousbombdiggitys

Walk off those calories on the easy 0.6-mile **Mt. Roosevelt Trail**. Enjoy great Black Hills views. For an even better view, climb to the top of the **Friendship Tower**. bit.ly/mtroosevelttrail

Spearfish is best known for **Spearfish Canyon**. The canyon includes three waterfalls, **Bridal Veil Falls**, **Roughlock Falls**, and **Spearfish Falls**. Watch for deer, mountain goats, and bobcats. In the fall, luxuriate in splendid foliage. bit.ly/spearfishcanyon

In Spearfish, enjoy Dick Termes' worlds. He calls his spherical artworks "Termespheres," and his **Termespheres Gallery** is a must-see. termespheres.com

Learn about history in five states at the **Western Heritage Center**. In August and September, enjoy the **High Plains Country Jamboree**. westernheritagecenter.com

Devour heavenly pizza at **Dough Trader Pizza**. Order the Heaven-Sent cheese bread and the King Leonidas Pizza, featuring fennel-infused sausage. Yum, yum! doughtraderpizza.com

Start your visit to **Belle Fourche** at the **Tri-State Museum**. Join the museum's jamboree in August and September. The **Great Western Cattle Trail**, the nation's longest cattle trail, passed through Belle Fourche. See exhibits about the cattle trail and other stories. Kids will love the **Dress-Up Trunk**. thetristatemuseum.com

The twenty-one-foot diameter **Center of the Nation Monument** is in a plaza below the museum. The actual center point is on private property. To visit the real center point, get directions in the museum. From the monument, join the **River Walk** beside the **Belle Fourche River** as it winds through town. bellefourchechamber.org/gcon

Enjoy delicious hand-cut steaks at the **Branding Iron Steakhouse & Social Club**. brandingironsteakhouse.net

Learn about a bizarre battle on the markers at **Crow Buttes** north of Belle Fourche. **M&R Travelers Rest** stands near Crow Buttes. Try M&R's version of South Dakota's Official State Nosh, chislic, deep-fried steak chunks with garlic butter sauce. Take home a souvenir from their store. facebook.com/crowbuttes

The Black Hills are calling, and you should answer.

Connect your trip:

Two hours north of Crow Buttes, enjoy scenic drives at **Theodore Roosevelt National Park**. Drive through the spectacular Badlands in the **South Unit**, near Medora, ND. The **North Unit**, an hour and a half from the South Unit, features an equally spectacular scenic drive. nps.gov/thro

Badlands Loop State Scenic Byway

Badlands State Scenic Byway is a surreal and otherworldly path through a unique landscape that was forged over millennia. This route is less than forty miles end-to-end, but it's an experience you'll never forget.

Sixty-five million years ago, this area of South Dakota was an ancient sea. Over time, the seabed compressed into a two-thousand-foot-thick layer of rock called Pierre Shale. Volcanoes dumped a blanket of ash. Then rivers flooded and receded, leaving sediment and fossils behind. Animals were captured in the layers: saber-toothed cats, miniature camels and horses, and giant beasts called *titanotheres*, which resembled the modern-day rhinoceros. Erosion chiseled away, and what remains is a magnificent landscape of jagged multi-hued ridges and deep gorges.

This landscape is extraordinary enough that it became a national monument in 1939 and a national park in 1978, and now one million people a year visit Badlands National Park.

Because this scenic byway travels through a national park, you'll need to pay for entrance. Your pass is good for seven days, which means you can take this route and then return after you've explored other South

Dakota drives. There are several overlooks, so even though you could technically drive the whole length in about an hour, where's the fun in that? Instead of rushing through, take your time and truly dig into this incredible drive.

Pro Tip: If you plan on doing any hiking, be sure to pack lots of water. There's a reason the Lakota called this land Mako Sico, or, Bad Lands. It's harsh and dry, and the erosion means any water source is not potable.

Your scenic drive begins north of Badlands National Park in Cactus Flat. Take Exit 131 from I-90. If you've got time, turn north first for a stop at **Minuteman Missile National Historic Site**, the first national park globally to commemorate the Cold War. The site is actually three locations: the visitor center, the control center, and a silo containing a Minuteman II missile. Upon launch, a Minuteman Intercontinental Ballistic Missile (ICBM) could reach the Soviet Union in only thirty minutes. This is one of only two places you can see a Cold War–era missile. nps.gov/mimi/index.htm

As you near the entrance to the Badlands, stop at **Prairie Homestead** to see an original sod house. Settlers on the Great Plains built homes with walls made of sod blocks and covered their roofs with the thick prairie. It was a good use of materials at hand, but not very permanent; Edgar and Alice Brown built theirs in 1909 and it's one of the few sod houses that remain. This seasonal attraction gives a glimpse into the rough conditions homesteaders would have experienced. Prairiehomestead.com

Shortly after you enter **Badlands National Park**, pull off at **Big Badlands Overlook** for a stunning view of the wall of buttes, pinnacles, and cliffs that make up this unique landscape and give the nearby town of Wall its name. This will be your first of several overlooks, and one you don't want to miss. nps.gov/badl/index.htm

Get out your hiking boots, because the next stop provides access to four trails. **Door Trail** is three-quarters of a mile on a boardwalk through a natural break in the wall. It's an easy trek, but not as easy as **Window Trail**.

At a quarter of a mile, that'll take only about twenty minutes. Early risers will get the best sunrise view in the park at either of these trails.

Notch Trail is one and a half miles of moderate to strenuous hiking. You'll climb a log ladder and follow a narrow ledge, but the view of the White River Valley is worth it. That is, unless you're afraid of heights. Stay off it during or after rain, because the trail will quickly go from moderate to treacherous.

Day hikers can pick up Castle Trail. It's five miles one way and a round-trip hike makes it the longest trail in the park. Plan on at least five hours on this relatively level path.

Your next pullout is the **Cliff Shelf Nature Trail**. Boardwalks and stairs take you half a mile into a juniper forest and there's a two-hundred-foot elevation change, so it's considered moderate. While rain might be bad for Notch Trail, it could create a pond off of this path, drawing deer and bighorn sheep.

It's time for a break, so enter the **Ben Reifel Visitor Center**, named for the first Lakota to serve in the US Congress. Inside, you can watch an orientation film and browse exhibits, including models and murals, that detail the area's history and geology. If you're hungry, you can get a bite to eat at the seasonal **Cedar Pass Lodge**. The restaurant has snacks as well as full-service dining. The lodge itself has been welcoming guests since 1928. Next door is also one of the park's two official campgrounds. **Cedar Pass Campground** has both tent sites and RV campsites with electrical hookups.

You won't be back on the road for long before another trail beckons. **Saddle Pass** is small but mighty: it's only a quarter of a mile, but it could take up to an hour because it climbs up the Badlands Wall. For an educational, and much gentler, hike, you'll want **Fossil Exhibit Trail**. It's the same length as Saddle Pass, but it's fully accessible and has fossil replicas and interpretive signs telling the story of many of the extinct sea animals. This trail is especially great for kids.

White River Valley Overlook is a wonderful place to see the tall formations collectively known as the Castle. Be careful, because not only are there steep drop-offs, rattlesnakes like to set up camp on the rocks and pavement to soak in the sun. This is a good place to see either sunrises or sunsets. You might also spy some American pronghorn.

Big Foot Pass Overlook is named for Chief Spotted Elk, who was also known as Big Foot. In 1890, the chief led a few hundred fellow Lakota through the rocky formations to avoid the US Army's 7th Cavalry. The Native Americans escaped notice for five days before the US soldiers intercepted them and diverted them to Wounded Knee. Interpretive signs at the overlook tell the tragic story. The view itself is magnificent, with layers of grays, browns, tans, and reds.

Panorama Point provides similar views to Big Foot Pass and is another rattlesnake hotspot, so be careful as you follow the boardwalk to the viewing platform. And for something completely different, **Prairie Wind Overlook** provides a sense of the vast grasses that used to blanket the plains states.

It's hard to believe, but at one point there was a freshwater stream in this dry land. Wilson Burns found it, built a homestead, and raised sheep. **Burns Basin Overlook** is named for the fortunate man, although the stream dried up long ago and wells now have to be dug several thousand feet deep. The **Homestead Overlook** tells the story of settlers like Burns, as well as the Native Americans those homesteaders displaced.

Conata Basin Overlook is like Badlands 101, with a grand view of the many layers and jagged peaks that make up this beautiful land. **Yellow Mounds Overlook** will definitely bring some color into your world. Mustard-yellow bases are topped with a stripe of purple and capped with domes of gray, and there are some red layers thrown in for good measure.

If you missed the Cliff Shelf Nature Trail near the Ben Reifel Visitor Center, what you'll see at **Ancient Hunters Overlook** will look similar. While the view, like every overlook in this park, is impressive, what's most interesting about this spot is what was found at your feet.

Archaeologists uncovered the remnants of what was most likely a base for Native American hunters, including pottery shards, arrowheads, and charcoal from campfires of long ago. If you notice road damage, it's because the land itself is a slide that broke off from the wall and is constantly moving.

Pinnacles Overlook is considered the best place in the park to watch the sunset, and like Big Badlands Overlook near the park's northeast entrance, the view illustrates the sheer magnificence of this unique landscape. To the east is the cragged and serrated wall; to the west, the sweeping Sage Creek Wilderness Area. This overlook might also provide your first glimpse of bison.

From this point, the Badlands Loop State Scenic Byway turns north towards Wall and the famous, or infamous, **Wall Drug**. However, before heading to that tourist destination, it's worth it to take **Sage Creek Rim Road**. Stop at the first pullout at **Hay Butte Overlook**. From this vantage point, not only can you see Hay Butte itself, a grass-topped mesa and one of the most recognizable formations in the park, but you're also likely to encounter bison and bighorn sheep. Be careful: neither of those wild animals are afraid of humans and their vehicles, but you should be cautious of them. They both roam freely in this section of the park, and bison are particularly dangerous. The largest North American mammal is not only big, but also fast. These beasts can get up to thirty-five miles an hour, and with a mature bull weighing up to two thousand pounds, they can do considerable damage. Stay at least a hundred yards away, and never ever try to feed or engage them.

The **Badlands Wilderness Overlook** sits on a transition between the wild rocky formations and a vast prairie. The view goes from jagged to undulating, offering a more hospitable environment. Soon you'll see prairie dogs popping up as they jump out of one burrow and scramble to another. **Roberts Prairie Dog Town** is a great place to watch them scurry.

Your final overlook is **Sage Creek Basin Overlook**. The Badlands eroded, leaving behind mixed grass prairie. You'll see a few trails, but be careful hiking them because these were formed by bison, not humans. Also in the distance is **Sage Creek Campground**. This primitive site is free and first-come, first-served. There are a couple of pit toilets and equestrian enclosures, but other than that ,it's you and the bison and prairie dogs.

At this point, you can take the twisting roads and curves back towards the Pinnacles Entrance and head north to Wall and I-90, or you can continue following Sage Creek Road until it dead-ends at SD-44. No matter which way you choose, you'll know you've experienced one of the most majestic, scenic, and awe-inspiring scenic drives in the country.

Eastern arts and culture

Eastern South Dakota's prairie landscapes contain friendly towns, glacial lakes, rushing rivers and unexpected outdoor spaces. Interstate 29 links most of the attractions in the eastern corridor, so it's easy to visit the historic sites, museums and scenic spots along the way.

This itinerary starts in Sioux Falls and ends in Watertown, just over one hundred miles to the north, with stops in Brookings and De Smet, home of author Laura Ingalls Wilder, in between. Drive the route in either direction or spend a day or two in each city.

Sioux Falls expertly weaves history, art and nature into its walkable downtown. It's named for the spot where the Big Sioux River spills down a series of reddish-pink quartzite stone ledges. experiencesiouxfalls.com

If you only stop at one spot in Sioux Falls, make it **Falls Park**, so you can see those falls up close.

The water churns at a rate of 7,400 gallons per second. experiencesiouxfalls.com/things-to-do/falls-park

Pose on the bridges, climb the **observation tower** for a bird's-eye view or watch the rushing water from **Falls Overlook Café**. The former hydroelectric plant now produces shareable appetizers, panini and creamy Stenland Family Dairy ice cream scooped into house-made waffle cones. fallsoverlook.com

Sioux Falls history, art, and entertainment are just a short drive or walk away. To travel in style, board the **Downtown Trolley** at the **Falls Park Visitor Center**. This hop-on, hop-off historic tour is free and ADA accessible. bit.ly/downtowntrolley

Admission to **The Old Courthouse Museum** is also free. It was built in 1889 from the same Sioux quartzite stone present at the falls. Accented with stained glass, it contains sixteen colorful murals, exhibits that detail the state's history, and a historical courtroom. bit.ly/oldcourthousemuseum

The Washington Pavilion of Arts and Science bursts with attractions. It includes the immersive **Kirby Science Discovery Center**, where visitors dig for dinosaur bones, shimmy through a mine shaft and feel the weather in 4D. Stroll through eight galleries at the **Visual Arts Center** or see a movie on a four-story screen at the **Wells Fargo CineDome**. The complex also houses the **South Dakota Symphony Orchestra, Sioux Falls Jazz and Blues** and other arts organizations that feature country music concerts, choral music, soloists, comics and musical theatre productions. washingtonpavilion.org

Step out into a city steeped in art and culture. The Beaux Arts–inspired **State Theatre** is a downtown jewel. **Levitt at the Falls** brings the community together at dozens of outdoor concerts each summer. levittsiouxfalls.org

The two sides of Dale Lamphere's sixty-ton stainless steel *Arc of Dreams* reach out from both sides of the riverbank. The work by the South Dakota Artist Laureate anchors **SculptureWalk Sioux Falls**, which features rotating sculpture installations that draw visitors downtown. sculpturewalksiouxfalls.com

Most of the sculptures are concentrated downtown along Phillips Avenue, a great shopping and strolling thoroughfare. Boutique **Hotel on Phillips** is located inside what was once a century-old downtown bank. The sixteen-ton bank vault now serves as the entrance to the **Treasury** cocktail lounge. hotelonphillips.com

The charmingly retro **Phillips Avenue Diner** is another blast from the past. It serves lunch counter classics such as chicken fried steak, cookie-studded shakes and quirky treats like a banana and peanut butter fluff Elvis waffle. phillipsavenuediner.com

Or try **Ode to Food and Drinks** for fresh seafood, keto, and low-carb main dishes. Sip craft cocktails on the patio along the Big Sioux River. odetofoodanddrinks.com

Request a river view balcony at **Hilton Garden Inn Sioux Falls Downtown**. Guests also have easy access to riverfront trails. bit.ly/hiltongardeninnsfd

It's a short drive to **Great Plains Zoo and Delbridge Museum of Natural History**. Open 361 days a year, it features animals you might see on safari, an award-winning snow monkey habitat, birding walks and hands-on enrichment activities. greatzoo.org

Butterflies flit overhead and sea creatures react to your touch at the **Butterfly House and Aquarium**. Find these and other hands-on exhibits on the city's south side. butterflyhouseaquarium.org

Stop at **Palisades State Park** near **Garretson**. Photographers, campers, hikers, and rock climbers flock to the spot where Split Rock Creek slices through dramatic, fifty-foot pink quartzite cliffs. gfp.sd.gov/parks/detail/palisades-state-park

Brookings is a college town—go Jackrabbits! Blend in with South Dakota State University gear from **Jackrabbit Central**. Several of the city's museums are right on the SDSU campus. visitbrookingssd.com

Start at the **South Dakota Art Museum**. It features works from Native American, Midwestern, and South Dakota artists and the largest collection of embroidered Marghab Linens in the world. sdstate.edu/south-dakota-art-museum

See South Dakota's agricultural history on display at the nearby **South Dakota Agricultural Heritage Museum**. The vintage machinery is a hit with both little ones and old timers. sdstate.edu/south-dakota-agricultural-heritage-museum

Then unwind in the botanical gardens and forty-five-acre arboretum at **McCrory Gardens**. The graceful flowers, waving grasses and thickets of trees and shrubs are a soothing escape. sdstate.edu/mccrory-gardens

Pose by the *I Love South Dakota Mural* at 312 Fifth Street or check out the **Centennial Cabin** in **Pioneer Park**. The park hosts outdoor concerts and the **Brookings Summer Arts Festival**. visitbrookingssd.com/directory/pioneer-park

The littlest travelers love the **Children's Museum of South Dakota**. Kids clamber up into a multilevel cloud structure, splash in a sensory water display, and catch walleye and sunfish in the sunshine. prairieplay.org

Take a break with SDSU ice cream from the museum's **Café Coteau**. Or treat yourself to burgers, shakes and homemade pie at **Nick's Hamburger Shop**, a Brookings favorite since 1929. nickshamburgers.com

Extend playtime at the **Brookings Inn**. Its Splash Zone Waterpark– complete with waterslides and a lazy river—is a family favorite. brookingsinn.com

Burn off more energy at **Dakota Nature Park**. The 135-acre site is crisscrossed with bike trails and perfect paddling and fishing ponds. Rent fishing rods, canoes, kayaks, snowshoes, adaptive bikes, binoculars, and GPS units at the **Larson Nature Center**. visitbrookingssd.com/directory/dakota-nature-park-center

Then take Highway 14 west to **DeSmet**, a tiny prairie town where literature and South Dakota history meet. Laura Ingalls Wilder, author of the *Little House on the Prairie* series, and her family were some of the city's first homesteaders. desmetsd.com/visitors/attractions

Start the literary pilgrimage at the **Wilder Welcome Center**. The gift shop is packed with souvenirs, art, and Laura-inspired gifts. **Prairie Bus Tours** whisk visitors off to tour Ingalls and Wilder family landmarks and locations that appear in the books. wilderwelcomecenter.com

Take a self-guided excursion to **Laura Ingalls Wilder Historic Homes**. Structures include the original **Surveyors' House** where the family lived in Laura's fifth novel, the **First School of De Smet** that Laura and her sister Carrie attended as well as the **original home** Pa Ingalls built in 1887. Or download the **Discover Laura** app for audio and visual tours and to see artifacts from the author's life. discoverlaura.org

The annual **Laura Ingalls Wilder Pageant** has brought history to life in open-air prairie theatre every July since 1971. Stop for breakfast, lunch, or fresh baked goods from **Ward's Store & Bakery**, just across the street from where Pa Ingalls' store once stood. desmetpageant.org

Then experience the rhythms of a settler's life at the **Ingalls Homestead** as you bounce across the prairie in a pony cart, scrub laundry, grind wheat into flour, and make your own jump rope or corncob doll. You can even stay overnight in a covered wagon. ingallshomestead.com

Let I-29 slowly lull you back to modern life as you head north to **Watertown**. As the city's name implies, this corner of northeastern South Dakota is dotted with glacial lakes and waterways to tempt outdoor enthusiasts. visitwatertownsd.com

Get some sun on the region's prettiest swimming beach and splash at crystal clear **Lake Kampeska** at **Sandy Shore Recreation Area**. You can rent a cabin with a dock right on the water. gfp.sd.gov/parks/detail/sandy-shore-recreation-area

Or visit **Pelican Lake Recreation Area**. Active types will like the archery range, canoe and kayak rentals, lakeside birdwatching, and five miles of trails sprinkled with wildflowers. gfp.sd.gov/parks/detail/pelican-lake-recreation-area

Architecture buffs should stop at the **Codington County Heritage Museum**. Art and history displays are housed inside the city's 1906 Carnegie Library. bit.ly/codingtoncountyhm

Redlin Art Center is modern, but equally grand. The free museum showcases 160 original paintings by Watertown native Terry Redlin. Redlin also designed the complex's thirty-acre conservation park. Dotted with picturesque bridges, waterways and walking paths, it's become a sanctuary for the wild creatures featured in Redlin's paintings. redlinart.com

If you want to see even more animals, stop at the **Bramble Park Zoo** to visit more than eight hundred primates, mammals, invertebrates and aquatic creatures. There's also a picnic area and playground for kids to enjoy. brambleparkzoo.com

Celebrate the end of your eastern South Dakota sojourn with inspiring local eats. Tempting bakery goodies like a raspberry cream cheese flip and chocolate croissants, blended coffee drinks, and salads and wraps make **Backroads Coffee House and Lunchboxx** a good bet for breakfast or midday dining. backroadscoffeehouse.com

Dempsey's Brewery Pub and Restaurant is a favorite for pizza and pub grub like chislic. These fried steak bits are a quintessential South Dakota snack. dempseybrewpub.com

More great eats

Roam Kitchen + Bar—Rotisserie chicken, smoked baby back ribs, and tender beef brisket are the centerpieces of this Sioux Falls restaurant. Pair your entrée with an impressive selection of beer, wine, and bourbon. roamkitchen.com

Original Pancake House—This breakfast and brunch spot in Sioux Falls has served up sourdough pancakes with lingonberries and real whipped cream and rich, eggy Dutch Baby pancakes since 1953. originalpancakehousesiouxfalls.com

Pheasant Restaurant and Lounge—The oldest full-service restaurant in Brookings sells diverse dishes like pheasant salad lettuce wraps, duck wings, and corn and sunflower hummus—and wine, olive oil and vinegar too. pheasantrestaurant.com

Harry's Haircuts and Hot Towels—Need to get a trim and grab a burger basket, hearty sandwich, or wings on your way out of Watertown? This strange (but kind of brilliant) barber/restaurant/bar combo has you covered. (605) 878-3311

Indigenous culture, art, and history on the
Native American National and State Scenic Byway

The **Native American National and State Scenic Byway** follows the Missouri River through the heart of central South Dakota. This river winds through the Crow Creek, Yankton, Lower Brule, Cheyenne River, and Standing Rock Sioux nations that share South Dakota's geography. bit.ly/nativeamericanbyway

These tribes are part of the Oceti Sakowin (Seven Council Fires), an alliance of Dakota, Lakota, and Nakota people often collectively called the Sioux. This road trip illuminates the history, art, and culture of these nations.

It visits places of stark, sometimes desolate beauty. Uncultivated prairies, rolling hills, and the chalky bluffs along some of the last undeveloped stretches of the Missouri River remind visitors that the land has always been central to Indigenous ways of being.

The 350-mile byway winds between the North Dakota and Nebraska borders, compelling travelers to slow down and feel the spirit of the place. A stop in Yankton has been added so travelers can follow the Missouri across the state. Start at the either end of this route if you have a few days to travel or break it up into sections. Many locations are rural and attractions may keep abbreviated hours, so plan accordingly.

Start along the Missouri River in **Yankton**. This river city was once the capital of Dakota Territory. visityanktonsd.com

Riverboat traffic is a relic of the past, but the Missouri still anchors the city. Walk or bike across its waters and into Nebraska on the **Meridian Pedestrian Bridge**. Then cool off at the **Meridian Bridge Plaza** splash pad, settle in for the **Music at the Meridian** outdoor summer concerts series and stock up on fresh produce at **Market at the Meridian** on Saturdays from May through October. visityanktonsd.com/businesses/meridian-bridge

The historical **Meridian District** between Fifth Street and the Missouri River is a smart stop for shopping and dining. Soak up Missouri River views (and classic cocktails and creative American fare) at the riverfront patio at **River's Edge**. facebook.com/riversedgeyankton

From there, it's a short walk to **Riverside Park**, with its playground, picnic shelters, ADA accessible fishing pier, and Missouri River boat launch. Walk off dinner on the **Meridian Trail Network**, which includes more than forty miles of paved and lighted paths. bit.ly/meridiantrail

The trail network stretches through Yankton and into the scenic **Lewis and Clark Recreation Area**. This is where the famous explorers Meriwether Lewis and William Clark met with the Ihanktonwan Dakota in 1804 during the Corps of Discovery's journey to the Pacific Coast. Learn about this first meeting at the **Lewis and Clark Visitor Center** across the bridge. It's a good spot for photos as well. gfp.sd.gov/parks/detail/lewis-and-clark-recreation-area

This is a popular boating, hiking, and fishing area blessed with cool blue water, chalkstone bluffs, and sandy swimming beaches. Many campsites feature scenic views. **Lewis and Clark Resort and Marina** offers additional amenities such as boat rentals, spacious rooms, and lakeside cabins. lewisandclarkresort.com/index.php#

There're more regional and Lewis and Clark history at **Dakota Territorial Museum in the Mead Cultural Education Center**. You can also learn about the state's history, see historic buildings, and even try on vintage clothing. meadbuilding.org

Paddle along the region's original transportation network on the **Missouri National Recreational River Water Trail**, which connects the state to Sioux City, Iowa. A popular thirty-nine-mile South Dakota stretch connects nearby Running Water and Fort Thompson. Its twenty-nine access points include boat docks, camping and scenic look-outs. Many are inside South Dakota state parks and recreation areas, so get a pass before you leave. mri.usd.edu/watertrail

The Chief Standing Bear Memorial Bridge links Niobrara, Nebraska; and Running Water, South Dakota. It honors Ponca leader Chief Running Bear, who won a landmark 1879 case that granted Native Americans the right to be considered people under the law. **Chief Standing Bear Overlook** marks the beginning of the Native American National and State Scenic Byway.

Then follow the river through the lands held by the **Ihanktonwan Nation (Yankton Sioux)**.

Stop for gaming including slots, bingo, and table games at **Fort Randall Casino**. fortrandallcasino.com

Architecture aficionados will like the **Charles Mix County Courthouse** in **Lake Andes**. It's the only Prairie Style courthouse in the state and was designed by Frank Lloyd Wright's student William Steele. Stop for hot lunch specials, homemade soups, and ice cream at **Inside Scoop** before you leave town. bit.ly/insidescoopSD

Lewis and Clark first encountered prairie dogs where **North Point Recreation Area** now stands. This waterfront spot features a playground, archery and trapshooting range, hiking, and golfing near **Fort Randall Dam**. The dam created **Lake Francis Case**, the eleventh-largest reservoir in the country. gfp.sd.gov/parks/detail/north-point-recreation-area

The ruins of **Fort Randall** sit just below the dam. The parade grounds and archeological remnants are all that remain of a site where soldiers surveilled Sitting Bull and imprisoned Chief Standing Bear for resisting relocation. nps.gov/mnrr/learn/historyculture/fortrandall.htm

Popular activities at **Randall Creek Recreation Area** just across the water include paddling, disc golf, and birdwatching. Bald eagles nest along the banks nearby, so keep your eyes to the sky. gfp.sd.gov/parks/detail/randall-creek-recreation-area

Indulge in hand-churned cherry nut or salted caramel mocha ice cream from **Little Brick Ice Cream** in **Platte**. Or pick up broasted chicken, wraps, and sandwiches for an impromptu picnic. facebook.com/lttlebrickicecream

Snake Creek Recreation Area is a pretty spot to enjoy your picnic lunch. The area is popular with anglers, boaters, and campers. gfp.sd.gov/parks/detail/snake-creek-recreation-area

Platte Creek Recreation Area is beautiful too. Both recreation areas are located in a region that contains burning bluffs, a geological oddity that baffled Lewis and Clark. The smoke rising from the riverside rocks is actually caused when the iron sulfide in the shale reacts with oxygen and water. gfp.sd.gov/parks/detail/platte-creek-recreation-area

One of the Native American National and State Scenic Byway's premiere cultural attractions is located down the road in **Chamberlain**. The city is just off of I-90. chamberlainsd.com

The **Aktá Lakota Museum** honors the art, culture, history, and lived experiences of Indigenous Northern Plains people. The educational complex offers fourteen thousand square feet of interactive displays, a meditative garden, and medicine wheel for directional prayers and a gallery featuring Indigenous artists. Learn a few words of Lakota online before you go and shop for traditional art like pottery, baskets, dolls, dreamcatchers, and star quilts before you leave. aktalakota.stjo.org

A sculpture of a woman holding a star quilt (***Dignity of Earth and Sky*** by Dale Lamphere) stands fifty-feet tall above the Missouri. Stop inside the nearby **Lewis and Clark Interpretive Center** to see the river from a fifty-five-foot keelboat, a re-creation of the one used by the Corps of Discovery. bit.ly/lewisclarkinterpretivecenter

Continue along the Missouri to visit the **Lower Brule Sioux Tribe (Kul Wicasa Oyate)** on the river's western banks. The **Narrows Historical Interpretive Area** includes both Lakota tipis and an Arikara earth lodge, illustrating the tribes who have made their homes here.

Hike the **Narrows Recreational Trail** up into the hills to see the Big Bend, the longest natural loop in any US river system. Then stop at the **Golden Buffalo Casino** in **Lower Brule** for a prime rib dinner, try your luck at one of two hundred slot machines, or to rest for the night. thegoldenbuffalocasino.com

The **Lower Brule Sioux Tribe Department of Wildlife, Fish and Recreation** also rents two seven-hundred-square-foot cabins with Wi-Fi, satellite television, and decks along the Missouri River. They're popular with anglers and hunters year-round. lowerbrulewildlife.com

The **Crow Creek Sioux Reservation** along the Missouri's east bank offers more incredible hunting and fishing opportunities. The Wildlife Management Department offers guided hunts and water sports are popular on the eighty-mile **Lake Sharpe** reservoir. See if you can spot the tribe's buffalo herd north of **Fort Thompson** on the way to play blackjack and poker, hit the slots, have dinner, or take in a show at **Lode Star Casino and Hotel**. lodestarcasino.com

Then you're off to **Pierre**. A central location, historical attractions and outdoor recreation draw travelers to the capital city. visitpierresd.com

The **South Dakota Cultural Heritage Center** details the history of the Nakota, Lakota and Dakota people and how the arrival of traders, trappers, miners and settlers changed the course of the plains through interactive exhibits and programming. The Smithsonian Affiliate is open seven days a week. history.sd.gov

The name of the capital and its sister city, **Fort Pierre**, are both pronounced like a fishing pier and not the French name. The latter is the oldest continuously occupied white settlement in the state. fortpierretourism.com

The cities are located between two Missouri River reservoirs (Lake Sharpe and Lake Oahe), so they're favorite destinations for outdoor enthusiasts. Explore 116,000 acres of wildflowers and natural prairie at the **Fort Pierre National Grasslands** or uncover fossils and climb into treehouses at more than sixty hands-on learning stations at **South Dakota Discovery Center**. sd-discovery.org

Hiking, birding, fishing, and cross-country skiing opportunities abound at **LaFramboise Island Nature Area**. The sandbar island is one of the region's most unusual landscapes. gfp.sd.gov/parks/detail/laframboise-island-nature-area

Farm Island Recreation Area features bike rentals, fishing, boating, and a swimming beach as well as trails that attract birders and hikers.

The Lewis and Clark Family Center details the explorers' visits to the region. gfp.sd.gov/parks/detail/farm-island-recreation-area

Book a cabin here or ask for the "fisherman's rate" at the **Ramkota** in Pierre. It includes pet-friendly lodging, access to the fish-cleaning shed and locked freezer, free ice, and a sack lunch to take with you in the boat. ramkotapierre.com

For a more upscale meal, take a **Sunset Paddleboat** dinner cruise down the Missouri River. The paddleboat is a relaxing throwback to an earlier age. sdriverboats.com

If you'd rather eat *by* the water instead of *on* it, dine on the riverfront patio at **Cattleman's Club and Steakhouse**. This friendly, paper-placement place has served up hearty steak and potatoes entrees since 1986. cattlemansclub.com/cms

Then join the locals at **Zesto** for dessert. They line up for fresh-made sherbet, ice cream, and seasonal favorites like peach cobbler from May through September.

Or drive to **Eagle Butte**, located on the **Cheyenne River Sioux Reservation** to use your dining dollars for a good cause at **Keya Café and Coffee Shop**. Every latte, smoothie, entrée, and dessert (from strawberry rhubarb cheesecake bars made with produce from the Winyan Toka Win Garden, to frybread tacos) promotes food sovereignty and benefits the young people on the reservation. The Cheyenne River Youth Project also operates **Waniyetu Wowapi Art Park**, where traditional and street artists create colorful murals under the endless sky. lakotayouth.org

The **HV Lakota Cultural Center** showcases local art and history. Look for colorful murals that depict historical events and Lakota traditions and a gift shop full of pieces from indigenous artists. You can even pick up supplies to make your own art here. lakotaculturalcenter.com

The **Timber Lake & Area Historical Society & Museum** in nearby **Timber Lake** houses rotating exhibits of local art, Lakota clothing and artifacts and fossils. Admission is free. The gift shop stocks many books about regional history. fourbands.org/timber-lake-area-museum

End your tour in **Mobridge**, on the **Standing Rock Sioux Reservation**, which stretches into North Dakota. Enrolled members are Upper and Lower Yanktonai Dakota as well as Hunkpapa and Sihasapa Lakota. standingrock.org/content/visit-us

Downtown Mobridge boasts ten large colorful and newly restored **Oscar Howe murals** that depict Dakota ceremonies, symbolism and spirituality. The Yanktonai Dakota painter created them as a WPA project in the 1940s. oscarhowetour.wordpress.com

Pick up fresh sourdough and sweet brioche donuts from **Filler's Bakery** if you roll into town early. It also sells *kuchen*, the fruit or cheese-filled cake that is the official dessert of South Dakota. fillers-bakery.business.site

The **Sakakawea Monument** overlooks the Missouri River just across from Mobridge. It honors the Shoshone woman who traversed these lands with Lewis and Clark on their journey west.

It stands near the **Sitting Bull Monument** which honors the region's most famous former resident. The Hunkpapa Lakota spiritual and tactical leader was killed while in custody across the North Dakota border, where a marker stands in his memory. Honor his legacy (and the conclusion of your trip along the Native American National and State Scenic Byway) by spending a few moments in silence and reflection along the shores of the Missouri River, just like you did at the beginning of your journey.

More great eats

Charlie's Pizza House, Inc—Specialty pizzas named for celebs like John Wayne, James Dean, and Betty White and the retro atmosphere make South Dakota's oldest pizza parlor in Yankton a throwback delight. (605) 665-2212 facebook.com/CharliesPizzaHouse

Branding Iron Bistro—Stop in Pierre for lavender lattes, delectable raspberry scones, and savory lunches like pulled pork sandwiches and a pear and blue cheese salad in a light, bright atmosphere. brandingironbistro.com

Number Nine Steakhouse—The menu at this Eagle Butte restaurant includes home-style favorites like country fried steaks, walleye, and fried chicken, and surprises like Mexican *menudo* soup. number09steakhouse.com

KT's Fireside Supper Club—This laid-back Mobridge eatery offers hand-cut steaks, rotating specials and hand-pattied burgers. Enjoy your dinner on the patio during warm weather. (605) 845-2936

Connect your trip:
The northern end of this byway links directly to the **Standing Rock National Native American Scenic Byway** just across the border in North Dakota.

South Dakota Scenic Byways
- **Badlands Loop State Scenic Byway**—39 miles
- **Native American National and State Scenic Byway**—350 miles
- **Peter Norbeck National Scenic Byway**—70 miles
- **Spearfish Canyon State and National Forest Service Scenic Byway**—19 miles
- **Wildlife Loop State Scenic Byway**—18 miles

Theresa L. Goodrich is an Emmy-winning author and the force behind thelocaltourist.com, a site dedicated to telling in-depth stories of magnificent, quirky, and unique places. A passionate member of the Midwest Travel Network, Theresa is slightly obsessed with writing, road trips, camping, and history. She's turned these interests into the Two Lane Gems *book series, first-person travelogues highlighting the beauty and diversity of the USA. In 2020, she published* Living Landmarks of Chicago, *a non-traditional guidebook featuring fifty of the Windy City's historic landmarks. She's driven, often literally, to inspire you to get off the interstates and explore the towns and communities that make this country, and especially the Midwest region, a constant and welcome surprise.*

Learn more about Theresa at theresalgoodrich.com.

Alicia Underlee Nelson is the co-host of the Travel Tomorrow *podcast, creator of prairiestylefile.com, and the author of "North Dakota Beer: A Heady History."*

She's a member of the Midwest Travel Network and has contributed to Thomson Reuters, USA Today, Food Network, AAA Living, Midwest Living, Matador Network, craftbeer.com and many other publications. When she's not chasing a story, you'll find her in the garden, on a yoga mat, or practicing a new language for an upcoming trip.

Roxie Yonkey has been writing about Kansas for thirty years, and has won numerous awards. Currently, she is Chief Exploration Officer at RoxieontheRoad.com and a Contributing Writer for TravelAwaits.com. Yonkey is on Facebook, Twitter, Instagram, Pinterest, and LinkedIn as @RoxieontheRoad.

Always interested in a new adventure, she loves to travel and enjoys road-tripping most of all. Join us on a great Kansas road trip in this book. It will show you how to enjoy the Midwest's many fun travel opportunities.

Roxie and her husband Eric have two cats, Dalbie and Lola. She enjoys reading, photography, gardening, repurposing pallets, and scrapbooking.

WISCONSIN

Wisconsin is an amazing state, founded in 1848. Known to many as either the "Badger State" or "America's Dairyland." as it has more dairy cows than any other state (1,500,000!), and produces more milk than any other state. Roughly 5.8 million people call it home.

Basic Wisconsin Facts:
- The state capital is Madison.
- The state motto is "Forward"—although "Eat Cheese or Die" came a close second.
- The state bird is the robin.
- The state flower is the edible wood violet.
- It is the only state that has highways named with letters besides numbers, like Highway M.
- There are seventeen highways and byways to explore.

That alone makes it fun to visit, but the eclectic mix of people who settled here create a diverse variety of food, experiences, and preservation of nature. I picked a road trip plan for each part of the state for you—covering the North, South, East, and West. I hope it encourages you to hop in your car and see it all for yourself!

Wisconsin's Great River Road: The Grand Adventure

Passing through thirty-three great small riverside towns, the 250-mile stretch of the Wisconsin part of the Great River Road makes for an incredible adventure. Following the Mississippi River, this National Scenic Byway is full of amazing things to see, people to meet, and items to tempt your taste buds. The entire route is marked by a green and white pilot's wheel and National

Scenic Byway signs, making it easy to stay on your journey. It starts on the Minnesota border at Prescott, Wisconsin, follows along Highway 35 to Iowa, with Kieler, Wisconsin being the last stop. It is very motorcycle-friendly.

First of all, with more than 250 miles of amazing things to see and do, you might want to set up a "home base" like we do. As the area is steeped in history, there are tons of charming older homes that have been turned into Bed & Breakfast facilities. A few of our favorites? The **Great River Bed & Breakfast** is a Swedish pioneer stone structure that lets you have a one-room cottage all to yourself. It is certainly historical, having been built in 1869, and is beyond charming. greatriverroadbnb.com

If hands-on activities are your thing, you might want to try the **Room to Roam Farm** where you lodge in a farmhouse and experience all the daily operations of the farm. You can try your hand at everything from feeding calves and working in the fields to exploring the beautiful nature around you while hiking or cross country skiing. (608) 687-8575

I would be remiss to not mention the **Historic Trempealeau Hotel**, which survived that terrible fire in 1888. Famous for its restaurant, bar, and decadent Walnut Burger, the Hotel is a mini community in itself. trempealeauhotel.com

Camping is our thing, and the area is perfect for immersing yourself in nature. The Great River Road makes that easy. Not only are there numerous bald eagle nesting sites, but two amazing State Parks: Perrot State Park, and Wyalusing State Park. Keep in mind that nesting is a seasonal thing, so you won't see little bald eagle babies in mid-August.

Seated on over 1,243 acres of bountiful nature, **Perrot State Park** lies among 500-foot bluffs and decked between the meeting point of the Trempealeau and the Mississippi River. The site features a wide array of historical sightings and resources, nature trails, lush vegetation, ancient artifacts, and breathtaking views.

Wyalusing State Park overlooks the Wisconsin and Mississippi Rivers, the park is roughly 2,700 acres and scattered with Native American burial grounds. As one of the oldest parks in Wisconsin, it offers bird-watching, camping, hiking, and canoe rentals. Wyalusing has more than fourteen miles of hiking trails spreading throughout Sand Cave, Mississippi Ridge, Turkey Hollow, and Sugar Maple Nature, to name just a few.

You will also find Nelson Dewey State Park of Cassville, Wildcat Mountain State Park of Ontario, Merrick State Park of Fountain City, and Kinnickinnic State Park River Falls of Pierce County along the Great River Road.

While it would be easy to simply enjoy the bounty that the nature of the area has to offer—there is so much more to see and experience as the Great River Road is full of wonderful historic gems like one of our favorites: Villa Louis. If you want to experience Victorian life during the nineteenth century then you must visit the estate of one of the most prosperous families of Wisconsin. **Villa Louis** was the country home for the famous Dousman Family and this estate sits pretty on the banks of the Mississippi River. The estate has undergone full and painstaking authentic renovation and today it has been restored to its splendor of the 1890s. Conducted tours are arranged on a daily basis wherein the guides are dressed in period clothing and help you to explore the everyday life of the Dousman Family. We even loved the artesian wells, which are still safe to drink from. villalouis.wisconsinhistory.org

You can take a short stroll to view the traces of the old river town and also view the remains of **Fort Crawford**. A museum has everything you could expectas it presents an authentic time capsule. Fort Crawford features some of the most amazing collections that have a vibrant place in history. You will learn about the second oldest city in Wisconsin, **Prairie du Chien**. A visit to the museum will allow you to experience the following exhibits and more . . . The city's experience during the War of 1812, the historic arrival of the 1857 railroad, and even Native American Artifacts and Spear Points from Al Reed. fortcrawfordmuseum.com

The appreciation of history doesn't stop there though, as there is also the **Fort Crawford Military Hospital**. It was one of the central points where wounded Civil War soldiers were treated, so there is considerable homage and respect owed to this facility. This National Historic Landmark gives you an insight to not only the history of medical progress, but the Military History of Fort Crawford and the Civil War.

There are plenty of places to grab a bite to eat in the area, such as **Muddy Water Pizza Pub**, **Fort Mulligan's Grill pub**, and even places like **Valley Fish & Cheese**. Our thoughts? If history is really your thing, then you will want to try **Pete's Hamburgers** for a quick lunch. Muddy-waters-pizza-pub. business.site; fortmulligans.com; valleyfishpdc.com

It all started in the summer of 1908 or 1909, when Pete Gokey was struck with the idea of starting a hamburger stand. He didn't have the traditional setting for an extravagant restaurant, so he had to make do with what he had. The setting was just a table with a kerosene oil stove mounted on top. He would, with the help of his assistant, pan-fry the burgers and sell them to festivals, fairs, and party-goers on the daily. It might not have been the fanciest of them all but the taste his customers were given was far above what others were providing. His continuous efforts in pleasing his hungry patrons made him an all-time favorite for food lovers. He put passion in his work and it turned a great profit for him in the end. That is how Pete's Hamburgers was born.

Things to keep in mind: This is a hamburger stand—not a dine-in place. You walk up, place your order, and find somewhere to eat. Pete's has hamburgers. That is it—along with chips and sodas. No salads, no hot dogs, no cheese. Pete's Hamburger Stand does take credit cards, but prefers cash. They charge a small fee if you use plastic. peteshamburgers.com

If Pete's Hamburgers turns out to not be your thing, check out the "Second-Best Burger in Town" at **Rowdy's Bar and Grill**. They have cheese, fries and pulled pork sandwiches . . . as well as chairs to sit on. Just look for the bar with the huge sign stating that they are the second-best burger in town. We didn't try it, but cracked up at the sign.

Remember the *Little House on the Prairie* book series for children? If you do, then the author is one of the first people to come to your mind; Laura Elizabeth Ingalls Wilder. This amazing woman was born on February 7th, 1867. She grew up to be a woman of character, history, and class, of course. The book series, which she produced and published between 1932 and 1943, were linked to her childhood days growing up in a pioneer family. Ingalls Wilder, through her life and work, became the inspiration on which the **Laura Ingalls Wilder Museum** of **Pepin**, Wisconsin was founded. It features a rich history of the writer's life and happenings during her years. The attributes and collections found in the museum tell the story of what life was like in that era.

You can visit the museum daily anytime from mid-May through to mid-October. Visiting the cabin will bring you back in time to what Laura's life was like. The museum features many replicas of things from the Ingalls' lives, as the rooms have been set up to authentically reflect their era. One of the rooms has a dress on display that was worn by Mary, who was also Laura's teacher. Also, you will get to see one of the bedrooms that has a trundle bed (like that which belonged to Carrie). There's hay that was twisted, supposedly by Laura and her father, to burn as heating fuel while they stayed in during the winter months. This is a low-cost adventure that your little pioneer fans will certainly love. lauraingallspepin.com

Looking for some fun spots nearby? **Villa Bellezza** is perfect if you are a wine lover and feel the need to complete your history with a sip. The **Breakwater Wine Bar** is another popular choice to chill with your friends and family. Have no fear, winery lovers, there are easily more than a dozen fantastic wineries to check out on the just the Wisconsin part of the Great River Road. Fifteen to be exact! villabellezza.com

Ellsworth is the place to get your Wisconsin cheese curd fix. The seat of Pierce County, it is known the world over as the "Cheese Curd Capital of Wisconsin." Keep in mind that real Wisconsin cheese curds do not come breaded and fried—they are either pale or golden versions of squeaky goodness just waiting to be bitten into. They host an annual Cheese Curd Festival that draws thousands of curd lovers to the village each year in June.

Wisconsin is steeped in Native American culture—and the reason so many of our town names seem so challenging to pronounce. Keeping the Native-given names was important to our settlers, a practice that dates back to the earliest days. In fact, the **Genoa Great River Road Interpretive Center** was recently built and dedicated. This brand-new facility hosts summaries of the area's history, wildlife, and Native American heritage through many vivid displays. Take a little time to learn about the people who first realized the benefits of using our Mississippi river for trade and lifestyle enhancements. bit.ly/greatriverroadcenter

Other great eats along the Great River Road:
Stockholm Pie and General Store. Stockholm is a tiny town with several interesting stores, including an Amish furniture store. But the highlight unquestionably is the **Pie Shop**—which has tripled in size during the last five years. You can get a slice or an entire pie, besides lunch, and a great espresso. Their treats and delicacies are made from scratch and also have that little "grandma homestyle." stockholmpieandgeneralstore.com

Hager Heights Drive In. This locally owned family restaurant takes great pride in serving their famous "broasted chicken." It is easy to stop by for a delicious meal or ice cream treat, just look for the giant rooster! facebook. com/Hager-Heights-Drive-In-140174882683829

Pearl Ice Cream Parlor. In a world full of frozen custard, the Pearl Ice Cream Parlor will allow you to savor a piece of history. Enjoy flavored fountain sodas, made from scratch. Thick, rich malts spun up on a Hamilton Beach, served with whipped cream, cherry, and the rest of what's in the tin. Handmade chocolates, sold by the piece or the pound, and a selection of nostalgic candies will take you back to another time. pearlstreetwest.com

Pier 4 Cafe and Smokehouse. If a bargain-priced pulled pork sandwich is your thing, this is the place for you. Maybe try the fantastic German Potato Pancakes or even the Mississippi Mud Pie. All smoked items are hand-rubbed and slow-cooked in an on-site smoker with the restaurant's own special blend of seasonings. pier4alma.com

This just gives you the tip of the iceberg when looking at all the incredible things that the Great River Road has to offer you—you will find amazing gift shops, biking trails, and even golf courses when you seek your own adventure.

Don't forget: you can link your trip by checking out
both the chapters on Minnesota and Illinois to see what
is on the other tails of the Great River Road.

Road Trip through Paradise:
Wisconsin Lake Superior Scenic Byway

The Wisconsin Lake Superior Scenic Byway is more than just a stretch of road; it's a whole experience worth living. The byway runs along the southern shoreline of Lake Superior and Bayfield Peninsula. The area features an array of geographical, recreational, cultural, and historical amenities you will love to bask in and enjoy as you traverse a seventy-mile space with plentiful nature-filled beauties such as forests, beaches, and lakes. There are also many attractions you will love, including the **Apostle Islands National Lakeshore** and Gaylord Nelson Wilderness Area. You will get a chance to connect with an amazing nature-lovers paradise as well as an area steeped in history.

So, where should you start? The journey begins at US Highway 2 and State Highway junction roundabout in the Town of Barksdale (Bayfield County) and west of Ashland city. As this route is only seventy miles long; you might not need a "home base" unless you are taking in one of the many fairs or outdoor festivals. This is a perfect journey for any time of the year, especially if you enjoy outdoor winter sports.

Chilling for the Night? After you have done your bit throughout the day and feel weary, the only best option is to have the perfect place to relax for the night. Along the Wisconsin Lake Superior Scenic Byway, here are a few places you should consider bunking:

The **Pinehurst Inn Bed & Breakfast** is an eco-friendly place with amazing accommodations to help you relax and unwind. It features comfortable guest rooms, views of the Apostle Islands, and healthy three-course breakfasts. Several of the rooms feature an old-style design as the main house was built in 1885. The Garden House was built in 2003. The rooms have amenities such as jetted tubs, fireplaces, TVs, and a deck. Could there be a better way to relax after cross country skiing? pinehurstinn.com

Being Wisconsin's first country Inn Bed & Breakfast, **Old Rittenhouse Inn** is located in Bayfield and offers more than twenty guest rooms in Victorian-style, and a private cottage. They also offer a full-service restaurant that provides breakfast, brunch, and dinner. Yes, you are in for a mouth-watering and satisfying treat as the restaurants serve up some amazing delicacies of locally grown products. rittenhouseinn.com

Another great place to stop by with the family and unwind in an ambiance of comfort is the **Island View Resort**. Situated on the hillside that overlooks Lake Superior, the ten one- and two-bedrooms are cozy, comfy, and have some amenities you will love. Add in the fact that you will be near some amazing places like delis, smoked fish shops, the marina, and the lake shore make for a winning locale. ivr906.com

If you are like our family, your road trip will never be complete unless you camp out with the gang on one of the amazing campsites around the area. When you think of secluded and scenic, then the **Little Sand Bay Recreation Area** should come to mind. It is located off Lake Superior and about fifteen minutes north of the historic trails of Bayfield. This amazing campground is controlled and operated by the Town of Russell and has things such as a boat ramp and dock, picnic area, and a swimming beach. There are more than forty-five campsites that include RV and trailer parking spots, tents, and group sites. townofrussell.org/little-sand-bay-recreation-area

Located on Onigamiing Drive in **Red Cliff**, the **Buffalo Bay Campground & Marina** is a great place to stay. The campsite sits adjacent to Legendary Waters Resort & Casino. It provides one of the most exciting and mesmerizing panoramic views of Lake Superior and the Apostle Islands. The campground features more than forty campsites and you can easily dock your boat on the marina. With Buffalo Bay Campground & Marina, no member of the family has to get left behind . . . not even your pets! Reach out to them for more details to include your pet-friendly camping arrangements. legendarywaters.com/campground-marina

You are in for a treat at **South Shore Campground**. The campsite will let you include your pets. You can experience a great time with both on-land and on-water recreational activities such as hiking, adventure trails, swimming, and more. southshorecampground.com

You can easily let your hair down and dive into the beautiful nature. There are several activities to partake in, including hiking, biking, scenic drives, geocaching, waterfalls, skiing, snowmobiling, beach-combing, ice caves, sled dogs adventure trails, and lots of shopping. It is also a haven for other activities such as hunting or bird-watching, and various water-based activities including fishing, kayaking, boating, or ice-fishing. Add in lighthouse tours, Apostle Island cruises, and shipwreck tours? How can you possibly miss this route?

Let's start with the **Apostle Islands National Lakeshore Visitor Center**. It is located between Fourth and Fifth Streets, in the old Bayfield County Courthouse, on Washington Avenue. There are hundreds of audiovisual programs and exhibits that you can interact with to brush up on natural history and recreational opportunities. While we talk about the **Apostle Islands**, you should check them out. nps.gov/apis/index.htm

The Apostle Islands consist of twenty-two small islands in Lake Superior, off the Bayfield Peninsula. It is home to some of the most beautiful and amazing sea caves in the world: The Apostle Island Sea Caves. The view becomes more scenic in the winter when these caves transform themselves into temples of ice. It is interesting to note that although they are called sea caves, they are actually lake caves.

The Sea Caves of Apostle Island are revered across the world as stunningly beautiful, and the eroded caverns just beneath the Apostle Islands are one of the most popular natural wonders of the US. During the warm summer months, the caves and tunnels are accessible only by boats, and many of them are too dangerous to enter by any means. However, the caves are much more accessible during the winter months. It is to be remembered that the trek across the ice is challenging. We recommend that you use sturdy boots and ski poles to maintain stability on the ice. If it had snowed the night before, then you should switch to snowshoes for easier hiking. It is a good idea to call the Ice Line for the latest updates at (715) 779–3397 and ask for extension 3.

Red Cliff is home to the **Red Cliff Band of Lake Superior Chippewa** and is worth a stop to steep yourself in Native American culture. Hit the **Legendary Waters Resort & Casino** to see the displays about the history and culture of the Anishinaabe people. Time your visit to hit the annual powwow in July or during their Chippewa Cultural Days. If you wander around the reservation, you will see a number of incredible murals that highlight the traditional Chippewa way of life, or take a walk on the trails of **Frog Bay National Tribal Park**. redcliff-nsn.gov

While in the Bayfield area, take a trip back in time at the **Bayfield Heritage Association** and learn the amazing history of the inhabitants of old, their industries, and events that gave rise to the beloved city. There is so much to learn through numerous educational exhibits. You can visit various sessions and join in as area historians detail interesting facts about Native American heritage, shipwrecks, and other subjects, such as lighthouse keepers. You can reach out to the team today at (715) 779-5958 to find out more about how you can book a visit to complement your adventure, or just drop by for a visit while on your tour. bayfieldmaritimemuseum.org

If you are looking for a location that collects, interprets, presents, and preserves historical nautical artifacts in the Bayfield region—the **Bayfield Maritime Museum** is the ultimate location. They share a rich history of the Apostle Islands in Lake Superior and host various exhibits and educational sessions throughout the year. So no matter when your vacation is, you will have a lot to look forward to. The best part? It is free! bayfieldmaritimemuseum.org

The **Washburn Cultural Center** prides itself on protecting and preserving a rich history that the city is known for in a brownstone structure called "The Old Bank Building." The center and historical museum was built in 1890 and is registered as both a national and state historical site. The Old Bank Building is preserved by the Washburn Cultural Center and serves as a community space where you can bond with locals, get enriched with educational resources, and much more.

At the Washburn Cultural Center, you can also access gift shops, antique and memorabilia shops, art galleries, and the **Washburn Area Historical Museum**. Check in advance of your visit for their various workshops, exhibits, classes, receptions, and more. washburnculturalcenter.com

Now, for satisfying your taste buds! No road trip is complete unless you dine on the dishes prepared by the local chefs and diners around the area. For the best in delicacies and mouth-watering dishes, you should ensure you complete your road trip with a visit to one of the following food spots . . .

Good Thyme Restaurant & Catering is located along State Highway 13, in Washburn. We can tell you that you are in for a treat like no other with their philosophy of "good food, good people, good thyme." They serve some of the most delicious and mouth-watering dishes from breakfast straight through to a night crunch. Try the Bruschetta Chicken! goodthyme.catering/restaurant

Eddie's World Famous Ribs is for all the ribs lovers. Think of all the BBQ dishes you have come to know and love; Eddie's World Famous Ribs is the place to stop for all of them. This fantastic restaurant is in Superior, and it is perfect for the entire family to chill and relax. The center cut grilled pork chops are worth trying, and kids can get a quarter rack of ribs. eddiesribs.net

Blue Wave Inn & Sandbar Restaurant is that amazing lakefront inn that caters to not only your taste buds but your mind, body, and soul in general. It is the perfect place to take the entire family and enjoy some of their delicacies prepared by local chefs from locally grown produce. We love locally sourced farm-to-fork style restaurants and this is one to hit! My favorite thing to do at fancy inns? Go there for lunch and enjoy the view. It is less expensive and this place has great sandwiches and wraps. bluewaveinnashland.com

Maggie's is a must-hit in **Bayfield**. You can't go wrong with the Maggie's Superior Sandwich: lake trout or whitefish, broiled or sautéed, served on a toasted brioche bun with lettuce, red onion, and tartar sauce. That is just one of their gems as they deliver the best of Bayfield's fruits, vegetables, and fresh fish to your table as they proudly support area fishermen, farmers, distillers, and brewers. Just look for the flamingos. maggies-bayfield.com

There's no limit to the amount of fun and adventure that awaits you along the Wisconsin Lake Superior Scenic Byway. We are sure you and the entire family will create memories that will last a lifetime as you stroll and experience the best that nature has to offer, from the mountain range to the lush green spaces and lakes. Take a moment to appreciate what it means to experience the true meaning of relaxation in an environment that creates an ambiance of peace and serenity. Let the seventy-mile stretch of historic beauty and elegance mesmerize your minds and leave you desiring more of what northern Wisconsin has to offer.

Door County Coastal Byway: Gateway to Nature's Paradise

The Door County Coastal Byway is a natural paradise, with sixty-six miles of mesmerizing beauty, freshness, and relaxing experiences. The journey begins just north of Sturgeon Bay, runs along State Highway 57, and also to one side of the Peninsula and Gills Rock. After a scenic drive, you head through State Highway 42 and back to the start of this adventurous trip. There is so much to behold and plenty of fantastic activities from nature walks along Lake Michigan to basking in the refreshing air of the Bay of Green Bay and the Niagara Escarpment bluffs. You're in for nothing short of a memorable experience as you traverse the agricultural lands along the adventure stretch, the local villages, or even the dense forest with lush green vegetation and wildlife. Need more? No problem, Door County Coastal Byway has it bountifully for you to explore.

Door County offers more than just an experience, but a way of life worth adopting. With a rich history of life in Wisconsin from the early days, you will experience a time-machine setting with every step you take. **Door County** has come a long way as it relates to the development of the features and amenities you have come to love. For a fact, this is one of Wisconsin's best places to visit whether you are on a "staycation" or a vacation. There are eleven lighthouses around the area; we are sure you will want to visit the locations of these beacons that saved countless lives during Wisconsin's developmental years. visitdoorcounty.com

The area features some of the most dog-friendly regions of the state, where you can practically let your fur-babies run free and explore the wildlife and nature. With lots of green and natural spaces, the state parks create an ambiance of relaxation as you enjoy the best of hiking, camping, swimming in the natural water sources, fishing, and so much more. It is almost like getting a glimpse of paradise on earth.

Incredible accommodations and mouth-watering delicacies await you at every restaurant and food joint around town. The diversity in food offerings, with both local and international cuisines, will have you wanting to return soon. Door County is one of Wisconsin's favorite spots for food lovers, and they don't just say it . . . they prove it! Ready for that vacation of a lifetime? Let's get going . . .

You may just have a day to get in as much of Door County as you can, and with the right planning, you can get more than you bargained for. For those who desire to explore the area for a few days, Door County can make your stay as comfortable as possible with locations like **Garden Gate Bed & Breakfast**, which provides you with a Victorian-style bed and breakfast setting. When you think of comfortable lodging with state-of-the-art furniture and amenities, warm hospitality, great food, and nature scene, then you are in the right place. Garden Gate provides your craving taste buds with the best in local and international cuisine prepared by professional chefs. doorcountybb.com

You could also stay at the **Roots Inn & Kitchen**, which is located in downtown **Sister Bay**. Designed in 1902, and only a short way from the major towns, it has a vast array of vintage amenities and features to help you explore the life of old Wisconsin. The rooms are the perfect place to relax and unwind and get you ready to dive in the dishes they serve—your taste buds will love you for it! rootsinnandkitchen.com

Eagle Harbor Inn is another excellent location to help you unwind after a day filled with fun and adventure. Being one of Door County's most exclusive bed and breakfasts, we can assure you, some of the best experiences lie beyond their gates. They feature luxurious resort amenities and are situated just minutes away from some of the state's most exceptional adventure locations. After a comfortable and restful night, wake up to the fresh smell of locally produced food being prepared for you to enjoy. eagleharborinn.com

Your vacation will not be as memorable as you desire it to be unless the entire family is a part of the trip, including your fur-babies. Give them the experience of a lifetime as you stroll through the **Rock Island State Park**, which will accommodate your pets. It features ten miles of hiking, camping, fishing, and sandy beach areas to give them enough space for frolicking and playing. You will also get the opportunity to unwind in a breathtaking environment that caters to relaxation, meditation, and good family bonding. There are so many historical spots to visit on the grounds. Some include Wisconsin's oldest lighthouse as well as the adjoining boathouse and **Great Hall of Chester Thordarson Estate**. It features a summer-escape area that was built by Thordarson, an Icelandic immigrant. To reach this amazing location, you travel across Washington Island and over to Karfi ferry, where you can bond with nature, your family and your pet. Don't forget to take food and water along for everybody; there are no stores. fori.us/chester.htm

Whitefish Dunes State Park will daze you with an amazing hiking trail up to Old Brady. You will see a beauty in boundless amounts, including beautiful wildflower patches, wooded trails, and massive dunes. Nature's best will greet you as water lovers explore the depths of the rivers and streams along the way that leads to a paw-filled wet sandy beach. bit.ly/whitefishdunes

Love the camping vibes? Then we are sure you will love the moment you step through the gates of **Egg Harbour Campground & RV Resort**. It features more than 160 wooded campsites and thirty-plus full-hookup sites. You can let your hair down and enjoy the hot pools, hikes, and so much more. eggharborcampground.com

Pets, especially dogs, love everything that spells adventure in the woods, and that is the experience that **Baileys Woods Campground** provides. Go fishing, go for nature walks, take a relaxing moment on the sandy beaches, or fill your eyes with some of the best offerings the locals have to offer. baileyswoodscampground.com

Are you into camping or touring with your RV and pet free? No vacation is complete unless you camp out for a few nights and experience life directly under the stars. For sure, the visit to this amazing area will not be complete unless you add **Peninsula State Park** to your camp-out list. It features a myriad of trails that you will love to explore. Our favorite is the Eagle Trail and a thrilling tour of the bottom of Eagle Bluff, where the 1868 Eagle Bluff Lighthouse was built—this will be a test of your agility, so be prepared to be up to the task. bit.ly/peninsulaSP

Strap up your boots as you get ready to face the deep adventure tour that comes with a visit to **Newport State Park**. This rustic park creates the perfect avenue for dense forest hiking with a three-mile trail that goes winding through the forest and rocky shoreline. Wet your feet with the water from the hills that nature chooses to grace your adventure with. It is also classified as Wisconsin's only Wilderness Park—perfect for a serious back-to-nature getaway. bit.ly/newportSP

Your journey through the Door County Coastal Byway will certainly grant you the opportunity to satisfy not only your adventure needs but also your taste buds. Are you looking for that farm-to-fork style restaurant? You are at the right place. There are so many places to grab a bite with family and friends as you traverse this route.

Are you a fish boil fan, or do you want to experience one of the most intriguing activities native to Wisconsin? Well, the **Door County Fish Boil** venues are the perfect place to take your family. Fish are caught from the local lakes and diced in small pieces or chunks and cooked in a large pot with red potatoes and onions. For many, the preparation takes on an elaborate setting where the restaurants usually invite the guests to witness the whole process. There are numerous spots around Door County to enjoy the best fish boils, and having done a little research, we have identified some of the must-visit locations.

Old Post Office Restaurant is an interesting waterfront dining spot that features some amazing delicacies and mouth-watering dishes. Their fish boils include fresh whitefish, which are sourced by fishermen daily. As you enjoy your delicious meal, you can bask in the beauty of the Eagle Harbor. oldpostoffice-doorcounty.com

Are you looking for a casual and affordable dining spot to enjoy some local Wisconsin dishes? Then, **Viking Grill & Lounge** is the place to be. All their meals are made from scratch each morning and include healthy and local products. Besides the fish boil, try the whitefish chowder. facebook.com/vikingfishboil

Established in 1896, the **White Gull Inn Restaurant** is one of the best places to enjoy a fish boil in Door County. You can even take your dogs along, but they will be allowed only for the outdoor activities. whitegullinn.com

Locally made pizza is hot in Door County too. We love **Wild Tomato Pizza** in **Sister Bay**. Committed to serving the entire world a bite at a time, they too provide delicious meals prepared from local, quality grown foods with their wood-fired pizza ovens. Grab a seat on their patio and indulge— you won't be sorry! wildtomatopizza.com

Morning Glory of Door County will have you licking your fingers with every bite you take. From their sunrise quesadilla to their sandwiches, you can look forward to only the freshest foods being prepared. It is one of the greatest little cafes on this stretch of the history and adventure trail of Door County Coastal Byway. facebook.com/MorningGloryFamilyRestaurant

Are you looking for a restaurant that has a "local" preparation style but with mouth-watering delicacies? Then, you ought to try renowned five star **The Fireside Restaurant**. As the name suggests, you can look forward to local delicacies with a fresh taste and cozy environment from breakfast servings to BBQ ribs. facebook.com/TheFiresideRestaurant

Start your day of exploration right by stopping at **Al Johnson's Swedish Restaurant**. With a mix of Swedish, local, vegetarian, and Scandinavian cuisine, you are in for more than you bargained for. Since 1949, they have been creating memories, down to the goats on the grass roof! Their adjoining Butik features lots of memorabilia such as books, jewelry, Swedish linens, housewares, and so much more. It is the perfect place to complement your Door County vacation tour. Whether you are looking to have breakfast, lunch, or dinner, Al Johnson's has got you covered. aljohnsons.com

Make sure you save room for dessert—with a visit to **Wilson's Restaurant**. It is the perfect spot for a late evening snack or even a Sunday evening chill-lax with the family over ice cream. wilsonsicecream.com

Aside from the nature trails or the fresh-food restaurants, you will love a historical tour of some of the landmarks. With eleven lighthouses to choose from, make sure to hit the **Cana Island Lighthouse**—one of Door County's most revered. Retrace the steps of your ancestors as you climb to the top of the tower to see the world from a different yet interesting angle. doorcounty.com/experience/lighthouses

What will be a visit without a tour of the **Alexander Noble House**? It is a ten-room authentic Greek revival farmhouse designed in 1875 and portrays a domestic life setting of early Wisconsin. So, who was Alexander Noble? He was one of the founders of Fish Creek after relocating from Edinburgh, Scotland, where he was born. He took on many roles that led to the development of the area, including being a postmaster, county board member, town chairman, and a blacksmith. Take a journey back to the late 1800s to early 1900s at this historical museum that still boasts some of the artifacts and furnishings of the early days. bit.ly/alexandernoblehouse

Take a tour of one of the saddest areas that are a rich part of Wisconsin history—the **Tornado Memorial Park**. In 1871, a deadly fire hit the country: the Great Peshtigo Fire. The area was named as a similar fire had already struck on the same day that caused extensive damage and broken lives. The area is known as "tornadoes of fire." doorcountypulse.com/fire-took-williamsonville

For museum lovers, you may want to visit the **Door County Maritime Museum**, a journey you begin after crossing the Michigan Street Bridge (also known as the Steel Bridge). It is one of the best small-town museums in the state of Wisconsin and provides a vast array of details. Learn how five naval ships were cranked out in a single day during World War II by Sturgeon Bay shipyards. You will also learn the tricks and trades of local inventors who managed to change the world of international shipping. bit.ly/doorcomaritimemuseum

No matter where in the world you come from, farm life is one of the most relatable experiences any family could have. **The Farm** features the historical rural setting of the region and lets you bond with the life nature created. It is perfect for the children and the young-at-heart adults who are looking for an exciting experience, to include feeding the animals, getting close and personal with farm life, and so much more. Ever see a baby chick break free into the world from its little shell? Well, come down to The Farm to behold this magnificent and amazing lifestyle. bit.ly/thefarmdoorco

Every minute you spend within the space of Door County Coastal Byway will create a memory for you that will last a lifetime. There is an endless amount of adventure for you to experience, from historical landmarks, to nature trails for you and your family (pets included), and, of course, the amazing delicacies you will find nowhere else. The experience creates an avenue for you to explore the life of Wisconsin from early history right through to what it is now. The locals will help you to understand why they call Door County home, and you will envy them when you come to the end of your vacation. For the food lovers around the world, let the diverse menus in the various restaurants along this adventure path satisfy you with the best mouth-watering dishes.

A Journey of a Lifetime: The Lake Geneva Adventure

From Kenosha to Racine, then to Lake Geneva, the seventy-seven-minute drive will be a satisfying and enticing journey. There are so many historical and educational sights to behold as you journey into the experience of a lifetime. The trip begins on Highway 32 South and takes you through a time machine as you encounter life from history of old. You will fall in love the moment you land, especially in Lake Geneva as the colors, scenes, people, history, food, and events will help you create fantastic memories with friends and family. Ready for a taste of the best of Wisconsin? Well, pack your bags and let us make the trip to the East-North Central region of the United States.

I know it seems goofy to think about where to spend the night on a 54.5 mile road trip, but there is so much to see, do, and taste along this stretch that you will want to stay a night or two so you have time to take it all in. Your stay will be perfect when you wake up in the area and open your windows to view the beauty that this surrounding area has to offer. There are so many places you can stay, but some offer particularly amazing features and amenities you don't want to miss out on. Waking up in one of the five luxurious rooms provided by **Lake Geneva's Baker House** will grant you the opportunity to experience a unique space with its personality, elegance, and exotic amenities. It is one of Lake Geneva's most prized locations when it comes to relaxation and enjoying some of the finer accommodations the city has to offer. The historic mansion features a lakefront garden which overlooks Geneva Lake and an exquisite dining area. It is also the perfect location for memorable events such as intimate weddings, anniversaries, birthdays, and so much more. Baker House is a home-away-from-home that you will certainly fall in love with. Bakerhouse1885.com

Didn't get a booking for Baker House? No problem! **Maxwell Mansion**'s doors are always open. This upscale-type historic mansion is blessed with antique furnishings, thus giving it a luxurious and rustic feel. It also features a barn-themed decor with amenities such as cocktail bars and lounges, up-to-date technology systems, and a ballroom. The mansion was built in 1856 in Lake Geneva and has been the central stop for many dignitaries and public figures for decades. It is surrounded by old oak trees—planted centuries ago—vegetation and floral gardens, outdoor fireplaces for the nature lover, a pool, and many other relaxation features. Indulge in the beauty and taste of sophistication and charm from an exquisitely-designed mansion. maxwellmansion1856.com

You can also take a step into a relaxing atmosphere at the **French Country Inn** with enchanting rooms to stimulate your fantasy. It features a peaceful retreat setting and is located close to Lake Geneva and Williams Bay. You can feel the refreshing cool breeze as it dazzles across Lake Como into every room on the premises. This Southern Wisconsin hotel features on-site Stefana's Restaurant, which serves some of the most intriguing delicacies around town. frenchcountryinn.com

Enjoy the best in hospitality that the Lake Geneva and Kenosha area has to offer as you make a stop at the **Racine Christmas House**. It's part of the Southside Historic District, and included inthe National Register of Historic Places, so you are in for a grand treat the moment you set your feet on their grounds. It is within walking distance of Lake Michigan and Downtown Racine and is situated in one of the cooler parts of Wisconsin. As you get away from the busy schedule of life, unwind in a setting where you can enjoy some amazing music by the lakeside. You can also host your special events on the grounds of Racine Christmas House as this bed abd breakfast has some of the most exquisite amenities to complement your experience. You are entitled to your full privacy from the third floor, where you get to overlook the best of nature. Their food? The best! ChristmasHouseRacine.com

By now you are aware that I am a camper. Make your first stop at **Big Foot Beach State Park**. You can camp out under the skies with your family as you bask in the refreshing atmosphere. Getting its name in recognition of Chief Big Foot, an early Potawatomi leader, there is so much history and fun that awaits you. Interestingly, Lake Geneva was once known as Big Foot Lake (English name). It is classified as one of the best beach parks in Wisconsin's Historic District. dnr.wisconsin.gov/topic/parks/bigfoot

Cliffside County Park has been voted one of the must-visit areas on your trip to this amazing city. It is seated on more than 230 acres of lush green space and has more than ninety campground sites to relax and unwind with the family. There are also a few secluded group campsites for those who desire a more exclusive camping experience. bit.ly/cliffsidecountypark

Are you ready to experience the best of nature's offerings in a single campground? Then, **Sanders Park** is your ultimate stop. It features some amazing picnic areas, nature trails, and exclusive and exciting campgrounds. There are also lots of play areas for both the young and young-at-heart, swimming areas, hiking trails, and so much more. This amazing campsite sits on roughly eighty acres of nature's offerings with natural resources and a hundred-mile bike trail. bit.ly/sanderspark

With all of that great outdoor exercise, one must keep up their strength. A visit to the **Simple Cafe** in Lake Geneva should be your top priority. Located just a few blocks away from the lake, in downtown Lake Geneva, it features some of the amazing delicacies that Wisconsin is best known for. The mission of Simple Cafe is to change the world one bite at a time, and we guarantee you that with four to five seasonal menus a year that showcase locally sourced gems, they hit that mark. In for some pastries? Try the offerings of **Simple Bakery** next door, and you will be coming back before you know it. simplelakegeneva.com

For a fact, pastries are a hot thing for Racine, Wisconsin, so coming here means you need to make a stop at one of the famous spots like **O & H Danish Bakery**. They make one of the best Kringle in town, and you will be licking your fingers for days. Racine is so serious about their Kringle, that many bakeries "compete" for the best title. Check out other amazing bakeries such as **Mars Cheese Castle** and **Racine Danish Kringles**. Try them all and decide on your own favorite! ohdanishbakery.com, marscheese.com, and kringle.com

There is no tour made complete without having a fantastic Wisconsin supper club experience. Stopping at the **Hunt Club Steakhouse** will make this experience a reality. It's one of the best restaurants in Wisconsin; the menu offers a diverse cuisine with homemade dishes and ingredients sourced from local farms. They really partner with their community to create quality consistency as they produce edible art. Ensure you have a bite of their mouthwatering steak before leaving to complete the trip. huntclubsteakhouse.com

In addition to the amazing campgrounds and lodging along this scenic trail, you also get to venture into some of the most incredible hidden gems such as **Safari Lake Geneva**. You get a zoo-experience without going to a traditional zoo. Located about five minutes away from downtown Lake Geneva, Safari Lake Geneva is a real-life wildlife preservative that features slightly domesticated animals from all around the world. It is a family-owned venture that allows animals to roam freely, and you get to be up close and personal with them as you feed peanut-free corn-based pellets from the safety of your own car. safarilakegeneva.com

Go from the amazing wildlife setting to a center where your blood will rush with excitement. **Lake Geneva Zipline Adventures** has everything you can think of when it comes to having a blast and letting your hair down. The team desires to create an outdoor adventure experience that lets you relax, unwind, and free your mind from the hustle and bustle of everyday life. lakegenevaadventures.com

Who said your kitchen should have the same menu for the rest of your life? Well, if you are the kind who doesn't know how to spice up your kitchen, let the **Lake Geneva School of Cooking** show you how. Gleaning recipes from the masterpiece, *Chef John Bogan Recipes From the Seasons of My Life cookbook*, the school offers you a real treat. Get a taste from every pot around the world in a single building as you build your culinary skills. lakegenevacookingschool.com

Romance and meditation can be experienced at the **Candle Mercantile**, where you get a chance to bask in the aroma of sweet fragrances. It features the unique experience of designing your signature scent from non-synthetic various oils—sourced from all over the world. Craft your scent, whether in candle form, spray, wax tarts, or diffusers with the guided help of friendly staff, all while munching on a charcuterie board or indulging in a glass of wine. You get to make your own fun souvenir. thecandlemercantile.com

History awaits you at the **Racine Art Museum** that features a myriad of fine art styles from professional artists all around the world. It will be as if you are venturing into a time machine as it holds both vintage and contemporary craft collections amounting to more than 9,500 pieces. To date, it holds the largest and most significant art collections in North America. You can't miss their annual Peeps Contest. ramart.org

Going from the serene historical museum to bonding with the animals at the **Racine Zoo** is more than you can imagine. Situated on more than twenty-five acres of rich land space, the Racine Zoo lies along Lake Michigan and is operated by the Racine Zoological Society. The zoo has a myriad of wildlife and protected species from all around the world. racinezoo.org

Time your journey to ensure you visit the **Bristol Renaissance Faire**, which hosts this amazing experience in a theme park in **Bristol**, just outside of Kenosha. Touted as the number one renaissance fair in the United States for eight years now, it features a recreation of the legendary visit of Queen Elizabeth I to the city of Bristol in the year 1574. It is a magnificent and educational event. If you wish, you may attend in costume. renfair.com/bristol

So, what are you waiting for? The adventure begins the moment you make up your mind to head out, and we guarantee—you will love it!

Dannelle Gay is the brains behind the popular Midwest Travel Blog: Traveling-Cheesehead.com and a valuable member of the Midwest Travel Network.

In addition to her love of all things travel, Dannelle also enjoys great food made from scratch, trying out new things, and spending time with her family

and friends. You may have also come across their work in: books such as her fifty-book series on Family Friendly Travel by State *or even* 101 Ways to Save Money Painlessly. *They have been featured on everything from Wisconsin Public Radio to Mom's Everyday, or across mutual travels. Above all, Dannelle hopes that travel teaches you more about other people and places, and that this book helps you do just that.*

Learn more about Dannelle at DannelleFraserGay.com

INDEX

L

Y

Z

CPSIA information can be obtained
at www.ICGtesting.com
Printed in the USA
BVHW070227151221
624021BV00011B/1055